JAMES OF VITERBO
ON CHRISTIAN GOVERNMENT

James of Viterbo (c.1255–1308) was one of the most distinguished intellectuals of the late thirteenth century. Combining an academic and an ecclesiastical career, he was professor of theology at the University of Paris from 1293 to 1300 and then, from 1302, successively Archbishop of Benevento and Archbishop of Naples. The celebrated papalist treatise, *De regimine Christiano* (*On Christian Government*), is his only venture into the field of political theory. The treatise was composed at the height of the conflict between Boniface VIII and Philip IV of France, probably during the spring and summer months of 1302. It is an exhaustive analysis of the distribution of power within the Christian community. Written from a standpoint of Thomist Aristotelianism, the work seeks to defend the view that the pope is the supreme judge of the world in spiritual and temporal matters alike and that temporal princes are to regard themselves as the servants and auxiliaries of the Church.

Dr R. W. DYSON is lecturer in politics at the University of Durham; he has also translated *Giles of Rome on Ecclesiastical Power* (Boydell & Brewer, 1986).

JAMES OF VITERBO

ON CHRISTIAN GOVERNMENT

DE REGIMINE CHRISTIANO

Edited, translated and introduced by
R. W. DYSON

THE BOYDELL PRESS

First published 1995
The Boydell Press, Woodbridge

ISBN 0 85115 397 6

The Boydell Press is an imprint of Boydell & Brewer Ltd
PO Box 9, Woodbridge, Suffolk IP12 3DF, UK
and of Boydell & Brewer Inc.
PO Box 41026, Rochester, NY 14604–4126, USA

British Library Cataloguing-in-Publication Data
A catalogue record for this book is available
from the British Library

Library of Congress Catalog Card Number: 94–47510

This publication is printed on acid-free paper

Printed in Great Britain by
St Edmundsbury Press Ltd, Bury St Edmunds, Suffolk

CONTENTS

Abbreviations   i

Preface   ii

Introduction   iii

PART ONE

ON THE GLORY OF THE ECCLESIASTICAL KINGDOM

The author's epistle to the lord Pope Boniface VIII   1

*The prologue of the work, in which is described the matter or
intention of the work and the cause in which the work has
been undertaken*   2

I   *That the Church is aptly and properly called a kingdom; and
why and in what way*   4

II   *That the kingdom of the Church is orthodox, that is, rightly
glorious; and in what its glory resides and consists*   11

III *That the kingdom of the Church is one; and in what way and
by what cause*   15

IV   *That the kingdom of the Church is catholic, that is, universal;
and in what way*   25

V   *That the kingdom of the Church is holy; and in what way*   30

VI   *That the kingdom of the Church is apostolic; and in what way* 37

PART TWO

ON THE POWER OF CHRIST THE KING AND OF HIS VICAR

I   *On the manifold power of Christ. Here begins the second part, in which is discussed the power of Christ the king and of His vicar*   41

II   *That Christ's power has been communicated to men; and why and in what way*   54

III   *To what men the power of Christ which could be communicated has been communicated. Priesthood and royal power distinguished*   60

IV   *On the differences between priestly and royal power in the prelates of the Church; and of the actions of each; and certain other comparisons of the one with the other*   72

V   *On the degrees and inequalities of priestly and royal power in the different persons who hold them. Here also is discussed the primacy of the Supreme Pontiff over all churches and rulers of churches*   82

VI   *On the differences and similarities of the two kinds of royal power: that is, the spiritual and the secular*   97

VII   *On certain other comparisons between these two kinds of royal power: that is, the spiritual and the temporal*   101

VIII   *On certain aspects of the powers discussed above which are especially worthy of note*   112

IX   *That in the highest spiritual power there is a fulness of both pontifical and royal power; and in what way*   128

X   *Containing certain objections relating to the foregoing remarks, and the solutions to these objections*   136

Bibliography   157

IN MEMORY OF
PROFESSOR H.S. OFFLER
1913-1991

ABBREVIATIONS

CC   :   *Corpus christianorum, series latina* (Turnhout, Belgium, 1954ff)

CIC   :   *Corpus Iuris Canonici*, ed. E. Friedberg (2 vols., Leipzig, 1879)

CSEL :   *Corpus scriptorum ecclesiasticorum latinorum* (Vienna, 1866ff)

NCE   :   *New Catholic Encyclopaedia* (15 vols., McGraw Hill, 1967)

PG   :   *Patrologiae cursus completus, series graeca*, ed. J.-P. Migne (Paris, 1857ff)

PL   :   *Patrologiae cursus completus, series latina*, ed. J.-P. Migne (Paris, 1844ff)

Reg.   :   *Les Registres de Boniface VIII*, edd. G.A.L. Digard, M. Faucon & A. Thomas (Paris, 1884ff)

i

PREFACE

This volume may be regarded as a companion to my *Giles of Rome on Ecclesiastical Power*. Once again, my objective has been to provide an annotated English translation of an important work of medieval political theory. As on the previous occasion, I have made as literal a translation as I could. My own editorial interventions, where they constitute any significant departure from the letter of the text, are printed in square brackets.

Broadly speaking, this translation is based on the critical edition published in 1926 by H.-X. Arquillière. That edition is, however, in many respects deficient (see Bibliography), and it has been necessary to depart from it rather frequently. For the most part, this has been done without comment, simply to avoid burdening the translation with a large number of purely technical footnotes. It may be remarked, however, that a new edition of the Latin text, based on a complete rehandling of the manuscript evidence, is much overdue.

My wife and daughter have, as always, been unfailing in their support and encouragement, as have my colleagues in the University of Durham. I mention especially Wendy Redhead, Jean Richardson, Julia Stapleton, Henry Tudor and Anthony Woodman. Whatever deficiencies this work exhibits are, of course, my own responsibility.

R.W. Dyson
Department of Politics
University of Durham
Michaelmas Term, 1994

INTRODUCTION

I

James of Viterbo,[1] surnamed Capocci, but almost always known by the name of his native city, was born in about 1255. While still a very young man (ca. 1270), he joined the Augustinian Order of Hermits and began his studies at the Order's house in Viterbo. He went to the University of Paris in 1275, and remained there reading philosophy and theology until 1282. He took his bachelor's degree in 1288 and his master's in 1293. In the latter year, after more than a decade in various administrative capacities in Italy, the Order again sent him to Paris, this time to fill the vacancy which had arisen in 1291, when Aegidius Romanus had resigned as Augustinian regent-master to become Prior-General of the Order. So far as we can tell, James was not the intellectual equal of Aegidius; but he was apparently a great success as a teacher. He held quodlibetal discussions and many *quaestiones disputatae*, notably XXXII *De praedicamentis in divinis*, VII *De verbo*, L *De Spiritu Sancto, De animatione caelorum*, and *De angelorum compositione*. In 1295, he was directed by the general chapter of Siena to concentrate his energies on the study of scripture. Thereafter, he produced commentaries on the gospels of St Matthew and St Luke and on the epistles of St Paul; although it seems that these commentaries have all failed to survive. He returned to Italy in 1300, to become definitor of the general chapter of Naples and to assume responsibility for the *studium generale* established in that city. On September 3, 1302, he became Archbishop of Benevento; three months later (December 12), at the request of King Charles II, he was named Archbishop of Naples. He spent the remaining years of his life in Naples, presiding over the completion of the city's Angevin Gothic cathedral. Venerable in deeds but not in years, he died in 1308. He was beatified by Pius X on June 4, 1914. He is known by the

---

1. For biographical details see: P. Glorieux, *Répertoire des maîtres en théologie de Paris au XIIIe siècle* (1933-34), II, 309ff; *La littérature quodlibétique* (1925), 214ff; D. Gutiérrez, "De B. Jacobi Viterbiensis vita, operibus et doctrina theologica", *Analecta Augustiniana* (1939); U. Mariani, *Enciclopedia Cattolica* (1949-54), VI, 333ff; P. Stella, *Enciclopedia filosofica* (1957), II,704f. Several modern sources say that James was appointed Archbishop of Naples in December 1303; but this is incorrect: see *Reg.* 4842.

scholastic titles of *Doctor gratiosus, Doctor inventivus,* and *Doctor speculativus.*

De regimine Christiano, somewhat misleadingly called by Professor Arquillière "le plus ancien traité de l'Église", is his only essay in political theory, written at the height of the crisis which was to bring the pontificate of Boniface VIII to its dramatic end. Before we consider the treatise as such, it will be useful to glance at the events which constitute this crisis.[2]

II

Boniface VIII's pontificate was, indeed, fraught with crisis from the beginning. He owed his very election to the extraordinary events of 1294. On July 5 of that year, the deadlocked cardinals freakishly chose as the next pope Peter of Morrone, a saintly ascetic who lived on the limestone slopes of Monte Morrone, near Sulmona in the Abruzzi.[3] Since the death of Nicholas IV in 1292, rivalry between the Orsini and the Colonna had repeatedly stalemated the election of a pope; and the choice of Peter was due partly to despair and partly to the calculations of Charles II of Naples, who saw here a chance to bring the papacy under his own control. Without experience in practical matters and untutored in the ways of the world, Celestine V, as Peter became, had not the slightest notion of how to function as pope.[4] At the invitation of Charles II, he took up residence in Naples.

---

2. Inevitably, this survey covers much the same ground as the corresponding section of my Introduction to *Giles of Rome on Ecclesiastical Power.* I have included it here for the convenience of readers; but I have taken the opportunity to expand it and correct a few errors pointed out by reviewers and other readers. The chief sources are: T.S.R. Boase, *Boniface VIII;* G.A.L. Digard, *Philippe le Bel et le Saint Siège de 1285 à 1304;* H. Denifle, "Die Denkschriften der Colonna gegen Bonifaz VIII und der Kardinäle gegen die Colonna", *Archiv für Literatur- und Kirchengeschichte des Mittelalters* (1885-1900), V, 493ff; H. Finke, *Aus den Tagen Bonifaz VIII;* J. Rivière, *Le Problème de l'église et de l'état au temps de Philippe le Bel;* R. Scholz, *Die Publizistik zur Zeit Philipps des Schönen und Bonifaz VIII.* The most useful collection of documents is P. Dupuy, *Histoire du différend d'entre le pape Boniface VIII et Philippe le Bel.*

3. G. Celidonio, *Vita di S. Pietro del Morrone, Celestino papa V, scritta su' documenti coevi* (1896); J. Leclerq, "La Renonciation de Célestin V et l'opinion théologique en France du vivant de Boniface VIII", *Revue d'histoire de l'Église de France,* XXV (1939), 183f; H.K. Mann, *The Lives of the Popes in the Early Middle Ages from 590 to 1304,* vol. XVII,247ff; R. Mols, *Dictionnaire de l'histoire et de géographie ecclésiastiques* (1912-), XII, 79ff; F.-X. Seppelt (ed.), *Monumenta coelestiniana (Quellen und Forschungen aus dem Gebiete die Geschichte,* XIX (1921)); L. Oliger, *Enciclopedia Cattolica,* III, 1258ff; J. Haller, *Das Papsttum* (1950-53), V, 91ff; A. Dieckmann, *Lexikon für Theologie und Kirche* (1957-65), II,1255f. An interesting oddity is the *Opus metricum* of Cardinal James Caetani Stefaneschi (ed. F.-X. Seppelt, *op.cit.,* 1-146).

4. This, at any rate, is the orthodoxy. But Celestine can hardly have been the nonentity or half-wit that he is sometimes depicted as. He had the strength of character and organisational ability to found a religious order - the Hermits of St Damian, called

There, he retired to a cell provided for him by Charles in the Castello Nuovo, to live on dry bread in the midst of luxury. While the Pope gave himself to prayer and meditation, the mundane business of the papacy was left in the hands of subordinates whose motives were by no means as unwordly as his own. Lacking plan and leadership, papal affairs slid daily deeper into chaos. On December 13, St Lucy's day, conscious of the absurdity of his position, Celestine took the unprecedented step of abdicating. It was rumoured that pressure and trickery had been used to put the idea of abdication into his mind; and it was rumoured that Cardinal Benedetto Gaetani had played a particularly deplorable part in organising the trickery.[5] Celestine spent almost the whole of the rest of his life in what was, by polite fiction, regarded as protective custody. He died in suspicious circumstances in the Castello di Fumone, on May 19, 1296. Cardinal Gaetani was elected as Pope Boniface VIII on December 24, 1294, and crowned in Rome on January 23, 1295.

Boniface's pontificate was to be dominated by two major episodes of conflict with Philip IV, called the Fair, of France. These episodes centred respectively upon two long-standing points of contention: the right of kings to tax the clergy within their realms (1296-97), and the issue of clerical immunity from the jurisdiction of secular courts (1301-03). But these controversies were of far more than merely local or transient significance. Both, and especially the second, touched crucially upon the most burning issue of all medieval political controversy: the question of how the relation between *regnum* and *sacerdotium*, the coercive power of the prince and the spiritual authority of the priest, is rightly to be conceived and observed.

In 1296, Philip the Fair was at war - an expensive war, waged with mercenary soldiers - with Edward I of England. Both kings sought to meet the costs of the war by imposing general, non-feudal taxes upon their clergy, and neither sought the pope's permission before doing so. Technically, this was a breach of canon law: the fourth Lateran Council of 1215 had expressly forbidden the taxation of clerics without papal consent. But both kings seem to have relied on the knowledge that, throughout the thirteenth century, popes had in practice been prepared to turn a blind eye to such taxation, especially when the taxes in question were being raised to support a 'just war'.[6] In 1296, however, two complicating factors were present. First,

---

Celestines after 1294 - which had some 36 houses by ca. 1285. Celestine was, no doubt, temperamentally unsuited to be pope; but his main weakness was as a judge of others: he was too ready to trust those unworthy of trust.

5. Hartwig, *Quellen und Forschungen zur Ältesten Geschichte der Stadt Florenz*, II, 221; Mohler, *De Kardinäle Jakob und Peter Colonna* (1914), 267; Ferreto Vincentino (ed. Cipolla, *Fonti per la storia d'Italia*, 1908), I, 64. But Aegidius Romanus, who wrote a treatise in defence of Celestine's abdication (*De renuntiatione papae* (1297), ed. Roccaberti, *Maxima Bibliotheca Pontificia*, II) insists (p.53) that Cardinal Gaetani was known to be opposed to Celestine's resignation. See also F.-X. Seppelt, *Studien zum Pontifikat Papst Coelestins V*, 1-13.

6. F.H. Russell, *The Just War in the Middle Ages* (1975).

the war between England and France was one in which each of two Christian kings claimed to be waging just war against the other. In such circumstances, some kind of papal intervention was only to be expected. In comparable circumstances, after all, Innocent III had intervened in 1204 when Philip Augustus had invaded King John of England's great fief of Normandy. Second, the taxes which the kings sought to exact were ruinously heavy, and the clergy upon whom they fell appealed directly to Rome.

Also, in a wider sense, the events of 1296-1303 took their colour from a conjunction of key personal and political contingencies. It has often been alleged that Boniface, driven by immense personal ambition, attempted to commit the papacy to new and greatly extended claims to authority in the temporal sphere. There is, in fact, little reason to think that this is so. The truth is that Boniface did not at any time - not, at any rate, in any document or on any occasion known to us - make any claim that had not already been formulated by his great predecessors Innocent III and Innocent IV. He was, however, almost entirely lacking in the tactical judgment and diplomatic subtlety which they had displayed. Much of our knowledge of Boniface comes from sources hostile to him; but it is obvious from the evidence of the documents which he himself has left behind that his undoubted abilities were in a measure vitiated by arrogance, intolerance and impulsiveness. He and his supporters were often vastly indiscreet and outspoken. It is said also that his temper was worsened by bouts of painful and debilitating illness. We should not, however, attribute the whole of Boniface's abrasiveness to merely personal quirks. It must be borne in mind that, during the months of Celestine's pontificate, the papal curia had become the virtual tool of Charles II of Naples. Boniface was, no doubt, anxious, and perhaps over-anxious, to stamp his authority upon his office from the start, and to re-establish a vigorous papal diplomacy upon an independent footing.

On the other hand, the governing factor in contemporary French politics was the determination that the French king should be the autonomous ruler of a unified nation state. It was this desire which had led Philip the Fair into war with Edward I over the territories which, as Duke of Guienne, the latter held in France. Philip realised quite well that this ambition could not co-exist with the pope's claim to act in the last resort as judge of the entire world and, in that capacity, to interfere in both domestic and foreign politics even to the extent of deposing temporal princes. We may conjecture also that the death of his father in the ill-fated crusade of 1285 against Aragon had left Philip with no great trust in Rome or sympathy for the political wishes of the Apostolic See. At all events, his resolve - or, perhaps, the resolve of the gifted and worldly ministers who advised him: Pierre de Flotte, Guillaume de Nogaret, Enguerrand de Marigny[7] - was to strengthen

7. In addition to the sources given at n. 2, see R. Holtzmann, *Wilhelm von Nogaret* (1898); J. Favier, *Un Conseiller de Philippe le Bel: Enguerran de Marigny* (1963).

the kingdom of France by all available means, and to tolerate no obstacle of whatever kind to that resolve.

The opening shot of the conflict was fired by Boniface on February 24, 1296, with the promulgation of the Bull *Clericis laicos*.[8] From the first, the Pope's tone was characteristically combative:

> Antiquity teaches that the laity have been exceedingly hostile to the clergy, and the experiences of the present time also clearly show this. For, not content with their own boundaries, they strive after that which is forbidden, and loose the reins for unlawful things.

Reaffirming the prohibition of 1215, the Bull went on to forbid the clergy to pay, and laymen to collect, taxes levied on clerical property without papal consent. The penalty of excommunication incurred by all who disregarded this injunction was not to be lifted, except by special papal dispensation, until the moment of death:

> For it is our intention that so terrible an abuse of secular power shall not be carried on under any pretext whatever, notwithstanding any privileges whatsoever...granted to emperors, kings and the other persons mentioned above.

Clericis laicos is the first of several instances of the incautious truculence with which Boniface was to conduct himself throughout his disputes with the French king. Scorning the possibility of negotiation, he chose at once to command the clergy of England and France to disobey their kings, and to assert his own right to correct the "abuse of secular power" of which he deemed those kings guilty. Almost any approach would have been less destructive than the one that Boniface actually chose. Having adopted this line - and this is the central point - he caused the quarrel to turn from the start upon the unadorned question of whether a king is or is not sovereign within his own realm.

Edward I contented himself with the expedient, effective enough in the long run, of outlawing the Archbishop of Canterbury, Robert of Winchelsea, and most of the clergy. Philip the Fair struck at the Pope directly. On August 17, 1296, he issued a royal ordinance prohibiting the export of bullion, precious stones and negotiable currency from France.[9] This shrewd move had the effect of depriving Boniface of the huge revenues of the Church in France, upon which the papal administration was heavily reliant. Indeed, it threatened the whole Italian banking system. The immediate result was an angry deadlock. In the Bull *Ineffabilis*,[10] promulgated on September 25, 1296, Boniface denounced the king and his 'wicked counsellors' and demanded that Philip's prohibition be removed at once, on

---

8. *Reg.* 1567.
9. Dupuy, *op.cit.*, 13.
10. *Reg.* 1653.

pain of excommunication. He reminded Philip that Edward I had complained of his sinful seizure of English territory and that, in matters involving sin, the pope has jurisdiction even in temporal matters.[11] For his part, Philip remained obdurate in his refusal to recognise any papal right of interference in the temporal affairs of his kingdom.[12]

By February 1297, his worsening financial situation had brought Boniface to a less uncompromising frame of mind. Still complaining, but ready to be far more conciliatory than he had been hitherto, he pointed out to Philip that *Clericis laicos* had not been intended to apply exclusively to France, but had been directed at all kings; and, at the same time, he conceded that, in an emergency so serious that there was no time to consult Rome, a king might tax his clergy even without the pope's consent.[13] This was not, however, enough to satisfy Philip. The Pope had, unfortunately, omitted to say who was to be the judge of when a sufficiently grave state of emergency existed, and had thereby left open the possibility of endless future recrimination. Accordingly, the king now sent his talented and pragmatic chief minister, Pierre de Flotte, to negotiate with the Pope face-to-face. Meanwhile, Boniface found himself under attack from other quarters.

Much animosity now existed between the Pope and his erstwhile allies, the powerful and influential Colonna family of Rome. The Colonna greatly resented Boniface's ceaseless and extravagant use of papal patronage to advance Gaetani interests in the Roman Campagna. In thirteenth-century Italy, such rivalries between families were apt to find expression in acts of brigandage. On May 3, 1297, an armed band under Stefano Colonna waylaid a party of Boniface's staff on their way to Rome from the Pope's native town of Anagni, and made off with a quantity of papal treasure worth, it was said, some 200,000 florins. When the news reached Boniface, he summoned the two Colonna cardinals, Giacomo and Pietro, and demanded the return of his property. This they promised to arrange. Never one to leave well enough alone, however, Boniface then insisted that Stefano

---

11. The doctrine that the pope has jurisdiction in temporal matters "by reason of sin" (*ratione peccati*) had received its definitive, although not its first, statement in Innocent III's decretal *Novit*, written in defence of his intervention in the quarrel between King John and Philip Augustus. Innocent maintained that even though the dispute over Normandy was on the face of it a temporal matter, papal interference was justified on three grounds: (a) because sin was involved, and the pope has jurisdiction over all sins; (b) because the Church has a special responsibility to keep the peace; (c) because oath-breaking, which is an offence over which the Church has a direct jurisdiction, had occurred during the dispute.

The *ratione peccati* principle was to become one of the most vital and potent elements of papal claims to supremacy in temporal affairs, for an obvious reason: given that the pope is, by common consent, the final arbiter of what is and is not sin, the degree of intervention which the principle can be used to justify is theoretically unlimited. See the remarks of Aegidius Romanus at *De ecclesiastica potestate*, III, V-VI (ed. Dyson, 172ff). See also M. Maccarone, *Chiesa e stato nella Dottrina di Papa Innocenzo III* (1940); F. Kempf, *Papsttum und Kaisertum bei Innocenz III* (1954); H. Tillmann, *Papst Innocenz III* (1954).

12. Dupuy, 27.

13. *Reg.* 2308-12.

be surrendered as a hostage and that the Colonna castles at Palestrina, Colonna and Zagarolo be handed over as sureties. When the cardinals declined to do anything of the kind, they were, without any kind of trial or formal process, excommunicated and expelled from the Sacred College, and the Pope preached a crusade against the Colonna. He was presently to congratulate himself on the thoroughness of his reprisals.[14] The city of Palestrina, it is said, was obliterated: every man, woman, child and beast slain, every building except the cathedral flattened, and the earth, like that of Carthage of old, ploughed with salt.

Giacomo and Pietro Colonna withdrew to the family stronghold at Longhezza. Here, they were joined by a number of leaders of the Franciscan Spirituals, who, though for different reasons, entertained grievances against Boniface every bit as intense of those of the Colonna. They despised the Pope's worldliness, venality and nepotism. They chafed at his uncongenial response to their convictions in regard to the poverty of Christ. Above all, they detested him for what they took to be his part in bringing about the abdication of Celestine V, the "angel pope" in whom they had reposed such hopes. The most energetic of their number, the famous Jacopone da Todi,[15] collaborated with the Colonna in drawing up a series of public diatribes, the so-called Colonna manifestos, against Boniface.[16] The Pope's enemies alleged that Celestine's abdication had been unlawful; that Boniface's own election had therefore been invalid; that Boniface had caused Celestine to be assassinated (a skull with an ominous hole in it was produced[17]); and that the Pope was a heretic and a simoniac. As time went by, so the accusations of the Pope's foes grew more furious and elaborate. Their polemical activities culminated in a plea to the chancellor, masters and scholars of the University of Paris to investigate Boniface's position and conduct with a view to his deposition by a general council of the Church. As de Flotte was travelling to Orvieto for his projected conference with Boniface, he was met by emissaries of the Colonna, who undertook to throw the family's influence in Italy behind Philip the Fair if the king would support their efforts to have the Pope removed. Faced with this menacing consort of foes, and possibly far from convinced that the legality of Celestine's abdication could withstand too close a scrutiny, Boniface was faced with little choice short of capitulation. At the end of July 1297, after a few face-saving manoeuvres, he issued the Bull *Etsi de statu*,[18] in which the provisions of *Clericis laicos* were formally withdrawn insofar as they related to France. The concession was repeated that the king might tax the clergy

---

14. *Reg.* 3416, 3922.
15. E. Underhill, *Jacopone da Todi, Poet and Mystic* (1919). More generally, see D. Douie, *The Nature and Effect of the Heresy of the Fraticelli* (1932); M.D. Lambert, *Franciscan Poverty: The Doctrine of the Absolute Poverty of Christ and the Apostles in the Franciscan Order* (1961); F. Bäthgen, *Der Engelpapst: Ideen und Erscheinung* (1943).
16. H. Denifle (ed.), *op. cit.*, V, 510ff.
17. F. Visca, *Celestino V ed il VI Centenario della sua incoronazione* (1894), 261ff.
18. *Reg.* 2354

without papal consent in an emergency; but the important proviso was now added that the king himself should be the final judge of when a state of emergency had arisen.

Manifestly beaten in this first phase of conflict, Boniface was, however, by no means ready to surrender unconditionally. It is said that his punctured morale (and, of course, the papal treasury) was much restored by the piety and generosity of the thousands of pilgrims who flocked to Rome for the centennial Jubilee of 1300. An eyewitness has recorded for posterity the image of two clerics standing day and night at the altar of St Paul's, collecting the donations of the faithful into heaps with rakes.[19] In any event, when, some four years after *Etsi de statu*, there occurred a further infraction of ecclesiastical liberties in France, the Pope returned enthusiastically to the fray.

In 1295, in circumstances of some acrimony and without consulting Philip, Boniface had appointed an old associate of his, Bernard de Saisset, as bishop of the newly-created Diocese of Pamiers.[20] On July 12, 1301 Bernard was arrested on charges of treason, blasphemy and heresy, tried in the presence of the king on October 24, and imprisoned. Philip then sent to Boniface asking him to approve what had been done (adding for good measure that the bishop had "very often affirmed that our most holy father Boniface is a devil incarnate."). The king was, in short, ignoring the clear canonical principle that a delinquent bishop should be tried only by the pope. So blatant was his disregard of this principle that it is difficult to avoid the conclusion that the trial of Bernard was a deliberate gesture of provocation, calculated to bring about a further and decisive contest for supremacy between the French crown and the papacy.

If the de Saisset incident was indeed intended as bait, Boniface swallowed it with obliging readiness. Not without some show of reason, but with his usual lack of diplomatic polish, he once more threatened the king with excommunication, demanded Bernard's immediate release, and revoked all the special privileges recently conferred upon Philip: that is, the concessions made in *Etsi de statu* and related documents. On December 5, 1301, he issued the Bull *Ausculta fili* (which, however, he took the precaution of first having vetted by the College of Cardinals), specifying in insulting detail his dissatisfactions, not only with Philip's treatment of the Church in France, but also with his general conduct as king.[21] He complained that the king was oppressing the nobles, clergy and people of his realm; preventing the Roman See from exercising its rights with respect to vacant benefices; compelling clerics to appear in his courts to answer charges unrelated to their feudal tenures and obligations; not permitting ecclesiastical penalties to

---

19. Chron. Asti, *Rerum Italicarum scriptores*, XI (ed. L.A. Muratori, 1723-1751), 191.
20. J.M. Vidal, *Histoire des évêques de Pamiers*, vol I: *Bernard Saisset (1232-1311)* (1926); R. Fawtier, *L'Europe occidentale de 1270 à 1380* (1940); J. Haller, *op.cit.*, V, 162ff; F.-X. Seppelt, *Geschichte der Päpste von dem Anfangen bis zur Mitte des 20 Jh.*, IV (1957), 26ff; H. Tüchle, *Lexikon für Theologie und Kirche*, II, 248.
21. *Reg.* 4424.

be carried out against those who molested the clergy; and not allowing ecclesiastical jurisdiction to be exercised in the monasteries of which he was guardian. All these complaints were prefaced by the following statement, unexceptionable in meaning but unfortunate in wording, and certainly unfortunate in timing:

> We shall indeed explain more clearly, son, why, moved by urgent necessity and prompted by conscience, we are directing these complaints to you. For, although our merits are insufficient, God has placed us above kings and kingdoms, and He has imposed upon us the yoke of apostolic service: to uproot and destroy, to disperse and scatter, to build and to plant, in His name and according to His teaching....And so let no one persuade you, dearest son, that you have no superior and that you are not subject to the head of the ecclesiastical hierarchy. For he who thinks this is a fool; and, if he obstinately affirms it, he is convicted as an unbeliever, and is outside the fold of the Good Shepherd.

It is said that, when *Ausculta fili* was handed to him, Philip at once burnt it. Whether he did quite this or not, it seems unlikely that its contents were made public in France. All the evidence that we have testifies that, to make assurance doubly sure, de Flotte caused the actual Bull to be suppressed and, in its place, circulated a forgery, *Deum time*, by means of which it was made to appear that the Pope had handled the king very discourteously indeed.

> Fear God and keep His commandments. We wish you to know that you are subject to us in spiritual and temporal matters alike. The collation of benefices and prebends does not belong to you in the least; and if you have custody of any vacant churches you are to keep their revenues for those who succeed to them. If you have conferred any such benefices, we declare the collations null and void, and we revoke any that you have made in point of fact.[22]

The tone of this bogus document - indeed, that fact that it was confected at all - will give some indication of the level at which the French side of the debate was being conducted. A similar remark applies to the equally spurious letter, *Sciat tua maxima fatuitas*, which the people of France were allowed to believe that their king had sent to the Pope in reply:

> Let Your Supreme Foolishness know that we are subject to no one in temporal matters; that the collation of churches and prebends belongs to us as of royal right, and that their revenues are ours; that the collations which we have made in the past and shall make in the future are valid; and that we shall stoutly defend their

---

22. Dupuy, 44; and see Holtzmann, "Philip der schöne und die Bulle *Ausculta Fili*", *Deutsche Zeitschrift* (1897-98), 16ff; Dupuy, 59, 79.

holders against anyone. All who believe otherwise we hold to be
fools and madmen.[23]

The existence of these documents lends much force to the conjecture that
Philip and his ministers were now actively seeking a decisive confrontation
with Rome.

Simultaneously with the promulgation of *Ausculta fili*, Boniface summoned
the senior ecclesiastics of France to a council to be held in Rome in
November 1302.   In *Ausculta fili* itself, Philip was invited to send
representatives to this council and informed that it would consider, not only
measures for strengthening the Church in France, but also ways of securing
"your guidance and peace and salvation, and...the good government and
prosperity of that kingdom." Philip forbade the French bishops to attend the
council and, in February 1302, summoned his "prelates, barons and other
faithful subjects" to advise him: the first convocation of what has become
known as the Estates General of France. The assembly was addressed on
April 10 by Pierre de Flotte. Apparently, his chief complaint was that
Boniface had claimed to be lord of France *temporaliter*: had, in effect,
asserted that the French kingdom was held of him as a papal fief.[24] This
complaint undoubtedly rested upon the forged *Deum time* and not upon the
words of the real *Ausculta fili*: "Let no one persuade you that you have no
superior and that you are not subject to the head of the ecclesiastical
hierarchy." It is obvious from the context that these words mean only that
the king is subject to the pope *ratione peccati*: a quite unobjectionable, and
certainly not a novel, statement.

The upshot of the meeting was an unexampled avowal of support, both lay
and clerical, for the king. The nobles wrote in terms of great reproach to
the College of Cardinals, castigating Boniface and refusing to acknowledge
him as pope. The bishops wrote to Boniface himself, taking a much more
deferential tone, but nonetheless voicing distress at his unprecedented claims
in relation to France and earnestly requesting him to abandon the proposed
council.[25]

In reply, the nobles received from the College of Cardinals a polite denial
that Boniface had ever claimed to be France's feudal lord, coupled with an
accusation that de Flotte had falsified *Ausculta fili* to give the contrary
impression. "We wish you to know with certainty that our lord Pope has
never written to the king that he is subject to him in temporal things and that
he holds the kingdom as a fief."[26] In a consistory held in Rome in the
summer of 1302, Boniface himself and a papal spokesman, Cardinal
Matthew of Acquasparta, repeated this denial and again bitterly accused de
Flotte of deception. "We have been practised in the law for forty years,"

---

23. Dupuy, 44.
24. G. Picot (ed.), *Documents relatifs aux états généraux et assemblées réunies sous
Philippe le Bel* (1901), Vf.
25. Ibid..
26. Picot, VII.

Boniface retorted, "and we know that the powers established by God are two. How should or can anyone believe that anything so foolish or stupid [as the contrary] is or has been in our head?"[27] But both the Pope and Matthew of Acquasparta reaffirmed the principle that the pope has jurisdiction even in temporal matters by reason of sin; and Boniface's statement ended on an unrepentant and provocative note:

> Our predecessors deposed three kings of France: they can read it in their chronicles, and we in ours; and one case is to be found in the *Decretum*.[28] And although we are not worthy to walk in the footsteps of our predecessors, if the king committed the same crimes as those kings committed, or greater ones, we should dismiss him like a servant.

In the event, neither the denials nor the assertions of Boniface and his supporters accomplished anything of value for the papal side. The council summoned for the end of 1302 was a humiliating failure. Less than half the French bishops were present (36 out of a possible 78), and no deliberations of any significance took place. Stung by this fiasco, Boniface issued, on November 18, 1302, the Bull *Unam sanctam*.

> Our faith urging us, we are bound to believe and to hold, and we do firmly believe and absolutely confess this, that there is one, holy, catholic and apostolic Church, outside whom there is neither salvation nor remission of sins....
> We are taught by the words of the gospel that within this Church and in her power there are two swords, a spiritual and a temporal. For when the apostles said, "Here are two swords"...the Lord did not reply that this was too many, but enough. Certainly, he who denies that the temporal sword is in the power of Peter has ill understood the words of the Lord when He said: "Put up *thy* sword into its sheath." Both, therefore, are in the power of the Church: that is, the spiritual sword and the material. But the latter is to be wielded on behalf of the Church and the former by the Church: the one by the priest, the other by the hands of kings and soldiers, though at the command and by the permission of the priest. And the one sword must be under the other, and temporal authority subject to the spiritual power....
> Therefore, if the earthly power goes astray, it will be judged by the spiritual power; if a lesser spiritual power goes astray, [it will be judged] by its superior. But if the supreme [spiritual power goes astray,] it will be subject to judgment by God alone, not by man, as the Apostle attests: "The spiritual man judges all things and is himself judged by no one." For although this authority was given to a man and is exercised by a man, it is not a human, but, rather, a divine power: given to Peter at God's mouth and

---

27. Dupuy, 77.
28. C.XV,q.6,c.3 (*Alius item*) (CIC I,756). This is the standard example of papal deposition: the dismissal of Childeric III in favour of Pepin. See below, p.xxiv.

established for him and his successors upon a Rock in Christ Himself, by Whom he was acknowledged when the Lord said to Peter, "Whatsoever thou shalt bind", and so on. Therefore, whoever resists this power so ordained of God resists the ordinance of God....

We therefore declare, state, define and pronounce that it is entirely necessary to salvation for every human creature to be subject to the Roman Pontiff.[29]

It must be noted that not even in this celebrated document does Boniface make any new or revolutionary claims for the temporal jurisdiction of the papacy. Once again, his error of judgment in publishing it - and undoubtedly it was an error of judgment - lay in his timing rather than in the Bull's content. To Philip the Fair and his counsellors, such forceful and public asseverations of the supremacy of the spiritual sword were the final straw. In response, Philip and his new chief minister Guillaume de Nogaret (de Flotte had lost his life at the battle of Courtrai in the summer of 1302) once more set in train a campaign of venomous intrigue against the Pope, reviving and embellishing the charges made five years previously in the Colonna manifestos of 1297.[30] Addressing the Estates General in the spring of 1303, de Nogaret once more urged that steps be taken for Boniface's deposition. Here, and during the ensuing months, Boniface was accused of every kind of crime and sin: of usurping the papal office, of adultery, blasphemy, fornication, heresy, homicide, sexual intercourse with the devil, simony, sodomy, sorcery and, believe it or not, omitting to fast during Lent. The steps taken to assassinate his character (although such childish tirades of accusation are by no means an unusual feature of medieval controversy) sometimes border on the ludicrous. In the heat of some moment or other, Boniface had said that he would rather be a dog than a Frenchman. Here, said his opponents, is clear proof of heresy: the Pope evidently believes that Frenchmen have no souls.

Boniface sought to exploit one last diplomatic possibility. Having at first opposed the election, in July, 1298, of Albert of Austria as emperor, he now (April 30, 1303) recognised his claim.[31] He made use of the occasion to restate, in the Bull *Patris aeterni*, the old theory that all national kings were subordinate to the emperor and that the emperor's power in turn came from the pope.[32] He also gained from the emperor an acknowledgement of the right of the pope alone to bestow the imperial crown and a promise that none of his sons should be elected German king without papal consent. These negotiations, however, were of no avail. On September 7, the papal residence at Anagni was entered by a contingent of armed men led by de

---

29. *Reg.* 5382; and see Rivière, *op.cit.*, 150ff; 394ff.
30. Dupuy, 102ff.
31. H. Henneberg, *Die Politischen Beziehungen zwischen Deutschland und Frankreich unter König Albrecht I* (1891); M. Lintzel, "Das Bundnis Albrechts I mit Bonifaz VIII", *Historische Zeitschrift*, CLI (1935), 457ff.
32. *Reg.* 5349-50.

Nogaret and Sciarra Colonna, a brother of the ex-cardinal Pietro.[33] Their apparent purpose was to kidnap Boniface and have him formally deposed by a general council choreographed by the French king. In a sense, they arrived in the nick of time. Boniface had already drawn up a solemn Bull of excommunication against Philip (*Super Petri solio*), intending to promulgate it on September 8.[34] The document did not in so many words declare the king of France deposed; but it pronounced null any foreign alliance that he might make and absolved his subjects from their allegiance to him. It was, in short, an invitation to any foreign prince whose loyalties lay with the Pope to invade France, and to the subjects of Philip the Fair to rebel against their king.

A pleasant, but almost certainly untrue, story is that, as his persecutors burst into the papal apartments, the aged pontiff confronted them in silent dignity, arrayed in full pontificals and holding a golden cross in his hands.[35] As he watched his possessions being ransacked and carted away by looters, he murmured to himself the words of Job: *Dominus dedit, Dominus abstulit; sit nomen Domini benedictum.* The Lord gave, and the Lord hath taken away; blessed be the name of the Lord.[36]

De Nogaret demanded that he relinquish the papal throne forthwith and submit himself to judgment. Boniface bared his neck and invited his assailants to cut his throat: *e le cape, e le col.* Here is my head; here is my neck. Sciarra Colonna was only with difficulty restrained from killing him there and then. Colonna and de Nogaret then wasted two days in wrangling over what their next move was to be. The hesitation proved fatal. The town of Anagni recovered from the shock of invasion and rallied to the Pope's defence. The invaders were repulsed and Boniface restored to liberty. But the Pope's already frail constitution had been irreversibly undermined by the stresses to which it had been subjected. He made his way back to Rome; on the way, it is said, he was harried by Sciarra Colonna's horsemen.[37] His

---

33. Understandably enough, this celebrated incident has acquired such an accretion of legend that it is not easy to distinguish truth from fantasy. Our knowledge rests mainly on three sources: a letter from William of Hundleby, proctor of the Bishop of Lincoln, sent to England on September 27, 1303 and now printed by H.G.J. Beck, *Catholic Historical Review*, XXXII (1947), 200ff; an anonymous account printed by G.A.L. Digard in *Revue des questions historiques*, XLIII, 557ff; and a fragment printed by L. Fumi in *Rerum Italicarum scriptores*, XV (New Series, edd. G.Carducci and V. Fiorini, 1900-   ), Pt. 5, 199ff. See also Holtzmann, *Wilhelm von Nogaret*, Ch, IV; Fedele, "Per la storia dell' attentato di Anagni", *Bullettino dell' Instituto Storico Italiano*, XLI (1921), 195ff.
34. Dupuy, 182.
35. Cf. Fedele, *op.cit.*, 203ff. The belief that Boniface was a very old man at the time of his death seems to originate with Ferreto Vincentino, who says (*ed.cit.*, 164) that he was eighty-six. This is probably an imaginative touch to add pathos to the drama. Boniface's own remark, in 1302, that he had been a lawyer for forty years, suggests that he was in his sixties in 1303. See also Finke, *op.cit.*, 1ff; Cf. Fedele, *Archivio della Società Romana di storia patria*, XXVII, 276; Boase, *op.cit.*, 6f.
36. This and the detail in the following paragraph are from William of Hundleby's letter.
37. Chron. Parmense, *Rerum Italicarum scriptores*, IX (New Series), 86.

health was in ruins, and the spirits which might have enabled him to recruit it were crushed. He died - cursing and blaspheming, his detractors gleefully alleged - on October 11, 1303. His body was found with frightful injuries. Were these injuries self-inflicted, as some said, in a final ungovernable rage, or were they the work of some unknown assassin? No answer is possible;[38] but Philip the Fair and his ministers could hardly have won a more complete victory.[39]

III

These, then, are the events in the light of which *De regimine Christiano* is to be read. It is not possible to assign an exact date to the work's appearance; but the following considerations may be mentioned.

The treatise seems at several points to echo the Bull *Ausculta fili*;[40] which fact, if it is a fact, establishes December 5, 1301 as a *terminus a quo*. If we assume, as is customary, that Boniface made James of Viterbo an archbishop as a reward for the loyalty attested by the appearance of the treatise, then September 3, 1302 is our *terminus ad quem*. It is, however, also possible to make out a case for a later date. James's appointment as Archbishop of Benevento may well have been a token of papal thanks for *De regimine Christiano*; but, then again, *De regimine Christiano* may equally well have been a token of its author's thanks to the pope for his preferment. James was, after all, a teacher and scholar of high distinction, and we have no business to assume that it was not for his achievements in these fields that he was honoured. In fact, his letter of appointment does seem to suggest that the appointment was made in recognition of his intellectual attainments and other sterling qualities, and not in requital of any particular favour.[41] Moreover, four of the six chapters of Part One of *De regimine Christiano* form a commentary on the Nicene Creed's description of the Church as one,

---

38. See Holtzmann, *Wilhelm von Nogaret*, 228ff; Gelasio Gaetani, *Domus Caietaniana*, I, Pt. I (1927), 178ff. But see Boase, *op. cit.*, 351: "When they opened his tomb in 1605, the body, well preserved, showed no signs of violence". See also Bottagisio, *Bonifacio VIII* (1926), 393.

39. The French campaign to discredit Boniface, and hence to consolidate the position of the French throne in relation to the papacy, nonetheless continued long after his death. The posthumous trial of Boniface was never brought to a formal conclusion; but, in April 1311, Pope Clement V was induced to declare that Philip and his allies "were and are not guilty of malicious accusation, and that they acted out of an estimable, just and sincere zeal and from the fervour of their Catholic faith." (*Regestum Clementi papae* (1887), 414. See Boase, *op. cit.*, 355ff.)

40. Anyone who wishes to make a comparison will find a translation of key passages of *Ausculta fili* in B. Tierney (ed.), *The Crisis of Church and State, 1050-1300*, 185f. Some apparent echoes in *De regimine Christiano*, below, are: I,III, p.21, line 36; p.22, lines 36ff; II,IV, p.77, lines 31f; II,V, p.92, lines 15f; II,VIII, p.113, para.2.

41. *Reg.* 4740.

holy, catholic and apostolic; but these are also the opening words of the Bull *Unam sanctam*. If it is partly James's intention to offer, in effect, a commentary on *Unam sanctam*, then November 18, 1302 becomes our *terminus a quo*. Also, the allusions to the empire and to the emperor's coronation in Part Two, Chapters V and VIII[42] may have reference to Boniface's belated recognition of the imperial claim of Albert of Austria; in which case our *terminus a quo* is April 30, 1303. In view of the fact that the work begins with a dedication to Boniface VIII that we have no reason to regard as spurious, our absolute *terminus ad quem* is October 11, 1303: the date of Boniface's death. But it is not out of the question that *De regimine Christiano* could have been completed well within the period demarcated by April 30 and October 11, 1303. Against a date within this period, however, and within the broader period between September 3, 1302 and October 11, 1303, weighs the fact that, in his dedicatory letter and in the Prologue, James refers to himself, not as the Archbishop of Benevento or Naples, but as a teacher of theology: which seems to re-establish September 3, 1302 as our *terminus ad quem*.[43] Clearly, the evidence is in all directions flimsy, and we cannot be dogmatic on the point; but it is at least reasonable to conjecture that the treatise was written during the early spring and summer of 1302: some little time after the promulgation of *Ausculta fili*, but somewhat before James's appointment as Archbishop of Benevento.

A certain amount of internal evidence suggests that, as he worked, James had available to him a copy, or perhaps a draft, of Aegidius Romanus's *De ecclesiastica potestate*. James's choice (at II,VII[44]) of harness-making as an example of an art which is subordinated to a higher end, and his use in this connexion of the unusual term *ars frenifactiva*, mirrors the similar reference of Aegidius at *De ecclesiastica potestate* II,VI.[45] Although he does not dwell on it at any length, James is obviously familiar with the famous *dominium* theory which Aegidius develops in such detail - that is, with the theory that all temporal property is ultimately held of the Church and can be taken away from the sinner by the Church. His brief summary of this at II,VII[46] is very reminiscent in its language of Aegidius' various expositions of it. Again, similarities of wording in his discussion of canon law at II,VIII[47] suggest that this discussion is a close compression of the lengthy analysis offered at *De ecclesiastica potestate* III,V-VIII.[48] Evidence apart, and on the assumption that *De ecclesiastica potestate* was written, or at least

42. See pp. 84, 125f.
43. In the dedicatory letter, James refers to himself as *theologiae facultatis professor*. This could be read as meaning that he was still at the University of Paris when he wrote; but this would indicate a date before the outbreak of the second controversy, which does not seem at all likely.
44. See p. 102.
45. Ed. Dyson, 58, paras. 7f.
46. See p. 109.
47. See p. 118.
48. *Ed.cit.*, 164ff; and see p. 118, n.10, below.

drafted, before *De regimine Christiano*, it is certainly not improbable that James knew Aegidius's work. The two authors were senior members of the same religious order. They would undoubtedly have known one another during James's student days in Paris: it may be, indeed, that it was on Aegidius's recommendation that James succeeded him as regent-master in 1293. Also, *De regimine Christiano* differs significantly from *De ecclesiastica potestate* in content and argument. James deals with the *dominium* theory and with canon law only briefly, whereas Aegidius has little to say about the Donation of Constantine,[49] with which James deals in several places (see below). These differences perhaps indicate that James was intentionally avoiding mere repetition of what his older contemporary had said or was intending to say. Although their approaches differ in no small degree, however, the objective of both authors is the same: to demonstrate that the pope is the supreme judge of the world in spiritual and temporal matters alike, and that secular princes are in all respects subject to his judgment.

De regimine Christiano has always been somewhat overshadowed in the minds of historians by the much more elaborate and forceful work of Aegidius Romanus, and the manuscript tradition by which the former has come down to us is exiguous. Nonetheless, *De regimine Christiano* seems to have been highly thought of in its own day. As we have mentioned, it is at least not unlikely that James of Viterbo's appointment to the Metropolitan See of Benevento was a token of papal gratitude for the treatise. Also, if imitation is the sincerest form of flattery, it is significant that when, in about 1330, the Franciscan scholar Alvaro Pelayo sought to defend Pope John XXII against Louis IV of Bavaria and Marsilius of Padua, his own treatise (called *De planctu ecclesiae*) should have embodied an almost verbatim transcription of much of the text of *De regimine Christiano*.[50]

We may note in passing that, content aside, *De regimine Christiano* differs substantially from Aegidius's *De ecclesiastica potestate* in style. James of Viterbo's writing, though not without difficulties of its own, is largely free from the repetition and over-elaboration which Aegidius's exhibits. Also, *De regimine Christiano* is in general terms much more coherent in structure than is *De ecclesiastica potestate*. Moreover, James's work entirely lacks controversiality of tone: Professor Arquillière describes it as "écrit en un style exempt de passion et impersonnel".[51] No one who did not know it on

---

49. He mentions it only in passing at III,XI (*ed.cit.*, 197, para. 3) as part of a discussion of Hugh of Saint Victor's statement that "certain temporal things have been granted to churches by the pious devotion of the faithful."

50. *De planctu ecclesiae* is, incidentally, an enormous work. Book One contains 70 chapters and Book Two 93. The edition published in Venice in 1560 runs, *cum indice copiosissimo*, to over 650 quarto pages closely printed in double columns. Not suprisingly, perhaps, no modern critical edition exists. See C.H. McIlwain, *The Growth of Political Ideas in the West*, Ch. VI.

51. *Le plus ancien traité de l'Église*, 16.

other grounds would be able to infer simply from the text that the treatise was produced during an international crisis of major significance.

Apart from scripture and the standard scriptural glosses, James's chief literary sources are: St Augustine (chiefly *De civitate Dei*); St Bernard of Clairvaux's treatise *De consideratione*; the *Etymologiae* and *Sententiae* of Isidore of Seville; and the Pseudo-Dionysius. There are also references to St. Ambrose, Aristotle, Boethius, the Pseudo-Cyprian to whom is attributed the work called *De duodecim abusionibus saeculi*, Pseudo-Cyril of Alexandria, Chrysostom, Gregory the Great, Innocent III, Origen, and Hugh and Richard of Saint Victor. James never mentions Aquinas by name, but he is clearly very familiar with St Thomas's work, and especially with the treatise *De regimine principum*. His general intellectual position has been succinctly described as "a Thomistic Aristotelianism [adapted] to serve the papal claims to direct power over the secular state."[52]

The treatise has two parts. The first and shorter part begins with an analysis of the Church as a community in the light of Book One of Aristotle's *Politics*. Then comes the commentary on *unam sanctam catholicam et apostolicam Ecclesiam*. It is in Part Two that the main substance of James's political doctrine is to be found. It is inevitable that a work called forth so directly by contemporary events should bear some marks of hasty composition; and James's arguments are, indeed, inclined to be a little diffuse. Some of his best arguments come in the final chapter of Part Two, which is clearly a collection of afterthoughts. With some rearrangement in the interests of logical order, however, the argument of *De regimine Christiano* may be summarised in a few paragraphs.

The Church is one, holy, catholic and apostolic. (When he speaks of the Church in this way, of course, James intends to refer to the whole community of the faithful, lay and clerical alike, and not to the Church in any narrow or 'institutional' sense.) She is the most self-sufficent of all human communities, containing everything needful to both the corporeal and spiritual wellbeing of mankind. Being the most self-sufficient of all communities, she is therefore also the most perfect of all communities. The most perfect community must be ruled in the most perfect way; and the most perfect form of government, because the most natural form, is monarchy. The Church, therefore, is a monarchy, a *regnum*, a kingdom: Christ is her king. He is, of course, no longer present in person; but He appointed Peter to be His earthly Vicar. Peter and his successors therefore rule the Church as kings in Christ's stead, having no less power than Christ Himself had. The pope is king of the whole Christian world in actuality and, potentially, of the world of unbelievers also.

Christ is both God and man. Inasmuch as He is God, He has all power. Inasmuch as He is man, He has all power except the power to create something from nothing; neither, as man, can He create, as distinct from give effect to, a sacrament. All the power which Christ holds as man He has

---

52. Ewart Lewis, *Medieval Political Ideas*, I,182.

communicated to mankind. There are, therefore, three kinds of power in the world: the power to work miracles; priestly power; and royal power. The power to work miracles need be mentioned only in passing. It is given according to no principle that we can fathom: it has no necessary connection with either priestly or royal power; sometimes good men have it, but it is not unknown for wicked men to be able' to work miracles, as Christ's own words testify.[53] We come next to priestly power. This is the power to sanctify and to mediate between God and man: that is, to pray, to offer sacrifice and to administer the sacraments. Finally, royal power is, distinctively, the power of *jurisdictio*, of judgment: "the principal and special action of royal power", James says, "is to judge."[54]

At this point, James departs from what we may perhaps be permitted to call the 'normal' papalist stratagem. One would expect that he will now say that only the clergy have priestly power, that kings have royal power, that priestly power is superior to royal power, and that kings must therefore submit to priestly, and, above all, to papal, authority.[55] His analysis is, however, rather more complex than this (although he is not, in fact, always consistent in it).

It is, he says, certainly true that only ordained priests can administer the sacraments. In a broader sense, however, every individual is responsible for the spiritual quality of his own life, and therefore for offering to God the sacrifices of prayer and a contrite heart; and, in this sense, every individual is a priest whether he is in holy orders or not. In this limited sense, even laymen have some measure of priestly power.[56] Royal power, on the other hand, is specifically the power to judge; and there is here, James suggests, an important distinction to be made between two kinds or manifestations of royal power: royal power over temporal things (*potestas regia temporalis*) and royal power over spiritual things (*potestas regia spiritualis*). Ordinarily, royal power over temporal things is exercised by the king, in the obvious sense of ruling over the secular affairs of his kingdom. Royal power over spiritual things, on the other hand, is primarily the power to judge in matters of sin: it is the power exercised by the priest when, making use of the keys which Christ entrusted to Peter, he judges the penitent and pronounces him worthy or unworthy to enter the kingdom of Heaven. Royal power, therefore, understood as a power of judgment, is not, after all, the exclusive preserve of kings. Priests have it also. It is not customary for them to be called kings, and it would not be proper for them to bear a title with such connotations of pride; but priests are, nonetheless, kings in reality: kings, we might say, in disguise.

---

53. *Matt*. VII,22f.

54. II,IV, p.73.

55. This is more or less the line of argument pursued by Henry of Cremona in his *De potestate papae* (see Bibliography).

56. This idea, and the related idea that all men are in a sense kings, is probably derived from Aquinas, *De regimine principum* I,14. On this, see M. Wilks, *The Problem of Sovereignty*, 136, n.2, and M. Maccarone, *Vicarius Christi* (1952), 213f.

Priestly power considered merely as a sanctifying or sacrificial power is inferior to royal power over spiritual things. This is so because priestly power lacks the characteristically royal dimension of jurisdiction (although, in practice, the two powers are usually found conjoined in the same person: the priest's function would be severely restricted if he did not also have a power of judgment[57]). Royal power over spiritual things, however, is a form of jurisdiction which is superior to royal power over temporal things: the kind of royal power wielded by priests is superior to that wielded by kings in the ordinary sense of the word precisely because spiritual things are in their very nature superior to temporal things. Properly understood, indeed, the two kinds of royal power are not ultimately separate at all. They differ only in the sense that royal power over spiritual things is more comprehensive than royal power over temporal things. Royal power over spiritual things includes or encompasses royal power over temporal things, whereas royal power over temporal things only is simply an imperfect or incomplete royal power. He who wields spiritual royal power stands in relation to those who wield temporal royal power as an architect does in relation to stonemasons and carpenters, or as a cavalry commander does in relation to the harness-maker. The analogy is not an exact one, but the point of it is clear enough.

It looks as though, in developing this line of argument, James is trying to forestall an objection which we nowadays most readily associate with a treatise written more than twenty years after *De regimine Christiano*: the *Defensor pacis* of Marsilius of Padua.[58] The objection in question is that the power of the priest, being in its very nature spiritual, has no grip, as it were, on temporal things, and therefore no claim to govern the things of this world. Priests have to do only with the spiritual order, and the spiritual order has reference only to the next world, where the sinner will be punished by God. In the world of the present time, priests can teach and admonish, but they cannot coerce. James does not, of course, say that priestly power considered as the power of orders is in any normal sense inferior to royal power over temporal things. On the contrary: "Royal power over temporal things,…inasmuch as it is temporal, is inferior to and lesser in dignity than the priestly, which is spiritual."[59] He does, however say that it is by virtue, not of priestly power simply as such, but of the higher type of royal power which it wields, that ecclesiastical power is superior to secular kingship. Moreover, bishops hold royal power over spiritual things in a more perfect -

---

57. See II,IV, pp.76f and 78 for this point.
58. *Defensor pacis* has been edited twice, by C.W. Previté-Orton (1928) and R. Scholz (1932-33); there is an English translation by A. Gewirth (1956). The work was completed in 1324 at the University of Paris. Marsilius was forced to relinquish his post at the University and became a staunch ally of the emperor Louis IV of Bavaria against Pope John XXII. See C.K. Brampton, "Marsiglio of Padua: Life", *English Historical Review*, XXXVII (1922), 501ff; C.W. Previté-Orton, "Marsiglio of Padua: Doctrines", *English Historical Review*, XXXVIII (1923), 1ff.
59. II,IV p.81.

that is, in a more extended - form than do lower priests; and the pope holds it in the most perfect form of all. The pope is, so to speak, the king of kings. No one at all, anywhere in the Church Militant, is exempt from the jurisdiction of the pope; from his decision there is no appeal, because there is no one to whom any such appeal could be made.

> He is the one Supreme Priest, to whom all the faithful owe obedience as to the Lord Jesus Christ.
> He is the universal judge who judges all the faithful of whatever condition, dignity and station, and who can himself be judged by no one.[60]

There is, indeed, a sense in which secular princes can concern themselves with spiritual things; but they can do so only in a very restricted and marginal fashion, and only under the supervision of the spiritual power.[61] The pope, however, can exercise royal power over temporal things - can, that is, give judgment in temporal cases - whenever it is necessary to the salvation of the faithful to do so. And, since the pope is obviously the final judge of what is and is not necessary to the salvation of the faithful, the conclusion clearly follows that the pope may intervene in any temporal case whatsoever, subject to no judgment but his own. This is, of course, a re-statement of Innocent III's *ratione peccati* principle. Needless to say, the Supreme Pontiff does not always act in his own person; but he can, without consulting anyone else, direct any subordinate to do whatever he judges to be in the interests of the Church.

The fact that, when he chooses to assume it, the pope may exercise supreme jurisdiction even over temporal things does not, of course, make the secular prince redundant. Although he has ultimate charge of all the affairs of the world, the pope chooses usually to act through the secular prince as his intermediary, just as God, though He can work miracles when He chooses to do so, usually governs the world through the agency of secondary causes. For one thing (and this frequent motif of medieval political thought originates with the Pseudo-Dionysius[62]), it is in the interests of order and dignity that there should be a hierarchy of powers in the world, just as there is in the universe as a whole. Also, it would not be suitable for the pope to concern himself regularly and generally with matters which are base, unworthy or trivial. His task is to wield the spiritual sword and to leave the material sword to others who are, in the words of St Paul, "least esteemed in the Church."[63] (This famous 'two swords' imagery comes from St Bernard's treatise *De consideratione*, written as a manual of advice to his protégé Bernard of Pisa, who became Pope Eugenius III in 1145). Both swords belong to the pope, however: princes wield the material sword subject to his

---

60. II,V p.86.
61. See II,VIII, pp.120f.
62. See W. Ullmann, *A History of Political Thought: The Middle Ages*, 30f.
63. *I Cor.* VI,4.

command and guidance. They are to regard themselves as servants and auxiliaries, whose task it is to defend the Church under the direction of the Vicar of Christ. This subordination is shown by the fact that secular powers are required to pay tithes to the Church.

James also gives considerable attention to the important papalist claim that the words of *Romans* XIII,1 - "the powers that be are ordained of God" - mean that kings are in some sense created or instituted by the Church or through the Church's agency, and can be removed by the Church: using the word 'Church' here in the more specific or 'institutional' sense. From James's point of view, of course, it is important to rebut the common royalist contention that royal power is derived from God directly: that coronation services are no more than a sign of this, and not a bestowal of power in themselves, and that the king is therefore answerable to God alone, without any intervening accountability to ecclesiastical authority. Like Aegidius Romanus, he relies on the authority of Hugh of Saint Victor's statement that it is the task of the spiritual power to institute the earthly power and to judge it if it is not good. But there are difficulties. Certainly, coronation services modelled on the Old Testament example of Saul's anointing by Samuel are intended to make the point that God gives power to the king through the Church. But what of the fact that, in the Old Testament, kings existed before there was any spiritual power? And what of the fact that, to this day, unbelievers are governed by rulers who are plainly kings, but whose power is not in any sense derived from the Church?

In dealing with questions of this kind, James purports to avoid the extreme view of Aegidius Romanus, that all temporal power is illegitimate and unjust unless it is regenerated through spiritual institution. There is, he says, a middle way: although it is a middle way which turns out to have implications every bit as radical as Aegidius's theory. All power, he says, comes from God, in the sense that everything comes from God. Even the power of tyrants is ordained of God, to prove the righteous and punish the wicked. It is, of course, undeniable that we see cases of earthly power which have not come into being through the Church: either because, at the time of their institution, there was no Church, or because the holders of such power have achieved it in parts of the earth where the Church has no influence. But these manifestations of political power are not, strictly speaking, wicked. They are natural: they arise from that natural inclination to society which mankind characteristically exhibits. Like all merely natural things, however, such power is imperfect. As such, it is tolerable, but it is not fully legitimate, and the Church could, if she chose, take such power away from those who hold it "because of their unbelief":[64] not specifically because they make bad use of their power, but simply because they are outside the community of believers. But, as St Thomas has said, the function of grace is not to abolish nature, but to perfect it:[65] James alludes

---

64. II,X, p.141.
65. *Summa theol.* I,q.1,a.8.

to this dictum several times, without attribution. Power in its perfected form, then - that is, in its fully legitimate form - is natural power perfected by grace: is, in practice, power validated or instituted by the Church. And the clear message is that what the Church can bestow, she can also withdraw:

> For the spiritual power has the task of judging the temporal power because it can and must correct and guide it, punish it, and impose on it a penalty not only spiritual, but temporal also, in the event of its sin and transgression, and proceed even to the point of deposing it if the quality of its fault so requires.[66]

All power in the full and perfect sense, then, comes through the Church, and all temporal power is removable by the Church. But James is aware that a dangerous complication is here presented by the famous *Donatio* or *Constitutum Constantini*: the Donation of Constantine.[67] This document, universally believed in the thirteenth century to be genuine - it was to be exposed as a forgery in the fifteenth century, by Nicholas of Cusa and Lorenzo Valla - probably originated in the papal chancery in about 755, in rather discreditable circumstances which we may briefly summarise.

By the middle of the eighth century, an anomalous state of affairs had for some time prevailed in the Kingdom of the Franks. The once vigorous Merovingian kings were now no more than ineffectual invalids, and royal power was wielded *de facto* by an official called the Mayor of the Palace. In 754, an approach was made to Pope Zachary by Pepin, Mayor of the Palace of the Merovingian king Childeric III. Pepin promised to defend the papacy against the grave threat of invasion posed by the Lombard king Aistulf if the Pope would declare Childeric deposed and proclaim Pepin king in his stead. This was done, and the last of the *rois fainéants* was discreetly packed off to a monastery. What right, however, has the pope to get rid of one king in favour of another? Some means of authorising such an act was necessary, and the Donation of Constantine was duly conjured into existence. Based on an earlier document called *Legenda Sancti Silvestri*,[68] the Donation apparently records how the Emperor Constantine, in gratitude for the gift of baptism and his miraculous deliverance from leprosy, gave to Pope Sylvester I "our palace,...our city of Rome, and all the provinces,

---

66. II,VII, p.104.

67. For the text of the Donation, see C.B. Coleman, *Constantine the Great and Christianity* (1914); C. Mirbt, *Quellen zur Geschichte des Papsttums* (1924). See also G. Lähr, *Die Konstantinische Schenkung in der abendländischen Literatur* (1926); W. Ullmann, *The Growth of Papal Government in the Middle Ages* (1962). The oldest surviving manuscript of the Donation, now in Paris (Bib. Nat., MS Lat. 2777), is of eighth century provenance. See S. Williams, "The Oldest Text of the *Constitutum Constantini*", *Traditio*, XX (1964), 448ff.

68. Ed. B. Mombrizio, *Sanctuarium seu vitae sanctorum* (1910), II, 508ff. See W. Levison, "Konstantinische Schenkung und Silvester-legende", *Miscellanea F. Ehrle* (1924), II, 181ff.

places and cities of Italy and the regions of the West, leaving them to the authority and governance whether of himself or his successors; and...we decree and grant that they shall...ever remain in the lawful possession of the holy Roman Church." Constantine has, in short, conferred imperial power on the pope, who therefore may in turn bestow it on lesser monarchs or remove it from them, as he sees fit.

It will be seen readily enough that, up to a point, the Donation of Constantine has its uses. By the time of Innocent III, however, as papal power came to be defined in terms of the pope's rôle as Vicar of Christ rather than heir of Constantine, the Donation had become something of an embarrassment. For, of course, the premiss that the pope owes his temporal power to the gift of a secular prince is exactly the opposite of what such papalist writers as James of Viterbo and Aegidius Romanus wish to assert. How, therefore, can the Donation of Constantine be accommodated with the theory of papal power which it is now wished to advance? This is a problem which Aegidius Romanus largely sidesteps. James flirts briefly with the idea that Constantine did not, in fact, give the empire to Sylvester after all, because it was never really his to give. The suggestion is not without promise, but not without snags, either: James does not rely on it, but favours a different view. When Constantine granted the empire to the pope, James argues, he in fact merely confirmed or proclaimed by means of human law what the pope possesses anyway under divine law; he showed his own deference and submission to the pope's authority; and he bestowed upon the papacy the power to do in fact what it could in any case do as of right - in short, he added power to the pope's authority: but he did not actually give the pope anything *de iure*, for, in that sense, the pope already had everything.

This attempt to make the Donation bear a construction other than the obvious one is not a success. We have no right to assume that it is a cynical or dishonourable attempt, but it has to be admitted that James's account of Constantine's intentions does not look very convincing when measured against Constantine's supposed actual words. Also, one cannot wholly escape the impression that James himself is here conscious of being on poor ground. In particular, his analysis of Augustine's dictum that kingdoms without justice are nothing but great bands of robbers[69] is rather weak: perhaps, it may be thought, self-consciously so. This is, however, one of only very few points in the treatise taken as a whole where James's argument falters through lack of conviction or coherence.

Taken as a whole, indeed, and having regard to the circumstances of haste and dudgeon in which it was written, we may fairly conclude that *De regimine Christiano* is a work of much subtlety and sophistication. It cannot really be called "one of the most impressive writings of the Middle Ages";[70] but it is interesting to wonder what James might have made of his material

---

69. II,X, pp.151ff.
70. Ewart Lewis, *loc.cit.*.

and arguments had he been able to devote more time to composition and revision. The treatise is likely to be found superficially less imposing as a piece of controversial writing than Aegidius Romanus's *De ecclesiastica potestate*: less imposing, that is, in terms of its scope and force and immediate impact. On a less superficial level of assessment, however, *De regimine Christiano* is in certain respects more telling and more skilful in its execution than its more celebrated companion. This is so precisely because James habitually takes what he calls "a middle way which seems to be more reasonable."[71] By this more reasonable and inoffensive way, he contrives, with mild logical steps, quietly to formulate a theory of papal monarchy which is every bit as imposing and ambitious as that of Aegidius, while being systematically less arrant and provocative. In this sense, James of Viterbo's work has the curious and beguiling property of combining moderation and extremism. For this, surely, he deserves credit.

We must note, however, that the arguments of James of Viterbo and Aegidius Romanus were, in a political sense, the papacy's last hurrah. Subsequent authors - notably Agostino Trionfo[72] and Alvaro Pelayo (*De planctu ecclesiae*) - went as far in their attempt to exalt the papacy's political rôle; but, as Professor McIlwain has remarked, they went no further, because it is not possible to go further.[73] The papal publicists of Boniface VIII's pontificate, unanswerable, it may be thought, on their own ground, were nonetheless fighting a rearguard action. To all intents and purposes, Boniface's death marks the end of the medieval papacy's vision of its own world-wide political authority. The struggles of 1296-1303 were, indeed, not so much a personal contest between Boniface VIII and Philip the Fair as a collison of two incompatible principles: on the one hand, the ideal, which had largely animated papal diplomacy since the time of Gregory VII, of a universal papal monarchy transcending territorial boundaries and uniting the Christian world in the peaceful and harmonious community of Christendom; and, on the other, the new conception, so rapidly supplanting older feudal loyalties, of the consolidated nation state, brooking no interference from without and acknowledging no sovereign but its king. The clash of these two principles personified in Boniface and Philip inflicted upon the vigour and credibility of the papacy a wound from which it was never fully to recover - which was, indeed, exacerbated by the calamities of the next hundred years: the "Babylonish captivity" of the popes at Avignon from

---

71. II,VII,p.103.

72. *Summa de ecclesiastica potestate* (1326); *Tractatus brevis de duplici potestate praelatum et laicorum*, ed. R. Scholz, *Die Publizistik*, 486ff. See M.J. Wilks, *The Problem of Sovereignty in the Later Middle Ages*. R.P. Russell's comment at NCE, I,1058 that *Summa de ecclesiastica potestate* is "reputed to be the earliest work of its kind on the Roman Pontiff" is presumably a reference to form rather than content. If not, it is difficult to see what he can mean. See also J. Rivière, "Une Première 'Somme' du pouvoir pontifical: Le Pape chez Augustin d'Ancone", *Revue sciences religieuses*, XVIII (1938), 149ff.

73. McIlwain, *op.cit.*,249.

1305 to 1377, and the Great Schism of 1378 to 1417. One final phase remained to be played out: the struggle which ensued between Pope John XXII and the emperor Louis IV after the disputed election of 1314.[74] For our purposes, however, it suffices to remark that this conflict served only to accelerate the political enfeeblement of the papacy and, above all, to refine the arguments of its opponents.[75] In the final analysis, it may be said that, "So far as any single event can mark the end of an era, the tragedy of Anagni symbolized the close of a period in papal history which had opened with an emperor standing barefoot before the gates of Canossa."[76]

oOo

74. C. Müller, *Der Kampf Ludwigs des Baiern mit der römischen Kurie* (1879-80); H.S. Offler, "Empire and Papacy: the Last Struggle", *Transactions of the Royal Historical Society*, V, 6 (1956), 21ff.

75. Not the least important consequence of this "last struggle" was the emergence of by far the two ablest opponents of papal absolutism: Marsilius of Padua (*Defensor pacis* (see n. 58, above); *Oeuvres mineures*, edd. and French translation by C. Jeudy and J. Quillet (1979)) and William of Ockham (*Opera politica*: Vol I edd. J.G. Sikes, H.S. Offler and R.F. Bennett (*ed. altera* (1974), H.S. Offler); Vol II edd. J.G. Sikes and H.S. Offler; Vols. III & IV ed. H.S. Offler (1940-   ). See also H.S. Offler, "The 'Influence' of Ockham's Political Thinking: The First Century", *Die Gegenwart Ockhams*, edd. W. Vossenkuhl and R. Schönberger (1990), 338ff. Much interesting and hitherto unavailable textological information appears in George Knysh, *Ockham Perspectives* (1994).

76. W.K. Ferguson, *Europe in Transition, 1300-1500*, 219.

PART ONE

ON THE GLORY OF THE ECCLESIASTICAL KINGDOM

The author's epistle to the lord Pope Boniface VIII

To the lord Boniface, most holy and reverend father in Christ, by divine providence Supreme Pontiff of the sacred and universal Church: Brother James of Viterbo, of the Order of Hermits of Saint Augustine, professor in the faculty of theology, though unworthy, kisses his blessed feet with all devotion, obedience and reverence.

Filial devotion to Holy Mother Church and to the Apostolic See over which you, the consecrated prince of the shepherds and kings of the earth, preside by the disposition of the Most High, has led me to undertake the following short work on Christian government. I have deemed it worthy to be offered to no one more than the Holy Father who, with wisdom and ardour, keeps watch over the liberty of the ecclesiastical government and the exaltation of catholic truth. If anything in it should prove acceptable, may he, by the fulness of the authority and the righteousness of the noble judgment conferred upon him from on high, graciously give approval, attributing it to God, the supreme author. And if there should be anything in it insufficient or worthy of blame, let him generously complete and amend it, with kindly indulgence towards my imperfection.

1

HERE BEGINS A SHORT WORK ON CHRISTIAN GOVERNMENT, CONTAINING TWO BOOKS

The prologue of the work, in which is described the matter or intention of the work and the cause in which the work has been undertaken

"They shall speak of the glory of Thy kingdom and tell of Thy power, so that Thy power and the glory of the majesty of Thy kingdom may be made known to the sons of men."[1]

The confession of our holy faith consists principally in two things: namely, in Christ the king and head, and in the Church, His kingdom and body. So it is that the subject-matter of the whole of sacred scripture, the first principle of which is faith, is taken by catholic commentators to be the whole Christ: that is, head and members. But while every true believer must rightly confess these two things for his own salvation, the teachers of the Church must also preach them for the saving instruction of others. However, because there are many things concerning Christ and the Church which must be truly believed and spoken, ecclesiastical teachers do not profess always to deal with all of them. Rather, they undertake to expound and treat of some matters specifically, when particular causes arise. And it is fitting at this time, and not without reasonable cause, for those who teach sacred doctrine to speak especially of the glory of the ecclesiastical kingdom and of the power of Christ the king which Christ Himself also delivered and bequeathed by communicating it to His vicar: that is, to Peter and, in him, to each of his successors.[2] For, as Isidore attests, when dissension appears, then must the assertion of truth be made manifest more clearly.[3] And, foreseeing the elucidation of these things which would be accomplished by the teachers of the Church, and directing his speech to Christ, and hence to His vicar, the psalmist says that, in due time, the teachers whom He has willed to be in the Church "shall speak of the glory of Thy kingdom", that is, of the Christian multitude and the ecclesiastical community. And these

---

1. *Psalm.* CXLIV,11f.
2. Cf. *Matt.* XVI,18f.
3. *Sententiarum libri tres* I,XVI,5 (PL 83,572).

2

same teachers shall "tell of Thy power," by which He guides, governs and rules: that is, by declaring it to others and resisting those who speak against it, "so that Thy power and the glory of the majesty of Thy kingdom may be made known to the sons of men", and especially to those of whom the same psalmist says, "for truths fail from amongst the children of men";[4] to whom he also adverts elsewhere, saying: "Children of men, how long will you be dull of heart? How long will you love vanity and seek after falsehood?"[5] For truth indeed fails amongst these; vanity is loved and falsehood sought by their idle speech; the glory of the holy Apostolic See over which the Vicar of Christ presides for the guidance of the universal Church is hidden: its excellence is oppressed and its power diminished. And although the luminaries of this world - that is, those who first taught the holy divine law - have not neglected the glory of the Church and the power of Christ, but have brought these things into the light by their assertions of truth, the teachers of our own time, however far removed from the perfection of their forebears, must themselves not neglect the same doctrines. This is especially so because of those persons who do not fully grasp the words of those who have borne witness to the truth, or who understand them less correctly, or who, disordered in will, strive to pervert them and wrench them from their sense. Nor is it idle that this should be done by many; for, as the great teacher Augustine says at *De Trinitate* I: "It is to advantage that many books, differing in style but not differing in faith, should be written even on the same questions by many authors, so that the subject-matter may reach many persons, some in this way and some in that."[6] I also, then, being a member of the fraternity of doctors of theology in number even if not in merit - for I have little wisdom and skill in speech - and leaning upon His help and grace, Who is the giver of speech and wisdom, have undertaken, with apprehension and modesty, some few and partial remarks concerning the matters just described, derived from the truth-bearing founts of scripture and assembled in orderly fashion within one convenient short work. In it, the glory of the ecclesiastical kingdom will be discussed first, and then the power of Christ the king and of His vicar, so that an orderly progression may be made from members to head and from lower to higher, according to the manner natural to the human intellect.

---

4. *Psalm.* XI,2.
5. *Psalm.* IV,3.
6. *De Trin.* I,III,5 (CC L,33).

That the Church is aptly and properly called a kingdom; and why and in what way

First, then, we must consider that the Church is most rightly, truly and aptly called a kingdom. Now the Church is a kind of community, because she is a congregation or association or convocation of many believers. For the community of men, though it may take many forms, is nonetheless chiefly divided into three kinds, as the blessed Augustine suggests at *De civitate Dei* XIX: that is, into the household, the city and the kingdom.[1] And these three names designate communities of men; for although the word 'house' [*domus*] may sometimes designate the dwelling-place of one family, just as 'town' may designate that of a whole populace and 'the world' that of the entire human race, as Isidore says at *Etymologiae* XV,[2] nonetheless, as the same author says at Book IX,[3] it is the whole family itself - which originates with two people, namely, a man and his wife, but also includes the children and servants - which is called a household [*domus*]. So too, although from time to time the word 'city' may be used to mean the dwelling-place of many men, it is nonetheless the multitude of men itself which is properly called a city. Hence Isidore, at *Etymologiae* XV, says that a city is a multitude of men united by the bond of society. And he adds that it is not the stones which are called a city, but the inhabitants.[4] Also, the blessed Augustine, at *De civitate Dei* I, says that a city is a concordant multitude of men;[5] and the blessed Gregory, at *Moralia* XVI, says that 'cities' [*civitates*] are so called from the fact that peoples dwell together [*conviventibus*] in them.[6] Again, though an area of territory and a collection of many towns may sometimes be called a kingdom, a kingdom properly so called is nonetheless an association of peoples and races: so named from the one who

---

1. E.g. *De civ. Dei* XIX,7; 13 (CC XLVIII,671; 679).
2. *Etym.* XV,III,1 (PL 82,541).
3. *Etym.* IX,IV,1ff (PL 82,348f).
4. *Etym.* XV,II,1 (PL 82,536).
5. *De civ. Dei* I,15 (CC XLVII,17).
6. *Moralia* XVI,LV,68 (PL 75,1153).

governs the multitude, that is, from the king; for, as Isidore says at *Etymologiae* IX, the word 'kingdom' is derived from 'kings'[7].

There exist amongst men, therefore, the three kinds of community just named: that is, the household, the city and the kingdom. If it should seem that there are other, intermediate, forms of these - for instance, a village community or a country estate or something of the kind - these are to be reduced to the foregoing types. Hence, Isidore says at *Etymologiae* XV that societies are of three kinds: namely, families, towns and peoples.[8] Now the setting up of these communities or societies has come about through the natural inclination of mankind itself, as the Philosopher proves at *Politics* I.[9] For man is by nature a social animal, and lives in multitudes; and this fact is due to natural necessity, because one man cannot live adequately by himself, but needs another's help. Hence also man has the gift of speech, with which he can explain his thoughts to another man and, by this means, communicate and live together with others more beneficially. Thus, because it is natural for men to live in society, there is therefore a natural inclination within men towards the communities named above: in a certain order, however; because the household comes first, then the city, and then again the kingdom.

And these three communities or societies are so ordered in relation to one another that one exceeds another both in multitude and in perfection. In multitude, indeed, because the city contains more men than the household, and the kingdom more than the city. And it follows from this that one also exceeds another in the extent of its territory, for many people need a greater area of land than do few: to dwell on, and for the cultivation of necessary food, and for the other things advantageous to human life which are extracted from the ground, and for the pasturing of the animals who serve the life of mankind. And from the fact that one exceeds another in multitude, it follows that one also exceeds another in perfection. For that community is the more perfect which contains the more men; and so the city is more perfect than the household and the kingdom than the city. For that community is the more perfect which is directed towards the greater good, and a good is greater in proportion as it is more common; and so because, in the city, the good of more people is sought than in the household, and in the kingdom the good of more than in the city, the city is therefore more perfect than the household and the kingdom is more perfect than the city.

Furthermore, the good which is aimed at in any kind of community is a sufficient provision for this life. Every community is instituted for the sake of this good, for one man by himself cannot provide himself with a proper livelihood without the help of other men; and so it is said at *Ecclesiastes* IV: "It is better that two should be together than one; for they have a good

---

7. *Etym.* IX,III,1 (PL 82,341); IX,III,18 (PL 82,344).
8. See n.2, above.
9. *Politics* I,1 (1252*a*ff).

5

reward for their labour."[10]   For the greater the extent to which many men are united with one another, the more able are they to provide for themselves the means of life by mutual aid.   And so a sufficiency of life is more easily found in a city than in a household, and more so in a kingdom than in a city.   Thus, the city is more perfect than the household and the kingdom than the city.   And because that which is prior in perfection is posterior in generation and time, the community of the household is therefore prior in generation and time to the community of the city, and the latter is prior to the community of the kingdom.   Also, of these communities, that which is the more imperfect is a part of the more perfect and is contained by it: the household is a part of the city, and the city is a part of the kingdom.   And, because the good of a part exists for the sake of the good of the whole, the more imperfect is therefore directed towards the more perfect as towards an end.   Hence the blessed Augustine, at *De civitate Dei* XIX, says: "Since the household ought to be the beginning or an element of the city, and every beginning has reference to some end of its own kind, and every part to the whole of which it is a part, it follows clearly enough that domestic peace has reference to civic peace."[11]   And because those things which are directed towards an end receive their measure from that end, the blessed Augustine therefore draws a further conclusion, saying: "And so it is that the head of a household ought to derive his precepts from the city's law, and so govern his household in such a way as to bring it into accord with the city's peace."[12]

Moreover, because of the way in which these communities are ordered, one may indeed take the name of another, with a qualification denoting defect or excess.   For example, the household is a kind of small city, and the city is a kind of large household;   so also the kingdom is a kind of large city, and the city a kind of small kingdom.   Hence, in ancient times, single cities had kings, and for this reason were called kingdoms.   Nor is it strange that even a single man, who is an element of the city in the way that a letter is of a text, as Augustine says at *De civitate Dei* IV,[13] should be called a little world, and that the world itself should be called a kind of great household.   But a more precise and full discussion of these three kinds of community belongs to another place.

However, the few remarks briefly set forth above have been made for the sake of the ecclesiastical community;   and of this we now intend to treat. For whenever the Church is called a kingdom she is also, by the same token, a kind of household and a kind of city;   although she is not a community of nature, but of grace, as her name itself suggests.   For she is called *ecclesia*, that is, 'called together', because she is called and brought together by God through grace.[14]

---

10. *Eccl.* IV,9.
11. *De civ. Dei* XIX,16 (CC XLVIII,683).
12. Ibid..
13. *De civ. Dei* IV,3 (CC XLVII,100).
14. Cf. Isidore, *Etym.* VIII,I,1 (PL 82,293).

And that the Church can be called by the names of the communities given above can be shown by the testimony of scripture. That she may be called a household is clear from the psalm where it is said of her: "I have loved, O Lord, the beauty of Thy house."[15] And again: "He maketh men of one manner to dwell in a house."[16] And then, at *I Timothy*: "That thou mayest know how thou oughtest to behave thyself in the house of God, which is the Church of the Living God."[17] And that she may be called a city is clear from the psalm where it is said to the Church: "Glorious things are said of thee, O City of God."[18] And the citizens of this city are the individual believers. This is a city founded upon a mountain, that is, upon Christ, or upon great justice.

And that the Church may be called a kingdom is made clear by the Apostle at *I Corinthians* XV. Here, speaking of Christ, he says: "Then cometh the end, when He shall have delivered up the kingdom to God and the Father."[19] As the Gloss on this passage says: "His faithful people, whom He has redeemed with His blood, are here called His kingdom, Whose kingdom is also the whole of creation."[20] But the kingdom of Christ is said to be the whole of creation in one sense, and the Church in another. For it is with respect to His divine power that the kingdom of Christ is said to be the whole of creation, whereas the Church is called the kingdom of Christ with respect to her possession of the faith which she has from Him, and through which He reigns over the faithful themselves. And although the Church may rightly be called by these three names designating the kinds of community, she is nonetheless more properly called a kingdom: partly because the Church contains a great multitude gathered in from many peoples and nations, and is spread and extended throughout the whole world; partly

---

15. *Psalm*. XXV,8.
16. *Psalm*. LXVII,7.
17. *I Tim*. III,15.
18. *Psalm*. LXXXVI,3; and see vs.1.
19. *I Cor*. XV,24.
20. Peter Lombard, *Collectanea in omnes de Pauli Apostoli epistolas*, PL 191,1679.

(i) In his numerous references to 'the Gloss', James usually has in mind one of the following:

(a) The *Glossa ordinaria* traditionally, but incorrectly, attributed to Walafrid Strabo and printed at PL 113 and 114;

(b) The *Glossa interlinearis* (6 vols., Antwerp, 1634);

(c) The *Collectanea* of Peter Lombard (PL 191 and 192);

(d) The *expositio continua* of St Thomas Aquinas on the four Gospels, usually called the *Catena aurea* (*Opera omnia*, Parma, 1852-73, vols. XI and XII).

(ii) On some few occasions, James makes reference to a scriptural gloss which cannot now be identified; or which, at any rate, I have not managed to identify.

(iii) His quotations from the glosses - and from scriptural and other sources - are frequently very inaccurate. Indeed, they are often more nearly paraphrases than quotations. This is no doubt largely due to the fact that he is quoting from memory; although he now and then introduces a nuance which makes the quotation suit the argument in support of which he has given it more closely than it otherwise would.

7

because all things necessary to the health and spiritual life of mankind are found in the ecclesiastical community; partly because she was founded for the common good of all mankind; and partly because, in the likeness of a kingdom, she contains within herself many congregations, mutually related in an ascending scale: for example, provinces, dioceses, parishes and colleges.

And this ecclesiastical kingdom is called the kingdom of Christ because He Himself is the founder and ruler of this kingdom and because He Himself has purchased it with His blood. And it is called the kingdom of Christ both inasmuch as He is God and inasmuch as He is man; and so the Apostle, speaking of the sinner at *Ephesians* V, says that "he hath no inheritance in the kingdom of Christ and of God",[21] that is, of the Son and of the Father; or of God, that is, of the Trinity, which is one God, and of Christ as man. (The kingdom of God is, however, also understood in other ways in sacred eloquence. For the kingdom of God is sometimes said to be Christ Himself, as at *Luke* XVII: "The kingdom of God is within you";[22] and sometimes holy scripture, according to *Matthew* XXI: "The kingdom of God shall be taken from you and given to another nation bringing forth the fruit thereof."[23]) And just as the Church is called the kingdom of Christ, so can she be truly called the kingdom of His vicar, that is, of the Supreme Pontiff: who, as will appear below, is truly called, and is, a king, and of a kingdom none other than the Church. Moreover, the Church herself is called the kingdom of Heaven because she orders and directs all men towards the heavenly goods which are sought in her as towards an end.

But the kingdom of the Church is differentiated. For one part of it lives by faith, being as yet a pilgrim on earth. And this part is called the Church Militant; for "the life of man upon earth is warfare."[24] And another part of it, already with God and seeing and enjoying Him, rejoices in Heaven; and this part is called the Church Triumphant, because of the subjection of all who oppose it.[25] One of these parts is temporal, the other eternal; the one lives in hope, the other in fulfilment; the one walks by faith, the other beholds God face to face; the one thirsts after God, the other attains Him; the one endures tribulations and perils, the other is secure in perfect peace; the one is cast into the depths, the other is raised up on high. And so the blessed Augustine, at *Confessiones* XIII, says that the one is signified by the waters that are beneath the firmament and the other by the waters that are above the firmament; for the waters are the peoples, and the firmament dividing the two signifies holy scripture.[26]

Moreover, because of this differentiation of the ecclesiastical kingdom, the expressions 'kingdom of Heaven' or 'kingdom of God' sometimes stand for

---

21. *Eph.* V,5.
22. *Luc.* XVII,21.
23. *Matt.* XXI,43.
24. *Job* VII,1.
25. Cf. *De civ. Dei* XIX,12 (CC XLVIII,675).
26. *Confess.* XIII,3ff (CC XXVII,243ff).

the Church of the present time, which strives on earth, as at *Matthew* XIII: "Every scribe instructed in the kingdom of Heaven is like to a man that is a householder";[27] and, in the same chapter: "The Son of Man shall send His angels, and they shall gather out of His kingdom all things that offend."[28] Elsewhere, however, they stand for the Church to come, triumphant in Heaven, as at *Matthew* XXV: "Come, ye blessed of my Father, inherit the kingdom prepared for you."[29] These are not two kingdoms, however, but one kingdom; because both parts have the one king, namely Christ, Who reigns in both, although in different ways. For in the Church of the pilgrims He reigns through faith, whereas in the Church of the blessed He does so through clear vision. This kingdom is one, therefore, by reason of its end and first principle, namely, unity; but it is divided by a difference of conditions. And this kingdom contains not only those men who are of the elect, but also all the holy angels; for there is one city, and one kingdom of God, composed of saints, angels and men, as Augustine says at *De civitate Dei* X.[30] Over against this kingdom of God stands the kingdom of this world, which is called Earthly because it appoints earthly goods as its end. This is also called the kingdom of the Devil, because the Devil reigns in it. "For he is king over all the children of pride", as is said in *Job*;[31] for he reigns over them through malice, just as Christ reigns over the just through grace. And this kingdom of the Devil contains wicked men and the wicked angels. But these two kingdoms differ in many ways. Hence the blessed Augustine, speaking of these kingdoms under the name of cities at *De civitate Dei* V, says: "These two cities are as distant from one another as Heaven is distant from the earth, as eternal life is from temporal joy, as solid glory from empty praise, as the fellowship of the angels from the society of mortal men, or as the light of the sun and moon from the light of Him Who made the sun and moon."[32] And at Book XIV he says that they differ as life according to the flesh differs from life according to the spirit, and as pride differs from humility.[33] Also, he says in the same book that "the two cities have been created by two loves: the earthly by self-love extending even to contempt of God, and the heavenly by love of God extending to contempt of self."[34] He also touches upon many other differences between these cities or kingdoms.

But these two kingdoms, insofar as they consist of men, are mixed together in this life; for the good are mingled with the wicked and the wicked with the good. Both make use of temporal goods in the same way, and are equally afflicted by evils until, at the last judgment, they will be separated

---

27. *Matt.* XIII,52.
28. *Matt.* XIII,41.
29. *Matt.* XXV,34.
30. *De civ. Dei* X,7 (CC XLVII,279f).
31. *Job* XLI,25.
32. *De civ. Dei* V,17 (CC XLVII,150).
33. *De civ. Dei* XIV,1 (CC XLVIII,414).
34. *De civ. Dei* XIV,28 (CC XLVIII,451).

and, as Augustine says at *De civitate Dei* XVIII, each will receive his end, to which there is no end.[35] For upon the Church's threshing-floor there is grain mixed with chaff, until Christ, the winnower of the threshing-floor, shall come and separate the wheat from the chaff: that is, the elect from the reprobate, the righteous from the perverse.[36] And this is a distinction represented by the wise and foolish maidens,[37] by the good and bad fish caught in the same net,[38] and by the vessels of honour and the vessels of shame.[39] And, because of this mingling, there are not a few who seem to belong to the kingdom of Christ because they are under the Church in number, who will be excluded from His kingdom at the end because they are not under the Church in merit. And within each city or kingdom, common use is made of those things which are necessary to this life; but each has its own very different end in making use of them, as Augustine says at *De civitate Dei* XIX.[40] And each kingdom has different laws of religion; and for this reason the kingdom of Christ is at odds with the Earthly kingdom and often endures anger and hatred and the assaults of persecution.

These two kingdoms began and are signified in Abel and Cain,[41] and in the two sons of Abraham.[42] Indeed, from the beginning of the human race there have always been men belonging to each kingdom, and the whole human race is contained within these two kingdoms; for each man necessarily belongs to one or other of them. And this distinction can be inferred from the distinction of light from darkness made at the beginning of the world.[43] Also, these two cities are indicated by the two cities of Jerusalem and Babylon. For Jerusalem, which means 'vision of peace', designates the kingdom of Christ, whereas Babylon, which is interpreted as 'confusion', implies the kingdom of the Devil.[44] And many more things might be said of these two kingdoms and their differentiation. What we have now said, however, is enough for what we intended to show at the outset: that is, that the Church is called a kingdom, and that she is the kingdom of God and Christ. And this will appear more fully below, when we come to treat of Christ's royal power.

---

35. *De civ. Dei* XVIII,54 (CC XLVIII,656).
36. Cf. *Matt.* III,12; *Luc.* III,17.
37. *Matt.* XXV,1ff.
38. *Matt.* XIII,47ff.
39. *II Tim.* II,20f.
40. *De civ. Dei* XIX,17 (CC XLVIII,684f).
41. Cf. *De civ. Dei* XV,1 (CC XLVIII,453).
42. Cf. *De civ. Dei* XV,2 (CC XLVIII,454f).
43. Cf. *Gen.* I,4.
44. Isidore, *Etym.* VIII,I,5f (PL 82,295); XV,I,4 (PL 82,527).

II

That the kingdom of the Church is orthodox, that is, rightly glorious; and in what its glory resides and consists

Now the kingdom of the Church is called orthodox, that is, rightly glorious;[1] and David touches upon its glory when he says: "Glorious things are said of thee, O City of God";[2] which can be understood equally of the Church Militant and Triumphant. Again, in the final chapter of Isaiah, it is said concerning Jerusalem, which prefigures the Church, that "you may flow with delights from the abundance of her glory."[3] And the Church is called glorious because of the good things which she possesses: a fitting glory, that is, known of many; for to be glorious is to be known clearly and with praise.[4] But while the Church may be called a kingdom, as is clear from what we have already said, we must consider what are the conditions, and how many they are, by reason of which a kingdom is called glorious, so that, when these have been found specifically in the ecclesiastical community, the kingdom of the Church may be called glorious with good reason: just as, in the authority cited above, the prophet speaks of "the glory of the majesty of Thy kingdom", that is, its great glory.[5]

For our present purposes, then, there are ten conditions which make a kingdom glorious.

The first condition is that it be rightly founded; and this is the case when dominion over the kingdom is achieved neither by violence nor fraud nor in any other unworthy fashion, but by legitimate authority: as came to pass in the kingdom of the Israelites, as we clearly read. And this condition is found in the ecclesiastical kingdom; for it was founded by God, in Whose hand are all laws and all powers. And although all kingdoms are founded by

---

1. Cf. Isidore, *Etym.* VII,XIV,5 (PL 82,294).

2. *Psalm.* LXXXVI,3.

3. *Isa.* LXVI,11.

4. Cf. Augustine, *Contra Maximinum* II,13 (PL 42,770); Aquinas, *Summa theol.* IaIIae,q.2,a.3.

5. Not, as the text seems to suggest, Isaiah, but *Psalm.* CXLIV,11, quoted at the beginning of the prologue.

11

divine providence, the kingdom of the Church nonetheless comes more especially and immediately from God: in the same way that all men exist under God's providence and power, but especially the just, in whom God is said to dwell through grace, and who are governed and protected by His special care; and, for this reason, they are specifically said to be in the hand of God.[6] Truly, therefore, the kingdom of the Church is glorious because its founder and ruler is God.

The second condition by which a kingdom is made glorious is antiquity; for the fact that it has long endured conduces to the repute and nobility of a kingdom. For so do we call those men noble and glorious whose forefathers were the rich and mighty men of old. We can observe this condition in the noble kingdom of the Assyrians, which was most ancient and, for that reason, much praised.[7] And this condition is found in the ecclesiastical kingdom, which, from the very beginning of the world, has encompassed the holy angels and the men who worship God.

The third condition which renders a kingdom glorious is that it be ordered; for multitude without order is confusion. Now the order of a kingdom consists in this: namely, that there are different ranks of men in it - different conditions, and such diverse offices as are necessary to promote both the advantage and beauty of the kingdom. We can note an example of this condition in the kingdom of Israel at the time of David and Solomon, and in the kingdom of the Romans, as is clear from what we read in the annals and histories of both kingdoms. And this condition is found in the kingdom of the Church, which is indeed most excellently ordered, having been ordered by Him through Whose wisdom all things are ordered.

The fourth condition is that it be made one through concord: of those, that is, who are within the kingdom. For dissension brings about the destruction of a kingdom, because, as the Lord says in St Matthew's gospel, any kingdom divided against itself will be brought to ruin.[8] On the other hand, then, the concord of a kingdom is a cause of its health, and hence of its glory. An example of this condition in times gone by is found in the kingdoms already cited: that is, the Israelite and Roman. And this condition prevails in the Church, who is united and made concordant by the bond of charity.

The fifth condition that pertains to the glory of a kingdom is that it be just and good: that is, that it be governed and live by just laws and good morals. With respect to the worshippers of God, an example of this kind of condition can again be observed in the kingdom of Israel; and, with respect to the gentiles, who do not hold to the worship of the true God, in the kingdom of the Romans. For amongst the Romans there were morals as praiseworthy as can be without faith. And this condition is found in the ecclesiastical

---

6. Cf. *Sap*. III,1.
7. Cf. Augustine, *De civ. Dei* XVIII,2 (CC XLVIII,593ff).
8. *Matt*. XII,25.

kingdom because it lives and is governed by most just laws and by morals of the highest kind.

The sixth condition required by the glory of a kingdom is that it be great and ample in respect of both number of men and extent of territory. An example of this condition appears clearly in the kingdom of the Romans; and this condition is found in the kingdom of the Church, which contains many persons and which is diffused and extended far and wide.

The seventh condition which contributes to the glory of a kingdom is that it be abundant and well supplied: that is, full of riches of all kinds. For a kingdom is directed towards self-sufficiency, and this cannot be achieved without riches. An example of this condition may be seen in the kingdom of Israel at the time of Solomon, and in the kingdom of the Romans at the time of Augustus Caesar. And this condition obtains in the kingdom of the Church, which is fruitful in the spiritual goods which are true riches, concerning which it is said to the Church in *Proverbs*: "Many daughters have gathered together riches; thou hast surpassed them all."[9] Also, there are temporal riches in the Church, and by making good and right use of these she merits eternal goods, just as, by abusing them, the congregation of the wicked deserves punishment. Hence, in this condition is contained the end of the ecclesiastical kingdom, which is blessedness; for, according to Boethius, this is a state achieved by the accumulation of all good things.[10] In this life, however, this kingdom is blessed but not perfectly so, by reason of a certain incomplete and unfinished state; whereas in the life to come, when filled with the abundance of the house of God, it will be fully blessed.

The eighth condition which pertains to the glory of a kingdom is that it be strong and firm: in order, that is, that it may not be vanquished, but, rather, may repulse all adversaries. An example of this appears in the kingdom of the Romans, whose fortitude was so great that they subdued all the kingdoms of the earth to themselves. And this condition is found in the kingdom of the Church, which remains unconquered and, standing victorious against its enemies, can be assailed indeed, but cannot be overcome.

The ninth condition that makes a kingdom glorious is that it be peaceful and quiet; for every multitude or community strives after peace as an end. We have an example of this in the kingdom of Israel at the time of Solomon, who is for this reason called the king of peace;[11] and in the kingdom of the Romans at the time of Augustus. And this condition is found in the kingdom of the Church, whose ruler is Christ, the author of peace, Who is our peace. For although that part of the Church which is a pilgrim on earth sometimes lacks temporal peace, she nonetheless has peace of heart, for she will come at last to an eternal peace.

The tenth condition from which the glory of a kingdom flows is that it should endure and be long-lasting; for every community must strive to be

---

9. *Prov.* XXXI,29.
10. *De consolatione philosophiae* III, pr.II (PL 63,723ff).
11. Cf. *I Para.* XXII,9.

long-lasting. We find an example of endurance in the kingdom of the Jews and in the Roman empire; and we find this condition also in the kingdom of the Church. For this is an eternal kingdom, which will not perish; for so did the angel foretell of Christ: "He shall reign in the house of Jacob for ever, and of His kingdom there shall be no end."[12]

The glory of the ecclesiastical kingdom therefore consists in these ten conditions; and if there are other conditions which might seem to pertain to the glory of this kingdom, these are contained within those already discussed. But although the Church now has some of these imperfectly, she will in time to come possess them to the full. Hence, by reason of that condition, she will be called, and she will be, fully glorious, having neither spot nor blemish nor any such defect.[13]

But we must speak more particularly and fully of these conditions; for, in our remarks so far, our observations and arguments have been by way of introduction. And because, amongst more distinguished authors, it is a more polished and useful method to reduce the many to the few, these ten conditions can therefore be reduced to four; that is, to the four which are touched upon in the Creed, where it is said: "And in one, holy, catholic and apostolic Church." And it is well that ten should be reduced to four, because the number four itself, when its parts are added together in succession, produces ten; for one plus two plus three plus four make ten. Hence, the ten-ness of the Commandments is reduced to the fourness of the gospels; for four is the number of stability, and, for this reason, we frequently encounter it in sacred scripture.[14] In the works of nature also, it is reflected in the elements, in the corners of the earth, in the seasons, in the humours and in many other things. We must, then, speak of the four conditions of the Church just stated, and of how all those conditions mentioned above are contained within these: in such a way, that is, that some of them can pertain to several of the four whereas several of them can be reduced to one of those four; as will become clear in what follows.

---

12. *Luc.* I,32f.
13. Cf. *Eph.* V,27.
14. Cf. Isidore, *Liber numerorum qui in sanctis scripturis occurrunt* V (PL 83,183f).

III

That the kingdom of the Church is one; and in what way and by what cause

First, then, we must show that the kingdom of the Church is one. And this is clear from the fact that every multitude in some way participates in unity: otherwise, the multitude itself would be disordered and divided, as the philosophers prove. Hence the blessed Dionysius, in the final chapter of *De divinis nominibus*, says that there is no multitude which does not participate in unity.[1] Rather, those things which are many in parts are one as a whole; those which have many accidents are one in substance; those which are many in number or powers are one in species; those which are many in species are one in genus; those which are many in processes are one in principle. Now the Church is a kind of multitude, of many persons. She must therefore be in some way one, as the very name 'Church' suggests. For *ecclesia* [in Greek] is the same as *convocatio* [in Latin]: that is, a 'calling together' of many persons to one and into one.[2] Moreover, as was said above, the Church is a kind of community; and unity is of the essence of any community: otherwise, it would not be a community. Again, there is a greater degree of similarity amongst those creatures which have intellect than there is between the corporeal and spiritual parts of the universe. Yet the whole universe, which contains so many different things, is one: is, so to say, a single realm of a single prince, God. So much the more, then, will the Church, containing only rational and intellectual creatures, be one.

Now we must further consider by what cause and in what way the Church is called, and is, one. As to this, we must first of all note that 'unity' and 'union' differ from one another, whereas 'one' and 'united' are similar; for unity excludes multitude, but union is found in a multitude. Strictly speaking, then, the term 'one' is applied to that in which there is no multitude, whereas that which contains many things is said to be 'united'. Therefore, since the Church is a kind of multitude, she is more properly called 'united' than 'one', and what binds her together is more properly

---

1. *De div. nom.* XIII,II (PG 3,987/988).
2. Isidore, *Etym.* VIII,I,1 (PL 82,293).

15

called 'union' than 'unity'. According to the common usage of speech, however, and in the scriptures, the two terms are used indifferently; and so they may be used indifferently here. In this treatise or work, then, whether we use the term 'one' or 'united', our task is to see by what cause the ecclesiastical multitude has its unity or union.

And if we seek the formal cause of its unity, this must be said to lie in three virtues: namely, faith, hope and charity, as will appear below. Whereas if we seek the efficient cause of its unity, it must be said that the unity of the Church has its being equally from the whole Trinity, as from an efficient principle: from the Father, I say, from the Son, and from the Holy Spirit. Sometimes, however, it is attributed to the individual persons [of the Trinity]. For sometimes it is attributed to the Father, inasmuch as He is the first principle of the Godhead, and unity has the nature of a first principle. Hence, according to Augustine, unity is to be attributed to the Father;[3] and this attribution is also found in St John's gospel, where it is said: "Holy Father, keep through Thine own name those whom Thou hast given me, that they may be one even as we are one."[4] Sometimes again, it is attributed to the Son, by reason, that is, of the nature which He assumed, according to which it is in a special way fitting for Him to be the head of the Church insofar as the Church consists of men: that is, for the sake of conformity with nature; for the unity of the members depends upon the head. And so the Apostle says at *Ephesians* IV: "We may in all things grow up in Him, Who is the head, even Christ, from Whom the whole body is united and joined together."[5] Also, it is sometimes attributed to the Holy Spirit, Who is love; for it is the special task of love to unite.[6] And so, on the words of the Apostle at *Ephesians* IV - "There is one body and one spirit" - the Gloss says that there is one body composed of many members, and one spirit by which we are made one body.[7] For it is for the sake of fellowship that we are made one body; and it is appropriate to say that the Holy Spirit does this, even though He acts in common with the whole Trinity. In order to make such fellowship known, those upon whom the Holy Spirit first came spoke in the tongues of all the nations;[8] for the fellowship of the human race is founded upon speech, and so the fellowship of Christ's members which was to be established among all the nations was prefigured in the tongues of the nations. Hence, it is well here to attribute unity to the Holy Spirit, Who is reciprocity and love; for the spiritual life of the soul indeed derives its being from love since, through it, the soul is united with God, Who is its life. And so it is that the Church is said to be quickened by the

---

3. *De doctrina Christiana* I,V (CC XXXII,9).
4. *Joan.* XVII,11.
5. *Eph.* IV,15f.
6. Ps.-Dionysius, *De divinis nominibus* IV,II (PG 3,751/52).
7. Cf. *Glossa ordinaria*, PL 114,595; Peter Lombard, *Collectanea*, PL 192,196. See also Gregory, *Hom. in evang.* II,XXX,1 (PL 76,1220).
8. *Act.* II,1ff.

Holy Spirit, by Whom she is also said to be made one.[9] For because, for living creatures, to live is to be, and because anything has it from the same cause that it is and that it is one, the Church therefore has life and unity from the same cause.

And having seen by what cause the Church is united, we must next consider the mode of her union or unity. Now the Church cannot be called one in the way that a man is called one, by reason of a unity of attributes and person (unless perhaps by analogy; for just as the many members of the body are one body, so are the many faithful one Church). Nor can she be called one by reason of a unity of the nature of species; for the Church includes not only men, but angels also, who differ in species from men. (In this work, however, we intend to consider the Church specifically as the congregation of faithful men which is called the Church Militant.) Rather, the Church is called one because she is a collection, just as many men form one people.

And in order that the way in which the Church is called one may appear more fully, a threefold mode can be assigned to the unity in respect of which she is said to be one. For, first, she is called one in respect of a unity of wholeness; for the Church is, as it were, a single whole whose parts are the individual believers. Also, individual churches or particular congregations are said to be parts of her. For in the human body also, by analogy with which the Church is called a Mystical Body, certain members are divisible, and are divided into other lesser members: as the hand into fingers, and the fingers into joints. But some members are indivisible, and are not divided into other members (although they may be divided into parts which are not called members): for example, the joints. In the same way, certain members of the Church are divisible - that is, particular churches and congregations; and some are indivisible: to wit, the individual believers. The Church, therefore, is one, as one whole constituted by many parts and as one body composed of many members. She differs from the natural body, however, in this regard: in that the members of the natural body all exist together at the same time, whereas the members of the Church do not all exist simultaneously. Rather, for as long as the number of the Church's sons is to be increased, some members are generated daily and successively.

Second, the Church is called one in respect of a unity of similarity; for in all the parts and members of the Church there is something with regard to which they resemble and conform to one another. Now this similarity of the Church's members is not to be understood according to the nature of genus and species; for such similarity is found also in those who are outside the Church as well as amongst those who belong to the Church. Rather, it is to be understood according to the gifts of grace. For the similarity between the Church's members is to be understood according to that by which they become and are called members of the Church; and someone is said to be a member of the Church not by reason of nature, but by reason of grace

---

9. Cf. *Rom.* VIII,1ff; *I Cor.* XII,1ff; *II Cor.* III,6.

(assuming, however, a nature which is capable of grace, of which kind is the rational or intellectual nature). And so the members of the Church resemble one another in respect of the gifts of grace; and, by reason of that similarity within the Church, they are said to be one. For similarity is a kind of unity. And those gifts of grace in respect of which the members of the Church resemble one another are faith, hope and charity, and the works which proceed from these. And the Church is said to be formally one from the fact that these gifts exist in the faithful themselves as certain spiritual perfections and forms. Of this mode of union or unity, the Gloss on *I Corinthians* X - "For we, being many, are one bread and one body"[10] - says that we are made one bread by the union of faith, hope and charity, and we are the one body of that head which is Christ through the performance of the works of charity; that is, we are all one Church united by the bond of faith, hope and charity, and by the common display of works.[11] The similarity of the members of the Church is therefore to be understood with respect to faith, hope and charity and the works which proceed from these. Hence, the similarity amongst the Church's members is to be understood with respect to knowledge, with respect to expectation, with respect to love, and with respect to the imitation of works. For the same people, and in the same fashion, have the same object of belief, hope and love - namely, Christ - and imitate His works.

Third, the Church is called one in respect of a unity of direction. For all the faithful are directed towards one end, which is salvation and eternal blessedness, and to one first principle and head: that is, to the whole Trinity according to the nature of its influence, but especially to Christ as man, by reason of the coming together in Him of nature and grace. For God gave Him to be head over all the Church, which is His body, as is said in *Ephesians*.[12] And of this mode of the Church's unity the Apostle says at *Ephesians* IV: "One body and one spirit, one Lord and one faith, one baptism."[13] For in what is said here, 'one body' implies a unity of wholeness; and 'one spirit' indicates a unity of purpose; and 'one Lord' indicates a unity of direction towards one first principle and head. And when it is said, 'one faith, one baptism,' this indicates a unity of similarity. To understand this, we must note that, as the Gloss on this passage says, 'faith' means both that which is believed and that by means of which it is believed; and in both senses we can understand that there is one faith in the Church.[14] There is one faith because we are commanded to believe the same things and to do so in the same way. For one and the same thing is believed by all the faithful, and so the faith itself is called catholic, that is, universal; and there is also one faith by means of which it is believed - that is, which exists in the soul of the believer; which is indeed one, not in

10. *I Cor.* X,17.
11. *Glossa ordinaria*, PL 114,536.
12. *Eph.* I,22.
13. *Eph.* IV,4.
14. Peter Lombard, *Collectanea*, PL 192,197.

number but in grace. For it is the same in all men, just as, when they have the same object of will, they are said to be of one will, and just as two similar objects are of one appearance. And by unity of faith is implied a unity of doctrine, the first principle and foundation of which is faith. And because faith is not living and completed without charity, unity of faith therefore implies a unity of charity, because all men love the same thing and the same charity is in them all, just as we said in the case of faith. And because, according to the Apostle in *Hebrews*, "faith is the substance of things to be hoped for",[15] unity of faith therefore implies a unity of hope: because, as we said in the case of faith and charity, all men hope for the same thing and the same hope is in them all. Moreover, because faith without works is dead and the love of charity is not idle, hope also rests upon good works; and so unity of faith, hope and charity implies a unity of action, because, by their works, the faithful imitate the same model, that is, Christ, and because they labour in the same way and together. And because charity is the end of teaching, what has been said above also implies a unity of teaching; for the same teachings are propounded by all. Moreover, since hope and charity have it as their object that they look to a final end, unity of hope and charity therefore implies a unity of direction towards a single end. And because God is worshipped in faith, hope and charity, what we have said therefore implies a unity of worship, by which the one God is worshipped in the same way. And unity of faith also implies a unity and communion of the sacraments which are contained within the faith. For the sacraments are the same for all who are in the Church. This unity is brought out more clearly by what is added, however: 'one baptism.' For by unity of baptism, which is the first sacrament and the gateway to all the sacraments,[16] the unity of the other sacraments is implied. And baptism is called one because it is the same for all men in point of both matter and form. Again, it is called one in the sense of 'equal', because, as the Gloss[17] says, it is given [equally] to each man; or it is called one because it cannot be repeated. And if anyone should ask how it is that the Church is one because the faith is one when the blessed[18] do not have faith yet nonetheless belong tó the Church, we must answer that this applies specifically to the Church Militant: to those who walk by faith. Again, it must be said that although the blessed do not have faith, they nonetheless have that to which faith gives place, namely, sight.[19] For what they see and what we believe in is the same; and so the whole Church, as comprehending present and future, can be called one in knowledge, even though the kind of knowledge possessed by each part is different. But although the Church is made one by faith, hope and charity, there is nonetheless a sense in which it is especially

---

15. *Heb*. XI,1.

16. Cf. Aquinas, *Summa theol*. III,q.63,a.6; q.68,a.6; q.73,a.3.

17. Peter Lombard, *Collectanea*, PL 192,197.

18. That is, those who have already died and gone to Heaven, who do not need faith because they see God face to face.

19. Cf. *II Cor*. V,7; Aquinas, *Summa theol*. IaIIae,q.67,a.3-5.

fitting to say that charity unites her. For charity is love, and, according to Dionysius at *De divinis nominibus* IV, love has a uniting and conjoining force.[20] For this reason it is called the bond of perfection by the Apostle;[21] for it binds and unites the members of the Church to Christ the head and to one another: by which fact the multitude of believers is said to be of one soul and one heart. Unlike the assemblies of the heretics, therefore, who are divided and at odds and cut off, the ecclesiastical community is one. For, as Dionysius says,[22] it is proper for the good to take one form and evil many, inasmuch as as the former is formed upon one pattern and the latter deviates from the pattern in many ways.

Although the Church is one, however, John nonetheless wrote to seven churches,[23] so that the Church might be shown to be filled with a sevenfold spirit, as is said in *Proverbs*: "Wisdom hath builded her house, she hath hewn out her seven pillars."[24] But there is no doubt that these seven are one; for the Apostle has said that the house of God is "the Church of the living God, which is the pillar and ground of truth."[25] Again, the number seven signifies the Church because this present life, in which she is a pilgrim, passes through seven ages.[26] Moreover, it can be said that, because in the scriptures the number seven is understood to signify wholeness,[27] the whole Church is therefore designated by the seven churches which, even though they are many, are nonetheless united in one. For just as many cities form one kingdom, so do many churches form the one Church.

Also, we must note the fact that the diversity and variety which appear in her do not impede the Church's unity; and, to say something of this diversity, it must be known that there are in the Church three principal kinds of diversity. First, there is a diversity of conditions, inasmuch as some are more perfect than others and stronger in merit. To this kind of diversity belong inequalities of grace and virtue in different persons, which is followed by an inequality of rewards. Of this, the Lord says: "In my Father's house there are many mansions."[28] And the Apostle says that "one star differs from another in glory."[29] To this diversity pertains the fact that some are called beginners, some proficient and some perfected. Again, there is a diversity of offices, which is seen in the fact that different persons are deputed to different tasks. According to Isidore, the word 'office' [*officium*] is derived from 'doing' [*efficiendo*].[30] For to each person there is

---

20. *De div. nom.* IV,II (PG 3,751/752).
21. *Coloss.* III,14.
22. Perhaps *De div. nom.* IV,XX (PG 3,783/84ff).
23. *Apoc.* I,4.
24. *Prov.* IX,1.
25. *I Tim.* III,15.
26. Cf. Augustine, *De civ. Dei* XXII,30 (CC XLVIII,865).
27. Cf. Isidore, *Liber numerorum* VIII (PL 83,186ff).
28. *Joan.* XIV,2.
29. *I Cor.* XV,41.
30. *Etym.* VI,XIX,1 (PL 82,252).

a proper and appropriate activity. To this diversity belongs the diversity of gifts by which men are rendered fit for offices. Of this diversity, the Apostle says at *Romans* XII: "Having different gifts according to the grace which is given us," and so on.[31] And in the psalm: "Distribute her houses,"[32] that is, according to the Gloss, "Allocate the various offices."[33]

Third, there is a diversity of rank, inasmuch as some are superior to others within the same condition or office.

And this threefold diversity which we have described is, as the learned teach, related to three things. For, first, it pertains to the perfection of the Church herself. For just as the plurality and variety of perfections pertains to the perfection of the universe, so that God's goodness may be made manifest in things in many and varied ways, so the diversity described above pertains to the perfection of the Church. And so the Apostle says at *Ephesians* IV: "He gave some to be apostles, some prophets, others evangelists, others pastors and teachers, for the consummation of the saints," - that is, for their perfection - "for the work of their ministry and for the edification of the body of Christ."[34]

Second, it pertains to the necessity of the tasks which are in the Church. For it is necessary that different men should be deputed to different tasks, so that these may be performed speedily and without confusion: just as, in the body, different members are necessary for the different functions. Hence the Apostle says at *Ephesians* XII: "Just as, in one body, we have many members, but all the members have not the same office," and so on.[35]

Third, it pertains to the Church's dignity and beauty, which consists in a certain order. For order creates beauty and comeliness and adornment; but order requires a certain diversity. As we have said, however, the diversity described above, which is found in the Church, does not take away or impede the Church's unity. Rather, the unity of the Church has need of such diversity, since it is the unity of an ordered and perfect multitude, and order and perfection require such diversity, as is clear from what we have said. And so from these considerations can be inferred a further twofold mode of unity with respect to which the Church is called one. For she is called one in respect of perfection; for, according to the Philosopher, perfection is a kind of unity, inasmuch as that which is perfect is said to be one.[36] And so, in the *Song of Songs*, after Solomon has said of the Church, "One is my dove," he adds, "my perfect one."[37] Moreover, she is called one in respect of order, just as the universe itself is said to be one by reason of a unity of order. For order itself draws the Church together and preserves the Church's unity. And so in the *Decretum*, dist. LXXXIX, it is

---

31. *Rom.* XII,6.
32. *Psalm.* XLVII,14.
33. *Glossa ordinaria*, PL 113,914.
34. *Eph.* IV,11f.
35. The correct reference is to *Romans* XII,4.
36. *Metaph.* V,16 (1021*b*10ff).
37. *Cant.* VI,8.

21

said that no corporate body can exist unless it is preserved by a great order of difference.[38]   And so it is clear that when we say that the Church is a kingdom and is called one, this implies another condition: namely, that she is ordered. For just as the universe is said to be ordered because there is in it an order of things which generate and are generated, which move and are moveable, and which cause and are caused, so the Church is ordered because, in her, there is an order of those who preach and those who hear, those who govern and those who are subject, and so of all the orders of the Church.

It must be noted also that just as the diversity of offices, conditions and ranks does not take away the Church's unity, so also the diversity of customs and rites found amongst the various particular churches does not prejudice it. For in respect of those things which are necessary to salvation, the Church is one is custom and rite; but, in other things, there can be different customs and various kinds of observance without detriment to her unity. Indeed, these may even be praiseworthy. Hence Boethius, in his work on the Christian faith, says: "Whatever is held in the Catholic Church has the authority of the scriptures, or of universal tradition, or at least of its own and proper usage. The whole Church is bound by this authority, and also by the universal tradition of the Fathers. Although the whole is bound, however, each separate church nonetheless exists and is governed by its individual constitution and its own conceptions, according to differences of locality or what seems good to each."[39]

The ecclesiastical community, therefore, is one; and the Lord, wishing to show this unity, appointed one man to be head of the Church: namely, Peter.[40] Outside this unity of the Church, neither grace, nor the remission of sins, nor spiritual life can be attained; and outside the unity of the Church neither the receiving of sacraments nor any other act can avail for eternal salvation. For just as health and life cannot inhere in a limb unless it acts within the unity of the body, so true health and life cannot come to anyone unless he is within the unity of the Church. Nonetheless, just as sometimes a withered limb is joined to the body by continuity although not by the influx of power, so there are not a few who by continuity of external converse are united with the Church but do not receive an influx of salvation and life from Christ her head and from His members.

The Church, then, is one; nor can she be divided into many parts. For is Christ divided?[41] God forbid! There is one Christ, then, and one Church, one head and one body, one bridegroom and one bride, one shepherd and one flock, one king and one kingdom, one prince and one dominion, one ruler and one commonwealth. The one Church is indeed that one seamless robe of Christ which was not divided.[42] She is herself the one ark of the

38. *Decretum*, dist. LXXXIX,c. VII (*Ad hoc dispositionis*) (CIC I,313).
39. *Brevis fidei Christianae complexio*, PL 64,1338.
40. *Matt.* XVI,18.
41. Cf. *I Cor.* I,13.
42. *Joan.* XIX,23; and Cf. Cyprian, *De unitate ecclesiae* VI (PL 4,518ff).

true Noah within which all who were gathered together under the one master were saved from the deluge, whereas those who were found outside all perished in the flood. Whoever separates himself from the unity of the Church in like manner ceases to be a member of the Church. Hence, those who are cut off from the Church's unity are justly deemed unbelievers, worthy to be regarded as enemies and to be punished temporally and eternally.

Moreover, from the fact that the Church is one and consequently ordered, there follows a further condition: namely, that she is firm and strong. For a united power is greater than a divided; and hence the Church is rendered strong and firm by her own unity. Also, her order makes her stronger; and for this reason she is said in the *Song of Songs* to be "terrible as an army set in order."[43] The Church is strong indeed, because she is firm against the assaults of her enemies, whether of demons or tyrants or heretics; and she is thus firm so that she may not weaken, but may increase and grow strong amidst the strife of enemies. Against demons she is strong in holiness and righteousness; against tyrants she is strong in patience; and against heretics and the world's philosophers she is strong in divine wisdom. She is the Tower of David, with battlements from which hang "a thousand bucklers and all the arms of valiant men":[44] not fleshly arms, but spiritual, as the Apostle says at *II Corinthians* X. "The weapons of our warfare", he says, "are not fleshly," that is, infirm, "but mighty through God to the pulling down of strong holds," that is, to the pulling down of the counsels of men or demons fortified by many wiles, "casting down imagination and every high thing", that is, the deep reasonings of the lawyers or philosophers, "that exalteth itself against the knowledge of God", that is, against that which is of God.[45] Of the strength and firmness of the Church it is said in *Matthew* XVI: "The gates of hell shall not prevail against it";[46] and the Gloss on this passage says that the 'gates of hell' are crimes and sins, or the teaching of the heretics by which men are led to damnation; or every one of the wicked spirits, that is, the demons: these are the gates of hell, over against which stand the gates of justice. Again, the gates of hell are the tortures and blandishments of persecutors. And the wicked works of the unbelievers, and their foolish utterances also, are the gates of hell because they show us the way of perdition. But none of these things prevails against her - that is, the Church; for they do not separate her from my love and faith, saith the Lord.[47] For she is the house of the wise man founded upon a rock, which neither the falling of the rain nor the force of the torrent nor the beating of the rushing winds overthrew, because it was founded upon the rock of faith, of the most solid truth.[48] For this house - that is, the Church - neither the

---

43. *Cant.* VI,3.
44. *Cant.* IV,4.
45. *II Cor.* X,4f.
46. *Matt.* XVI,18.
47. Aquinas, *Catena aurea*, on *Matt.* XVI,18.
48. Cf. *Matt.* VII,24ff.

rain of false teaching corrupts, nor the blast of the Devil overthrows, nor the assaults of the flood of violent men disturbs. Finally, the Church is strong because, like a fortified city, she has the protection and custody of the angels. Also, she has Christ Himself, the Angel of Great Counsel,[49] as her chief guardian and helper, of Whom it is said in *Revelation* that "the city had a wall great and high";[50] and the Gloss[51] on this passage says that we may properly understand the wall to be Christ, who encompasses holy Jerusalem herself round about, and now defends her on all sides against the assaults of demons and wicked men and their crimes.

And from the three conditions of the Church described above there follows a fourth condition: namely, that she is at peace. For unity is a cause of peace, because peace is an effect of love, whose task it is to unite. Order also is contained within the nature of peace; for, according to Augustine at *De civitate Dei* XIX, peace is the tranquillity of order, and the peace of men is an ordered concord, and the peace of a city is an ordered concord of the citizens with respect to those who rule and those who obey.[52] Also, fortitude leads to peace; for from fortitude comes forth victory, and from this follows peace. And so Augustine says at *De civitate Dei* XIX that victory is the subjection of those who oppose us, and that, when this is achieved, there will be peace.[53] The Church, therefore, who is one and ordered and strong, also lives at peace. During this pilgrimage, however, where she is disturbed in many ways and often, she does not have perfect and full peace. But in time to come she will be fully at peace, when there will indeed be no discord, no opposition, no disturbance of her order. Hence, Isidore says that now, by reason of her present pilgrimage, the Church is called Sion, because she awaits the promise of heavenly things after the appointed duration of this pilgrimage; and so she has received the name 'Sion', which means 'waiting'. But she is called Jerusalem, which means 'vision of peace', because of the peace of the heavenly realm to come.[54] For then, set free from all adversity, she will possess the peace which is Christ in immediate contemplation. And so it is said to Jerusalem in the psalm: "He maketh the peace in thy borders."[55] These, then, are our remarks on the unity of the ecclesiastical kingdom.

---

49. Cf. Hilary, *De Trinitate* IV,24 (CC LXII,127).
50. *Apoc.* XXI,12.
51. *Glossa ordinaria*, PL 114,746.
52. *De civ. Dei* XIX,13 (CC XLVIII,679).
53. *De civ. Dei* XIX,12 (CC XLVIII,675).
54. *Etym.* VIII,I,5f (PL 82,295).
55. *Psalm.* CXLVII,14.

IV

That the kingdom of the Church is catholic, that is, universal; and in what way

Our next task, then, is to observe that the kingdom of the Church is called catholic, that is, universal, and in what way. The Church is indeed rightly called universal [*universalis*], because her founder is the Lord of all [*universorum*], of Whom it is said in *Job*: "All things are the work of His hand";[1] and in *Proverbs* it is said: "All the ends of the earth shall be converted to the Lord, and all the kindreds of the gentiles shall adore in His sight."[2] But the Church is called, and is, universal in many ways.

First, she is called universal with respect to place. For she is not found only in Judea, as the synagogues are, but in the whole world; for the sound of the preaching of the gospel and of her doctrine has gone forth to the whole world,[3] and so it is said at *Malachi* I: "From the rising of the sun even to the going down, my name is great among the gentiles, and in every place there is offered to my name a clean oblation."[4] Of this universality Isidore says at *Etymologiae* VIII: "*Ecclesia* in Greek means *convocatio* in Latin, because she calls [*vocet*] all men to herself."[5] Also, the Church is called catholic, that is, universal, because she is not confined to certain restricted parts like the assemblies of the heretics, but is spread at large throughout the whole earth. And in his work on the Supreme Good, the same author says that heresies are found either in certain corners of the world or in one nation, but the Church is catholic: just as she is extended throughout the whole world, so also is she made up of the fellowship of all nations.[6]

Second, the Church is called universal with respect to the standing of her people; for she brings together all sorts of men and excludes none. She does not despise differences of custom, for she calls Jews and gentiles

---

1. *Job* XXXIV,19.
2. The correct reference is to *Psalm.* XXI,28.
3. Cf. *Psalm.* XVIII,5.
4. *Mal.* I,11.
5. *Etym.* VIII,I,1 (PL 82,293f).
6. Isidore, *Sentent.* I,XVI,6 (PL 83,572).

25

equally; nor differences of race, for she calls Greeks and barbarians, Scythians and Indians; nor differences of rank, for she calls both slaves and free men; nor differences of sex, for she calls both women and men; nor differences of fortune or external goods, for she calls both poor and rich, noblemen and commoners; nor differences of intellect, for she calls the learned and the unlearned, the wise and the simple, philosophers and plain folk, orators and jesters. Universally, indeed, she despises no diversity of men, but receives all. For God is no respecter of persons.[7] Rather, He Who is the maker of all is also the saviour and sustainer of all, and He desires that all men may be saved. Hence also, when Christ sent forth His disciples, He said: "Go ye into the whole world and preach the gospel to every creature",[8] that is, to every man.

Third, the Church is called universal with respect to time; for she began at the foundation of the world and will endure to the end. Hence she is said to have begun from Abel himself.[9] Isidore, to be sure, says that "the Church began in the place where the Holy Spirit came down from Heaven and filled those who sat in that one place";[10] and, so far as her fulness of persons and graces is concerned, she did indeed begin in that place, for then was come the fulness of the time in which God sent His Son. In respect of her increase, and with respect to the explicit and revealed faith, she began then. In an absolute sense, however, she began at the beginning of the human race. For she is said to have begun in Abel by reason of his innocence; and those [innocent persons] who have lived both before and after Christ, of all of whom Christ is the head, have made up the one body of the Church. "For those who went before and those who came after cried out, Hosanna: blessed is He Who comes in the name of the Lord."[11] And the faith of those who went before was the same as that of those who came after; for the former believed that there would come to pass that which we now believe to be accomplished. Moreover, in the fact that the Church is called universal with respect to time, two further conditions of the ecclesiastical kingdom are implied: that is, antiquity and permanence.

Fourth, she is called universal with respect to condition. For she contains both those whose condition is one of knowledge, and those who are in a condition of pilgrimage, as we have said above; and not only men, but angels also. Hence the Church, so understood, is properly called the congregation of all those of whatever kind who are Christ's members. The Church, then, by reason of [her present] condition, is called the congregation of those who believe; and, as to her future condition, she is called the congregation of those who know.

---

7. Cf. *Act*. X,34.
8. *Marc*. XVI,15.
9. Cf. Augustine, *De civ. Dei* XV,1 (CC XLVIII,453).
10. *Etym*. VIII,I,4 (PL 82,295); Cf. *Act*. II,1ff.
11. *Marc*. XI,9.

Fifth, the Church is called universal with respect to doctrine; for there is in her a universal doctrine concerning all things necessary to salvation and beneficial to the whole human race.

Sixth, the Church is called universal with respect to her healing power. For she has a universal cure for all the sins of all people, and she contains sufficient and universal remedies for all men: that is, the seven sacraments, which derive their efficacy from the one saving remedy by which all men are delivered: that is, from Christ. And so the Church is called universal because she contains the universal way of the soul's deliverance, namely Christ, Who says of Himself: "I am the way, and the truth and the life."[12] Hence Augustine, speaking of the Christian religion at *De civitate Dei* X, says: "This is the religion which contains the universal way of the soul's deliverance. This is a kind of royal road, which alone leads to the kingdom which does not fail, like other temporal dignities, but stands firm upon eternal foundations. For what else is the universal way of the soul's deliverance if not that by which all souls universally are delivered and, by the same token, without which no soul is delivered? This, I say, is the universal way of deliverance for those who believe, concerning which the faithful Abraham received the divine assurance: 'In thy seed shall all the nations of the earth be blessed.'"[13] This is the universal way spoken of in the prophecy: "That we may know Thy way upon the earth, Thy salvation in all nations."[14]

The Church is called universal, then, in all the ways of which we have spoken; and of her universality, considered in relation to some of the things set forth above, Isidore, in the book *De origine officiorum*, says: "The Church is properly so called because she calls all men to herself and unites them in one body. And she is therefore called catholic because, established throughout the whole world, she is catholic either insofar as there is in her a general doctrine for the instruction of all men concerning the visible and invisible things of heaven and earth; or because men of every kind are subject to the obligations of piety: rulers and ruled alike, orators and jesters."[15] For the Church must be gathered in from men of every kind: even from those who seem to turn away from faith and humility through the contempt and pride of this world. Again, she is called universal because she has a general cure for all the sins which are committed by body and soul. Also, in the book *De Trinitate*, Boethius says of the Church's universality: "There are many who lay claim falsely to the dignity of the Christian religion; but that faith is the most greatly and singularly esteemed which, both because of the universal character of the precepts and rules by which the authority of that same religion is established, and because its worship has spread almost to all the ends of the earth, is called catholic or universal."[16]

---

12. *Joan.* XIV,6.
13. *De civ. Dei* X,32 (CC XLVII,309ff), quoting *Gen.* XXII,18.
14. *Psalm.* LXVI,3.
15. *De ecclesiasticis officiis* I (*De origine officiorum*), I,3 (PL 83,740).
16. *De Trin.* I (PL 64,1249).

And the rules of those who teach the Christian religion are called universal because they are enjoined, not upon one people, as was the Law of the children of Israel, nor upon one sex, like circumcision upon males, but upon every people and each sex: in short, upon all sorts and conditions. For one faith, one baptism, one rite of sacrifice, one charity and one hope is preached to all men. Moreover, they are called universal rules because no falsehood or iniquity is mingled with them at any time or in any circumstance whatsoever. Again, they are called universal rules because they contain and order the whole life of man and everything of whatever kind that pertains to it. Also, in his book on the Christian faith, that same Boethius says of the Church's universality: "Therefore Christ gave to His disciples the form of baptism, the saving truth of His teaching, and the power to perform miracles, and bade them go and bring life to all the world, so that the message of salvation might no longer be preached to one nation only, but to all the earth."[17] That heavenly doctrine, therefore, is spread throughout the world: peoples are united; churches founded; a single body is formed which occupies the breadth of the world. And how wonderful a thing it is that the Church should be spread and scattered throughout the world, and for this reason be properly called universal, appears from this fact: that the Church has not grown great through force of arms or civil power or magic arts, as certain liars have said, whom Augustine splendidly denounces at *De civitate Dei* XVIII,[18] but through the preaching of the gospel, through miracles of divine power, through examples of virtue, through the patience, perils and labours of the saints and the shedding of their blood, and through many kinds of suffering and tribulation. What is more, we note what manner of men they were who first preached the gospel, through whom the world came to believe and the Church increased on earth. For they were not mighty according to this world; they were not wise in the wisdom of the earth; not noble; not wealthy. Rather, they were weak, illiterate, common men, and poor fisherfolk. The Church, then, is catholic, that is, universal; and those who withdraw from this universality are, because separated, rightly called heretics and not catholics. And from the fact that the Church is called universal another of her conditions can be deduced: namely, that she is well supplied and self-sufficient. For the more universal a multitude is, the more sufficient it is for the mutual aid of those who are contained within that universality. Again, the Church can be called universal in another way, by reason of the fulness of spiritual goods which is in her, proceeding from the fount of Christ; and so, again, from the fact that she is called universal her plenteousness and abundance can be inferred. And we must not forget that, just as the universality of the Church does not take away her unity (as is clear from the previous chapter), neither does the unity of the Church take away her universality. On the contrary, the fact of her unity is given in that very universality; for, as Isidore says at

---

17. *Brevis fidei Christ. comp.*, PL 64,1337.
18. *De civ. Dei* XVIII,53 (CC XLVIII,653).

Etymologiae VIII: "'Universality' is synonymous with 'oneness', for [that which is universal] is bound together by unity."[19] And in logic also, that which contains many things in one is called a 'universal' because it is a 'oneness' consisting in many things and composed of many things. The intellect infers this from the resemblance and conformity of many things; for every resemblance is a unity. Thus, on the one hand, the Church is one because universal and, on the other, is universal because one. And so, by reason of this unity and universality, she can with equal truth be called a commonwealth. For a commonwealth is the property of a people, "and a people is a multitude associated by common agreement as to what is just, and by a communion of wellbeing", as is clear from the definition of Cicero, to which Augustine frequently alludes.[20] According to this definition, indeed, no community is more truly called a commonwealth than the Church; for only in her is there true justice and true wellbeing and true communion.

---

19. *Etym.* VIII,I,2 (PL 82,295).
20. *De civ. Dei* XIX,21 (CC XLVIII,687f);   24 (CC XLVIII,695);   Cf. II,21 (CC XLVII,53).

V

That the kingdom of the Church is holy; and in what way

But we must show, further, that the kingdom of the Church is holy, and in what way. To this end, we must first consider what holiness is. And the blessed Dionysius proposes a definition of holiness at *De divinis nominibus* XII, where he says that holiness is a free and perfect and entirely unblemished purity from every defilement;[1] and the Church is rightly called holy according to this definition because she is cleansed of every defilement, and there is in her a purity having the three conditions just prescribed. For there is in her a purity which is free, because she is free from the bondage of any kind of defilement. There is in her a purity which is perfect, because she lacks no aspect of purity; for that which lacks nothing is perfect. And there is in her a purity which is unblemished, because she cannot be polluted by anything coming from without; for a blemish arises from some extraneous cause. And in order that something may be said more particularly concerning the Church's holiness, we must note that, as is clear from the definition given above, holiness requires an absence of defilement, and that there are two kinds of defilement which affect rational creatures. One kind arises out of fault, and the other out of error or ignorance; and there is a distinction to be drawn in each of these cases according to the distinction between fault and error. The rational creature is delivered and purified from the defilement of fault by grace, through which comes the remission of sins; and he is cleansed from the defilement of error and ignorance by sacred doctrine, the first principle of which is faith, and the effect of which is to purify the heart. And because holy scripture directs her and grace assists her in doing her work well, the Church is therefore called holy because of her good works and the virtues which are the foundation of good works. And because grace is conferred in the sacraments, the Church is therefore called holy because she is sanctified and purified by grace; for the sacraments are the remedies of sanctification against the defilement of every sin. And because God dwells in us through grace, the Church is therefore called holy because she is sanctified by the divine presence and

---

1. *De div. nom.* XII,II ((PG 3,969/70).

30

indwelling. Hence the psalm: "Holiness becometh Thy house";[2] and *I Corinthians* III: "The temple of God, which you are, is holy."[3] And this [spiritual] temple is signified by the material temple which, for this reason, is called a church, the consecration of which by a bishop is a symbol of the sanctification of the faithful by Christ, Who is the Holy of Holies, as also is said at *I John* II: "Ye have an unction from the Holy One",[4] that is, an inward unction from Christ Himself, of the fulness of Whose unction we all receive, and by which "we are anointed above our fellows."[5]

Now this holiness and sanctification of the Church comes equally from the whole Trinity, of Whom it is said in *Isaiah*: "Holy, Holy, Holy, Lord God of Hosts."[6] Sometimes, however, it is attributed to the Father, because of His authority as the first person [of the Trinity], as at *John* XVII: "Father, sanctify them in truth."[7] And sometimes it is attributed specifically to the Son, because of His assumption of the humanity under the aspect of which He suffered; for we are sanctified by His Passion. And so, at *I Corinthians* I, it is said of Him that "He of God is made unto us wisdom, and righteousness, and sanctification, and redemption."[8] Also, the Apostle says at *Ephesians* V: "Christ loved the Church, and gave Himself for her, that he might sanctify her" (that is, having first purified her from sin by the righteousness of a goodly life) "and cleanse her with the washing of water in the word of life," (that is, with what gives life; for He makes the element a sacrament by entering into it, so that the man sanctified by it receives eternal life) "that He might present to Himself a glorious Church, having neither spot" (of any criminal sin) "nor blemish" (of any false show of purity and simplicity) "nor any such thing": that is, no sin for which she might be condemned, but that she might be holy through good works and unblemished in her abstinence from evil.[9] Sometimes, however, it is attributed to the Holy Spirit, as at *Romans* I, where it is said that [Jesus was "declared to be the Son of God with power, according to the Spirit of Sanctification, by the resurrection from the dead."[10] For] the Spirit of Sanctification is the cleanser of all impurity, a holy love and the first of gifts, in Whom all the gifts are given to us by which every impurity is taken away. The Church is holy, therefore, because purified of every sin and iniquity and adorned with virtues and good works. Hence, in the second person [of the Trinity,] He gave Himself for us, that he might redeem us from every iniquity and present to Himself an acceptable people, a retinue of good works.

---

2. *Psalm*. XCII,5.

3. *I Cor*. III,17

4. *I Joan*. II,20; Cf. *Heb*. IX,12.

5. *Psalm*. XLIV,8.

6. *Isa*. VI,3.

7. *Joan*. XVII,17.

8. *I Cor*. I,30.

9. *Eph*. V,25ff; and see Peter Lombard, *Collectanea*, PL 192,214.

10. *Rom*. I,4. The evident omission here is clearly due to homoeoteleuton: specifically, the occurrence of the phrase *spiritus sanctificationis* twice within a couple of lines.

Moreover, the Church is holy because purged of all error by sacred doctrine, which is both pure and purifying, and of which it is said in the psalm: "The law of God is without blemish, converting the soul."[11] In it, whatever is useful to salvation is easily found, and whatever is harmful and contrary to salvation is condemned. Whatever resists it is beyond all doubt wholly false, and it says of itself in *Proverbs*: "All my words are just; there is nothing wicked or perverse in them"[12] - nothing wicked in faith; nothing wicked in morals. In this sense, then, we may take it that the Church is called holy with respect to the celebration of the sacraments, by which we are cleansed from sin; and with respect to the fulness of grace through which we perform good works; and with respect to the truth and goodness of the doctrine by which we are enlightened and instructed, which contains nothing false or worthy of condemnation, but the whole and saving truth. Indeed, all the Church's instruction in doctrine is holy, whether derived from either of the testaments of scripture, or from apostolic tradition, or from the ordinances of the Fathers and holy councils, or from approved and rational custom.

The Church, therefore, is holy in precepts, holy in the sacraments and mysteries, holy in works, and holy in observances. There is in her a religion pure and unblemished in the sight of God and the Father; and it is her task "to visit the orphans and widows in their tribulation and to preserve herself unblemished from this world."[13] It is said of her at *Revelation* XXI: "And the city itself was pure gold, like unto clear glass."[14] And again: "I saw the holy city, the new Jerusalem, coming down out of heaven."[15] This city, as the Gloss says, is the whole company of the just, called 'holy' because of their righteousness, 'Jerusalem' because of their vision of eternal peace, and 'new' because descending from heaven purged of what is old.[16] For he who lives righteously in this world, he who lives blessedly in eternity, knows himself to have everything from God. Also, the Church is called holy because raised up from earth. For 'holy' is *hagios* in Greek, which means 'not earthly';[17] and the Church is truly said to be not of this earth because she has set her heart "on things above, not on the things of this earth",[18] and her "conversation is in heaven"[19] in mind and spirit, and will in time to come be so in place also.

---

11. *Psalm.* XVIII,8.
12. *Prov.* VIII,8.
13. *Jacob.* I,27.
14. *Apoc.* XXI,18.
15. *Apoc.* XXI,2.
16. See Ch.I, n.20(ii), above.
17. This etymology seems to be incorrect: see the authorities cited at *Theological Dictionary of the New Testament*, ed G. Kittel; trans. & ed. G.W. Bromiley (Grand Rapids, Michigan, 1964), I, p.88; See also W.F. Arndt and F.W. Gingrich, *A Greek-English Lexicon of the New Testament and Other Early Christian Literature* (Chicago & London, 1958), ad loc..
18. *Col.* III,2.

The kingdom of the Church, then, is holy above all other kingdoms. Indeed, no other kingdom is holy; for the kingdom of the Romans, which, as we read, was praised above all others for its justice and virtue, was nonetheless unclean beyond all doubt: for demons were worshipped in it, and there were many wicked laws and numerous vile practices, as Augustine relates in the book *De civitate Dei*.[20] But to explain the Church's holiness still more fully, we must examine the various senses of the word 'holy' as Isidore distinguishes them in the book *Etymologiae*. For she is called holy in three senses. In one sense, she is called holy because purified by the shedding of blood; and, in this sense, 'holy' [*sanctum*] is derived from 'blood' [*sanguine*]. And so Isidore says at *Etymologiae* XV: "The word 'holy' comes from the 'blood' of sacrificial victims; for nothing was called holy by the men of old unless it had been consecrated and sprinkled with the blood of a sacrificial victim."[21] And so those who wished to be purified were touched by the blood of the sacrificial victim, as he says at Book X.[22] In this sense, the Church is holy insofar as she belongs to men because they have been purified by the blood of the true victim Who is Christ; and this is clear from the pronouncements of the Apostle cited above. And the commemoration of this victim is enacted daily in the sacrament of the altar.

In a second sense, 'holy' is the same as 'firm', as Isidore says at *Etymologiae* XV.[23] She is called 'holy' [*sanctum*] because she is firmly established [*sancitum*]. For to establish [*sancire*] is to make firm and to defend against injustice by the infliction of punishment. Thus, the laws are said to be 'established' [*sanctae*], and the city walls are said to be 'made firm' [*sancti*]; and, in this sense, the Church is said to be 'holy' [*sancta*] because made firm by divine sanction [*sanctione*] and eternal law. Nor is it lawful to defile her; for, as the Apostle says: "If any man defile the temple of God, him shall God destroy."[24] The Church is indeed confirmed in goodness and against wickedness; and this is so by virtue of the grace of which it is said in *Hebrews*: "It is best that the heart be established with grace."[25] She is confirmed in her union with God because she adheres to God with firmness, so that neither death nor life separates her from God's love.[26] In this life, however, she has an imperfect firmness, whereas in time to come she will be perfectly firm. And she is made firm principally by God, as is said at *I Corinthians* I: "He shall also confirm you to the end without blame";[27] and at *I Peter* V: "He will confirm and strengthen

---

19. *Philip.* III,20.
20. E.g. *De civ. Dei* II,22ff (CC XLVII,55ff).
21. *Etym.* XV,IV,2 (PL 82,543f).
22. *Etym.* X,241 (PL 82,393).
23. *Etym.* XV,IV,2 (PL 82,544).
24. *I Cor.* III,17.
25. *Heb.* XIII,9.
26. Cf. *Rom.* VIII,39.
27. *I Cor.* I,8.

you";[28] and in the psalm: "I have made firm the pillars thereof"[29] - that is, the apostles and their successors who, like pillars, sustain the edifice of the Church; for their task is to confirm the others who are within the Church. And this is especially the task of the Supreme Pastor of the Church: of the Vicar of Christ, I say, and the successor of Peter, to whom it was said by the Lord: "When thou are converted, confirm thy brethren."[30] And in *Exodus* it is written: "In Thy sanctuary, O Lord, which Thy hands have made firm";[31] that is, in the Church, who, according to the Apostle, is the pillar and foundation of the truth.[32] For she is firm in the sacraments and firm in what she teaches. For although her statutes may vary according to the diversity of places, times and persons, those things which are necessary to salvation are nonetheless established and made firm in the Church.

She is called Holy in a third sense because she is devoted to the divine services and to divine worship. It is in this sense that we speak of holy vestments and holy vessels and holy places and holy days. Hence, holiness, so understood, is that virtue which exhibits due worship to God, which Andronicus defines when he says that "holiness is the virtue which makes us faithful and leads us to perform our just obligations to God."[33] And the Church is holy in this sense because she is dedicated to the worship of the one true God: indeed, in her alone is there the true worship of God.

Now to worship God is to show Him due honour and due service, whether inwardly or outwardly. The worship of God, then, is of two kinds: namely, inward and outward. For God is worshipped inwardly through faith, hope and charity, and outwardly by external observances. And in order to give a summary of those things in which the worship of God consists, we must notice that devotion of mind belongs to the worship of God, for by this we subdue the will to God and have a will which is prompt to serve Him; and that prayer pertains to the worship of God, for by this we ascend to God in mind and ask of Him what is fitting and wholesome; and that adoration pertains to the worship of God: both spiritual and inward, which is performed in spirit, and bodily and outward, which consists in the humbling of the body through genuflexions, prostrations and other such bodily signs. To the worship of God belong the praises and canticles and psalmody performed in the Church; and to the worship of God belongs the offering of sacrifices, which must be offered only to the one true God.

But in the Church there is offered the one especial sacrifice which is both supremely real and supremely efficacious: that is, the sacrament of the body and blood of Christ. In this sacrifice He is truly contained and received, Who offered Himself as a sacrifice and victim to God in a pleasing

---

28. *I Pet.* V,10.
29. *Psalm.* LXXIV,4.
30. *Luc.* XXII,32.
31. *Exod.* XV,17.
32. *I Tim.* III,15.
33. Ps.-Andronicus Rhodius, *De affectibus*, as quoted by Aquinas at *Summa theol.* IIaIIae,q.81,a,8.

fragrance.[34] He Himself is both priest and victim, Whose one and true sacrifice was prefigured in all the sacrifices of old.[35] This sacrifice was indeed offered once in ransom; but it is continually renewed in the Church through the mystery according to which it is indeed consecrated and offered by the ministry of the priests for the salvation of the people and of themselves. There are, moreover, other spiritual sacrifices which the faithful offer, and are obliged to offer, to God. A contrite and humble heart is a spiritual sacrifice indeed;[36] the chastisement and mortification of the flesh is a spiritual sacrifice; every work of mercy is a spiritual sacrifice; the defence of the truth, the unity of love, each act of virtue everywhere, and every good work offered to God and directed towards blessedness: these are spiritual sacrifices. The blessed Augustine shows this at *De civitate Dei* X,[37] where he says of the many kinds of sacrifice - offerings and tithes and first fruits, which are given over to the use of those who are ministers of the divine worship - that these things pertain to the worship of God. For although all the faithful worship God, some of them are nonetheless appointed especially to conduct the ministry of divine worship.

The building and dedication of temples and altars pertain to the worship of God; also the anointings and washings, incensings and sprinklings, consecrations and blessings which are performed in the Church, whether of places, ministers, vessels, vestments, or of any other things of whatever kind which are in any way applied to God's worship. Also, to the holiness of the Church pertains not only the worship which is offered to God, but also that offered by men to the angels and saints, even though this worship is different in nature from that which is offered to God.

The Church, therefore, is rightly called, and is, holy. To this state belongs that condition of the ecclesiastical kingdom by virtue of which it is called just and good; for it lives by the highest laws and by holy morals. Also, to this state belongs its perpetuity, for, in one sense, the word 'holy' means 'firm'. Indeed, perpetuity, firmness and permanence are of its essence; and so to this state also belongs the firmness of the Church, by virtue of which she cannot be conquered or overthrown. Also, to the Church's holiness belongs that condition by virtue of which she is said to be well supplied; for the Church is called holy by reason of her abundant supply of spiritual goods and gifts. Indeed, there is no spiritual gift which is not contained within the holiness of the Church, and these spiritual gifts are the true riches by which the Church is rendered well supplied. These riches are the canon of the scriptures and the many commentaries on them, the free gifts of grace, and the virtues, gifts and various works of merit in all of which the Church abounds through Him, Who is the Lord of all riches, in Whom are all the

---

34. Cf. *Gen*. VIII,21.
35. Cf. *Heb*. VII,27; IX,11ff.
36. *Psalm*. L,19.
37. *De civ. Dei* X,5 (CC XLVII,276ff).

treasures of grace and wisdom. The kingdom of the Church, then, is holy, and sanctified by Him Who says: "Ye shall be holy, for I am holy."[38]

---

38. *Levit.* XI,46.

VI

That the kingdom of the Church is apostolic; and in what way

Finally, then, it remains for us to consider that the Church is, and is called, apostolic.   In the first place, indeed, the Church is called apostolic because she has her origin and beginning in the apostles;   for, in the time of the revelation of grace, these were the first of the Christian people.   And just as they were the first in time, so also were they foremost in spiritual perfection. Hence the apostle Paul, speaking of himself and the other apostles, says: "We have the first fruits of the spirit."[1]   The Gloss adds here that they received the Holy Spirit both first in time and also more abundantly than others.[2]   In *II Thessalonians* he says: "God hath chosen you first unto salvation"[3] - that is, [the salvation] of ourselves and every nation.   Hence, it is said at *Luke* VI that "Christ chose twelve, whom He called apostles":[4] whom, as the Gloss says, He destined to be the sowers of the faith, so that the means of the salvation of mankind might be spread throughout the whole world.[5]   And because, in every genus, that which is first and perfect is the cause of all the things which come after it, therefore, secondly, the Church is called apostolic because propagated by the apostles and spread by the word of their preaching to the very ends of the earth.   For "their sound hath gone forth into all the earth and their words unto the ends of the world."[6]

These fathers and progenitors of the faithful, then, these founders and builders of the Church: what doctrines have they planted by their miracles, examples, and effusions of blood!   And because to one who has produced something there also falls the task of governing it, the Church is therefore called apostolic in a third sense, because governed and administered by the apostles.   These, therefore, are the Church's ordainers, dispensers, teachers, princes, pontiffs, kings and lords: these are the twelve gates of the city of which it is said in *Revelation* that the city "had a wall great and high, having

---

1. *Rom.* VIII,23.
2. Peter Lombard, *Collectanea*, PL 191,1444.
3. *II Thess.* II,12.
4. *Luc.* VI,13.
5. Aquinas, *Catena aurea*, on *Luc.* VI,13.
6. *Psalm.* XVIII,5.

twelve gates."[7] The Gloss here says that by 'gates' we are to understand the holy apostles through whose faith and doctrine we enter into the holy city.[8] For no matter how many men are converted to Christ, they are led into the holy city by their teaching. These are the twelve foundations of that same city, as is written in the same place: that "the walls of the city had twelve foundations."[9] For although Christ is the first and chief foundation of the Church, the apostles are nonetheless her secondary foundations. Hence the Gloss on that passage at *Ephesians* II - "They are built upon the foundation of the apostles"[10] - says: that is, upon Christ, Who is the foundation of the apostles and prophets.[11] For no one can lay down another foundation deeper than that which is laid down, and which is, in Christ. For the apostles and prophets are called foundations, as in the psalm: "Her foundations are upon the holy mountains."[12] Christ, however, is the first and greatest foundation. For just as He is called the Holy of Holies and the Shepherd of Shepherds, so is He called the Foundation of Foundations.

Of these secondary foundations of the Church - of the apostles, that is - the Apostle says at *I Corinthians* XII: "God hath indeed set some in the Church: apostles first," [and so on][13] - first, says the Gloss, in dignity and time, preaching on Christ's behalf, and as the ordainers and judges of all men.[14] And at *Hebrews* XII: "You are come to the Church of the first-born"[15] - that is, the Gloss says, of the apostles, who were the first to believe, and by whose faith others have been set free.[16] To these blessed apostles there have succeeded in the Church the bishops and prelates; and the successor of the foremost and first of them, namely Peter, is the chief prelate and Supreme Pontiff, the shepherd and ruler of the universal Church, who is called pope [*papa*], that is, the father of fathers [pa*ter* pa*trum*], or the shepherd of shepherds [pa*stor* pa*storum*]. Or, again, he is called apostolic in a special sense, because he has succeeded to the headship of the apostles: because he presides over the whole Church which is called apostolic.

Now seventy-two disciples were ordained by the apostles;[17] and these are said to be the second contingent of those first designated as apostles by the Lord. And to these have the lesser clergy succeeded in the Church. The Church, therefore, is rightly called holy and apostolic. Here, however, a question must arise: Why is she rather called 'apostolic' than 'prophetic'?

---

7. *Apoc.* XXI,12.
8. *Glossa ordinaria*, PL 114,746f.
9. *Apoc.* XXI,14.
10. *Eph.* II,20.
11. *Glossa ordinaria*, PL 114,592; Peter Lombard, *Collectanea*, PL 192,186.
12. *Psalm.* LXXXVI,1.
13. *I Cor.* XII,28.
14. *Glossa ordinaria*, PL 114,542; Peter Lombard, *Collectanea*, PL 191,1657.
15. *Heb.* XII,23.
16. Peter Lombard, *Collectanea*, PL 192,508.
17. But the seventy-two disciples mentioned at *Luc.* X,1 were appointed by Jesus Himself; the seven deacons of *Act.* VI,1ff were ordained by the twelve.

To this, we must reply that this is because of the greater fulness of grace that was in the apostles, and their more enlightened and far-proclaimed teaching, which has been spread throughout the whole world. And so we have it in *Deuteronomy* XIX.[18] Thus our Lord Jesus Christ, our Saviour, provided, so that the truth which was formerly contained in the proclamation of the Law and the prophets might issue forth from the trumpet of the apostles for the salvation of all men. In this sense, the apostles are the sons of the prophets and patriarchs of old. Hence the psalm: "Instead of thy fathers, sons are born to thee: thou shalt make them princes over all the earth."[19] And so, therefore, from the fact that the Church is called apostolic from the apostles, we are to understand also the patriarchs and prophets whose sons the apostles are, both by fleshly begetting and by emulation of their works.

But another doubt arises with regard to what we have said: namely, why [in the Creed] is the Church called apostolic, from the apostles who are Christ's members, albeit noble and distinguished ones, yet she is not called Christian from Christ, Who is the head of the Church? To this, we must reply that, whereas the Church is undoubtedly said to be Christ's and is called Christian [elsewhere], just as we speak of the Christian people, in the Creed she is instead called apostolic because, by this, two things are meant: namely, both the band and company of Christ's apostles, and also Christ Himself. For 'apostles' means 'those who are sent'; and to be sent implies a sender. Hence, because the apostles were sent out by Christ, Christ Himself is also implied in the fact that the Church is called apostolic. Moreover, Christ Himself is truly called an apostle, because He was sent out by the Father, according to that passage in *John*: "As the Father sent me, I also send you."[20] And so at *Hebrews* III it is said of Christ: "Consider the apostle and high priest of our confession"[21] - that is, Whom we confess. For why, as the Gloss says here, should we deny the apostle Whom God has sent us?[22] For this reason, then, the Church is called apostolic not only from the apostles of Christ, but also from Christ Himself, the supreme apostle.

Moreover, by the fact that the kingdom of the Church is called apostolic we are given to understand a further condition of this kingdom: namely, that it is properly instituted. For the first institutor of this kingdom is Christ, and then the apostles. For they are her institutors who are also her founders and propagators. And this ecclesiastical kingdom cannot be other than rightly or legitimately founded, for she has both holy and perfect men as her institutors: the apostles, I say - the princes of peoples, gods of the earth, mighty witnesses to the faith, vicars of Christ, friends of God, vessels of the Holy Spirit. These received the fulness of the gifts of the Spirit so

---

18. The sentence seems to be incomplete and the reference makes no sense. This is presumably one of those unaccountable accidents which befall manuscripts as they are copied and recopied.

19. *Psalm.* XLIV,17.

20. *Joan.* XX,21.

21. *Heb.* III,1.

22. See Ch.I, n.20(ii), above.

that they might institute and propagate the Church: the speech of all tongues, to instruct all nations; the power of miracles, to confirm their teaching and convert the unbeliever; the authority to remit sins and to lead men into life, binding and releasing them; fortitude of soul against tyrants and against all the world's woes and joys; and wisdom of spirit against the wise men and lawyers of this world.

Also, from the fact that the kingdom of the Church is called apostolic we can infer another of its conditions: namely, firmness. For those same apostles who are the lords and princes of the Church are also her patrons and intercessors, her guardians and defenders. Also, as has been said above, they are her foundations. And therefore the Church is firm and strong because directed by such government, supported by such foundations, and protected by such patrons.

But we must not overlook the fact that, although the Church is called apostolic from all the apostles, she is nonetheless especially so called from the head of the apostles, Peter: because, that is, although she is founded upon all the apostles, she is nonetheless founded especially upon Peter, who is indeed the Church's head and foundation after Christ and on Christ's behalf. Hence at *Matthew* XVI it is said to him by Christ: "Thou art Peter, and upon this rock I will build my Church":[23] that is, in one sense, "upon thee", as Augustine explains.[24] (There is, however, another interpretation of "upon this Rock": that is, "upon Him Whom thou hast confessed," for the Rock was Christ,[25] or "upon this faith and confession";[26] and Augustine says this in a certain sermon on the See of the blessed Peter, expounding the text just cited.[27]) Thus, the Lord named Peter as the foundation of the Church; and the Church therefore rightly venerates this foundation, upon which the ecclesiastical edifice has risen to so great a height.

Truly, therefore, is the kingdom of the Church glorious in majesty and majestic in glory; for she is most rightly called one, holy, catholic and apostolic. And with this we bring to a close the first part of this work, in which the glory of the ecclesiastical kingdom has been briefly treated.

oOo

---

23. *Matt.* XVI,18.
24. Perhaps *Epist.* LIII,2 (CSEL XXXIV(II),152f).
25. *I Cor.* X,4.
26. Chrysostom, at Aquinas, *Catena Aurea* on *Matt.* XVI,18.
27. The expression "in a certain sermon" [*in quodam sermone*] suggests a reliance on memory. What James probably has in mind here is not a sermon, but *Retractationes* I,XXI (CC LVII,62).

PART TWO

ON THE POWER OF CHRIST THE KING AND OF HIS VICAR

I

On the manifold power of Christ. Here begins the second part, in which is discussed the power of Christ the king and of His vicar

After these things, then, we must treat of the power of Christ the King, and consequently of the power of His vicar: that is, the Supreme Shepherd of the Church Militant. But, as is written in the psalm: "Who shall declare the powers of the Lord?"[1] Certainly, no one worthily. But we should not on that account abstain from proclaiming the power of Christ to such an extent as the feebleness of human intellect and speech can achieve. First of all, however, we must distinguish the manifold forms of Christ's power inasmuch as Christ is both Son of God and Son of Man: one nature in two persons, true God and true man. And, according to His twofold nature, two forms of power belong to Him: the one divine, indeed, inasmuch as He is the Son of God and God in His own nature; and the other human, inasmuch as He is man and the Son of Man. His divine nature He receives from the Father by eternal generation, by which, just as He receives it that He is God, and one and the same with God the Father, so also does He receive it that He is the same in power as, and equal in might with, God the Father.

But it is not now our intention to consider divine power with respect to its emanation from person to person [of the Trinity], according as there is in the Father the power to generate the Son, and in the Father and the Son the power to breathe forth the Holy Spirit. Rather, we shall deal with that power which is in God in relation to His creatures, which power indeed belongs to the Son of God, not in a different way from that in which it is in the Father and the Holy Spirit, but in the same way and equally. Hence also, just as the Father is omnipotent, so also is the Son omnipotent, and both are infinite in power. It does not, however, serve our present purpose to treat more fully of the omnipotence of God and the infinity of His power.

---

1. *Psalm.* CV,2.

41

Rather, in the matter before us it is enough for us to proceed by distinguishing Christ's divine power in relation to His creatures. For God's power in relation to creatures takes two forms: one pertaining to their creation, and the other pertaining to the government of created things.

Now this power may be differentiated according to a comparison of its different modes of action (for, considered with reference to the essence in which power is founded, it is one power, just as it is one essence). By His creative power, God brings forth natural things in order that they may be; for this - that is, this bringing into being - is a creation from not-being. And, by His governing power, He directs and conducts the thing so brought forth to its end. For this is what it is to govern: namely, to conduct something to its proper end. For a ship is said to be governed when it is steered and directed into a safe harbour by the industry of the master. And to God's creative power pertains both the creation of natural things themselves, according to the perfection of their being, and also the disposition of them according to the degree of their perfection of being.

Moreover, the governing power of God is differentiated according to its effects. For, as learned men propound, the effects of government can be taken to be of three kinds. One kind has reference to the end itself which it is intended to secure by government; and this end, indeed, is assimilation to the likeness of God.[2] In this sense, then, clearly, one of the effects of government is assimilation to the likeness of the Supreme Good which is God. In another sense, the effects of government can be considered with regard to those things by which a creature is brought to resemble God; and, in this sense, there are in general two effects of government: namely, the preservation of things, and the movement of them towards the good. For a creature resembles God in proportion as two things are achieved: that is, a creature is good in proportion as it approaches that good which is God; and a creature also resembles God in being the cause of goodness in others in proportion as it moves another creature towards goodness. And, in a third sense, we can consider the effects of government with regard to particular cases; and its effects of this kind are such that they cannot be numbered by us.

In the first sense, then, governing power is not differentiated; for, in that sense, it has only one effect. In the other two senses, however, it is differentiated. Its differentiation within the last sense, however, will not be discussed, because it does not lie within human comprehension by reason of the infinite number of its effects in relation to ourselves. We must, then, consider the distinct forms of governing power within the remaining sense. So, then: it is differentiated according to its two effects, which are the preservation of things in being and the movement of them towards the good.

Now government in the sense of preservation is indeed necessary to all things; for they would fall away into nothing if they were not preserved by the power of God. And so the blessed Augustine says at *De genesi ad*

---

2. Cf. Ps.-Dionysius, *De coelesti hierarchia* III,If (PG 3,163/164f).

litteram VIII: "The power and omnipotent and all-swaying might of the Creator is the cause of the continued existence of every creature. If this virtue by which the things which have been created are governed were at any time to be withdrawn from them, they would at the same time vanish from sight and the whole of nature would collapse together."[3] Now God preserves all things in general inasmuch as the existence of all things depends on Him, just as the light in the lower atmosphere depends upon the light of the sun. In this sense, God is said to be essentially in all things, because all things depend on Him not only when they are made, but also after they are made. And, specifically, He preserves something by removing the causes of its corruption. (Although not all things are subject to corruption, for certain things are indeed incorruptible.)

Now government in the sense of causing motion is differentiated; for the movement of God in things is of two kinds. In one sense, it is general: He moves things according to the order of nature which He Himself has instituted. In another, it is special, because sometimes He moves something in a fashion which is beyond the order of nature and beyond the causes known to us; and such motion and the effects which flow from it are called miracles. To this mode of government belongs, in a certain sense, the justification of the ungodly and the infusion of spiritual gifts; although the former is also the work of the Creator. But we must consider that God is called the king and ruler and lord of all with respect to both His creative power and His governing power; for it is the task of a king both to found a kingdom and to govern what he has founded. But because it is not always the case that he who is called a king has founded the kingdom, whereas government always pertains to the king's office, someone is therefore called a king specifically in respect of the task of government. The name 'king' [*regis*] itself, which is derived from 'ruling' [*regendo*], suggests this.[4] So also, God Himself is properly called a king by reason of His government.

But although He may be called, and is, the king of all creatures, there is nonetheless a special sense in which He is said to be the king of intellectual or rational creatures. For these are governed by Him in a special way by reason of their dignity, in respect of which they surpass all other creatures in intellectual splendour and in the freedom of will by which they do not merely act, but act as having dominion over their actions. For they are governed by God not only in the sense of being moved by the working of God within them, but also in the sense of being led by Him towards the good, and led away from the bad, by His teachings and prohibitions, His promises of reward and His threats of punishment. Non-rational beings, however, are not governed by God in this way; for they are only acted upon, and do not act, because they do not have freedom of will. Hence also, it belongs to the rational creature alone to govern itself by intellect and will, even though this government may not be sufficient for it because, since

---

3. The correct reference is to *De Gen. ad litt*. IV,12 (CSEL XXVIII(I),1O8).

4. Isidore, *Etym*. IX,III,4 (PL 82,342).

the creature may be deficient in intellect and will, it needs to be governed and ruled and perfected by some superior: that is, by the intellect and will of God. Generally speaking, then, and in sum, these are our remarks concerning the divine power of Christ in relation to His creatures: He is the creator of all things inasmuch as He institutes and disposes them; and He is the governor of all things inasmuch as He preserves and moves all things.

But there is in Christ a certain knowledge and will which belongs to Him specifically as man, aside from that which He has as God. And, as we have already mentioned above, we must speak of power in this sense also. For, apart from His divine power, there is in Christ another power which belongs to Him inasmuch as He is man and according to His human nature. It is not, however, our intention now to speak of Christ's human power insofar as, whether as an active or a passive power, it pertains to His body, but of His human power insofar as it belongs to His soul.

Now the soul of Christ can be considered in three ways. In one way, it can be considered according to its own nature and natural virtue; and, so considered, it has power to produce those effects which by nature belong to the soul: that is, governing and quickening the body and performing other natural tasks according to the powers with which it is naturally endowed - namely, sensing according to the power of sensation, moving according to the power of movement, desiring according to the power of appetite, and understanding according to the power of the intellect.

In another way, the soul of Christ can be considered according to the nature and virtue which have been superadded to its own natural capacities by grace; and, so considered, it has the power to bring about all those effects which belong to the soul - that is, to dispose and govern human actions - yet also to illuminate, by grace and the fulness of knowledge, and in a manner appropriate to rational creatures, all rational creatures who lack its perfection.

In a third way, it can be considered as a instrument which is itself united with the Word of God;[5] and, so considered, it has an instrumental power to bring about all miraculous transformations consistent with the purpose of the Incarnation, which is to make all things new,[6] whether in Heaven or on earth.

Now the power of Christ's soul considered in the three ways just set forth, pertains only to the power of government, which alone is capable of being communicated, and is communicated, to creatures, as will appear below. Creative power, however, which belongs only to God and is not communicated to any creature, is not found in Christ's humanity. Moreover, we must leave aside the power of Christ's soul considered according to the first way; for this kind of power is not peculiar to Him, but is shared with other men. Rather, we shall discuss the power of Christ according to the other two ways, for these are peculiar to Christ. For it

---

5. Cf. Aquinas, *Summa theol.* III,q.13,a.2.
6. Cf. *Apoc.* XXI,5.

belongs only to the soul of Christ to be personally united with the Word of God and to be full of grace. Other souls are indeed united with God according to contemplation and love, but not hypostatically.[7] Also, they participate in grace according to a certain measure; but they do not have the measureless grace of Christ, to Whom the Spirit is given without measure.[8] Hence, the power which belongs to Christ as man by reason of His union with the Word and His fulness of grace and wisdom is peculiar to Him. And this power is so full that He may in a sense be called omnipotent by reason of it. Not, however, in the absolute sense in which He is called omnipotent inasmuch as He is God; and so we must consider the two ways in which Christ is called omnipotent inasmuch as He is man.

In one way, He is, in fact, called omnipotent in the absolute sense, because of His hypostatic union with the Divine Word, by reason of which union those things which belong to Him as God are also said to belong to Him as man. And it is in this way that we are to understand what Christ says of Himself in the last chapter of *Matthew*, speaking in His human voice: "All power is given to me in Heaven and on earth."[9] For all power is given to Christ as man by reason of the union through which it was brought about that He should be omnipotent even though a man, just as He might be called God even though a man: not because He is omnipotent in different ways as Son of Man and Son of God, or divine in different ways, but because He is God and Man in one person. And, after the resurrection, He said that all power was given to Him because this fact had by then become known to men, whereas, before, it was known only to the angels.

In another way, Christ is called omnipotent, not in an absolute sense, but in relation to some specific thing and with respect to it, by reason of the universal power which He has over the transformation of creatures and over the government of all rational creatures. And He is called omnipotent in this sense not only because of His union [with the Word of God], but because of the power which belongs to Him according to His human nature, whether by virtue of grace or because it is the instrument of the Word which is united with it. Hence, according to this, it is possible to understand the Lord's words, quoted above, in another way, when He said, "All power is given to me in Heaven and on earth": that is, power over both angels and men, because He also illuminates the highest angels;[10] or power in the Church both Triumphant and Militant; or power with respect to the miraculous works which He can perform in all creatures, which is what is meant by "in Heaven and on Earth".

---

7. The expression 'hypostatic union' refers to the substantial union of the divine and human natures in the one person ('hypostasis') of Christ. It was adopted as a *terminus technicus* of Christian theology by the Council of Chalcedon in 451. For discussion and explanation see NCE, Vol. 7, s.v. "Hypostatic Union" (and related entries).

8. Cf. *Joan.* III,34.

9. *Matt.* XXVIII,18.

10. Cf. Ps.-Dionysius, *De coel. hier.* VII,III (PG 3,209/210).

It is, however, especially pertinent to our argument to discuss the power of Christ which belongs to Him by virtue of grace, by which power He influences rational creatures, and by reason of which He is called the head of the Church and we His members. For just as the natural head influences the other members as the first and chief and most perfect member, so does Christ influence other rational creatures inasmuch as He is before all in dignity and perfection because of the fulness of grace and wisdom which He receives from His union with the Word of God. And He is called the head universally, of angels and men alike, because of His excellence and influence, although He may be called the head of men in a specific sense by reason of the conformity and resemblance of nature according to species.

In order, then, to discuss this power, we must consider that, just as the influence of the natural head is of two kinds - the one an interior force of sensation and movement flowing from the head to the other members, and the other exterior, that is, a certain external government according to which man is directed in his outward acts by the vision and other senses which are in the head - so also does Christ, Who is a spiritual and mystical head, exert two kinds of influence. One kind is inward, by which He enlightens us with wisdom and justifies us through grace. For His humanity, because united with divinity, derives the power to justify and influence from the fulness of grace and wisdom; and because His humanity is the instrument of divinity itself, His actions bring salvation to us by the power of His divinity inasmuch as they create grace in us both by merit and by a certain efficacy. As to the other kind, He influences us as it were externally, by governing and directing us by outward teaching: by word and example, and by other acts such as judging, feeding and purifying.

And because Christ is a head, influencing and presiding and governing, it is also fitting for him to be a king; for He is the king of angels and men because He is their head. Hence, those who are set over a people are called the heads of the people, and they therefore have royal power and dignity. There is, however, a further consideration: that it is fitting for Christ to exert influence in the manner of a head, but it is also fitting for Him to unite and reconcile in the fashion of a mediator.[11] For He is said to be a mediator between God and man because He unites men to God by exhibiting the teachings and gifts of God to men, and by giving satisfaction to God and interceding with Him for men. Now every act flows from some power; and so the office of mediator presupposes some power in Christ. And this is a priestly power; for He is a priest because He is a mediator. There is in Christ, therefore, both priestly and royal power. Both are directed towards the salvation of men and pertain to their government, although in different ways. But it is fitting for Christ to be a priest, just as He is also a mediator, only according to His human nature; whereas it is fitting for Him to be a king, just as he is also a head, according to both His divine and human natures. For He was anointed with both priestly and royal unction from the

---

11. Cf. *I Tim.* II,5.

moment of His conception; not with a material or visible, but with an invisible, oil. And just as He receives grace and wisdom from His union with the Word of God, so also does He receive power. Hence, from what has now been said, we can infer the following differentiation of Christ's power: namely, that a certain power belongs to Him only inasmuch as He is God, namely, creative power; for this is not communicated to Him as man, unless perhaps it may be said to be communicated to Him in the sense that justification is called a kind of creation, or, rather, re-creation, the cause of which justification is Christ's meritorious humanity, which brings it about in the manner of an instrument. Nonetheless, we do not on this account say that the power of creation, or [the power of bringing] the sacraments, which are the instruments of grace [into existence], have been communicated to Him [as man]. For the kind of power which belongs to Christ solely as man is priestly. Nonetheless, a certain power belongs to Him both as God and as man: namely, royal power and the power to perform miracles; although these belong to Him as God in one way and as man in another. For they belong to Him as God as to their originator, and they belong to Him as man as to a minister.

Now it may be objected that every power which belongs to a creature belongs also to God because every perfection of a creature reposes pre-eminently in God, and a power to act must be a perfection, and that therefore priestly power must belong to Christ as God. To this, we must reply that, inasmuch as it is a power and a perfection, priestly power pre-exists in God pre-eminently; but what is implied in the exercise of such power does not pertain to God, because it involves imperfection. For it pertains to the priestly office to make offerings, to pray and to mediate between God and man; and so subjection and subordination are introduced into the priesthood, neither of which things pertains to the divine perfection even though they may belong to the dignity of a creature. God can, however, be called a priest in a large sense, inasmuch as He is the sanctifier of men; because the word 'priest' [*sacerdos*] is derived from 'sanctifying' [*sanctificando*].[12]

In confirmation of what has just been said, authorities may be adduced from many places in scripture by which Christ's power and lordship may be shown, and how He is the head of the Church, and His royal and priestly dignity, and that both may belong to Him, and also the manner and excellence of His priesthood. Indeed, in *Colossians*, the Apostle says of Christ: "He is the head of the body of the Church";[13] and the Gloss[14] here says that He is the head of His body according to the nature of man: that is, of the Church, which is united with Christ by grace and nature as with a head. It is well said, therefore, that He is the head of the body of the Church, because He is related to the Church as the head is to the body.

---

12. Isidore, *Etym.* IX,III,4 (PL 82,342).
13. *Col.* I,18.
14. *Glossa ordinaria,* PL 114,610; Peter Lombard, *Collectanea,* PL 192,264.

For He tends the Church and rules her, and all the Church's spiritual senses are in Him, just as all the body's senses are in the head. And, as the Gloss[15] says later, the operation of all things is subject to the head because it is set on high in order to govern; for the head is, so to speak, the seat of the mind, which governs the body because all the senses are located there. But that Christ is the head not only of men but of angels, the Apostle explains in the same epistle,[16] speaking of Christ as the head of every principality and angelic power, as the Gloss says.[17] And of the lordship and power of Christ over all things, and of the manner in which He is the head, the same Apostle says in *Ephesians*: "He", that is, God the Father, "hath put all things under His feet, and gave Him to be the head" over the whole Church which is His body.[18] And the first part of this verse is derived from that passage in the psalm[19] upon which the Gloss[20] says that Christ surpasses all things not only in dignity but also in power, because all things are wholly under Him (for 'under His feet' signifies entire subjection): all of which things are subject to Him because made by Him. Alternatively, 'under His feet' means 'under His humanity', which is signified by 'feet'; for just as the feet are the lowest part of the body, so is Christ's humanity the lowest part of His nature. The angels adore even this, however; and so all things are under Christ even as man.

Moreover the Gloss on the following words, "He gave Him to be the head over all things to the Church", says: "Over all things to the Church, whether in Heaven or on earth."[21] For these things are subjected to Him as to the head from which they derive their origin. For they were made by Him according to His divinity, and so He is the head of the Church by reason of His godhood, inasmuch as the Father gave Him to be the head by begetting Him before all things. Also, and specifically, He is called the head with respect to His humanity, according to which the Church is conjoined to Him by both nature and grace. For there is in Him a fulness of grace, and of that fulness we receive.

As to what we have said, however - that all things are subject to Christ: we must consider that, whereas all things are subject to Christ now with respect to the power which He has received from the Father over all things, not all things are yet subject to him with respect to the exercise of that power. They will be in time to come, though, when His will concerning all men shall be fulfilled: salvation for some and punishment for others; and so all men will then be under Him, whether willingly or under compulsion and unwillingly. Of this lordship and power of Christ it is said at *Hebrews*

---

15. Peter Lombard, *Collectanea*, PL 192,263f.
16. *Col.* I,16ff.
17. Peter Lombard, *Collectanea*, PL 192,263.
18. *Eph.* I,22f.
19. *Psalm.* VIII,8.
20. Cf. *Glossa ordinaria*, PL 113,856.
21. *Glossa interlinearis* on *Eph.* I,22.

I: "Whom He hath appointed heir of all things";[22] on which the Gloss[23] says that, although He possesses all things with the Father, He is nonetheless rightly said to have been appointed heir in respect of His humanity, according to that passage which says: "I shall give thee the heathen for thine inheritance."[24] Therefore, because God the Father has now appointed Christ to be the unalterable heir of all things, that is, the possessor of every creature, not now is Jacob the Lord's portion and Israel His share, but indeed all the nations of the world.[25]

Again, in the same epistle the Apostle cites, in relation to Christ's royal power, that passage from the psalm: "Thy throne, O God, is for ever and ever; a sceptre of righteousness is the sceptre of Thy kingdom."[26] Expounding this, the Gloss says: "O God the Son, Thy throne, that is, Thy royal dignity, or Thy judgment seat, endureth for ever and ever, because it will forever rule and its judgment will be forever exalted."[27] Hence, in the Gospel: "These shall go away into everlasting punishment, but the just into life eternal."[28] And rightly does Thy throne endure, because the sceptre of Thy kingdom, that is, the rod and discipline by which the good are governed and the wicked smitten, is a sceptre of righteousness: that is, a straight and unbending rod, elsewhere called a rod of iron,[29] by which, if it shall be willing to cleave to it, misshapen wickedness may be guided.

At the same time, with regard to His priestly and royal dignity or power, the Apostle cites that passage from the psalm which says: "God, thy God, hath anointed thee with the oil of gladness above thy fellows."[30] Expounding this, the Gloss says: "O God the Son, Thy God - that is, the Father - hath anointed Thee Himself, and not by ministers after the fashion of men, because godhood hath no need of such."[31] Who, then, is the God anointed by God? You are to understand this to mean Christ. For 'Christ' means 'anointed': "For *chrisma* in Greek means 'anointed' in Latin."[32] The name 'Christ' therefore means 'anointed'; nor were kings and priests anointed elsewhere than in the kingdom of the Jews. Therefore, by the fact that he [St Paul] says that He [Christ] was anointed, he signifies that He is king and priest. But He [God the Father] has anointed Him, not with a visible and corporeal oil, but with the Holy Spirit, Whom scripture signifies by the name 'oil of gladness'; and this above His fellows, that is, above all

22. *Heb.* I,2.
23. Peter Lombard, *Collectanea,* PL 192,402.
24. *Psalm.* II,8.
25. Cf. *Deut.* XXXII,9; *Psalm.* LXXVII,71; *Glossa ordinaria,* PL 114,643; Peter Lombard, *Collectanea,* PL 192,402.
26. *Heb.* I,8, quoting *Psalm.* XLIV,7.
27. *Glossa interlinearis* on *Heb.* I,8.
28. *Matt.* XXV,46.
29. Cf. *Psalm.* II,9.
30. *Heb.* I,9. quoting *Psalm.* XLIV,8.
31. *Glossa interlinearis* on *Heb.* I,9.
32. Isidore, *Etym.* VII,II,2f (PL 82,264).

the saints. For all the saints are partakers of the Spirit, and so all are anointed as Christians; but Christ is anointed in a manner peculiar to Himself.

Again, concerning the priesthood of Christ, the Apostle specifically cites, in the same epistle, that passage from the psalm: "Thou art a priest forever, according to the order of Melchizedek."[33] And the Gloss, expounding this, says of the pontificate of Christ: "God the Father says, Thou art a priest, that is, teaching, praying and making offerings."[34] Behold the two kinds of priestly office. Thou art a priest, not in time, as Aaron was, but for ever, and this according to the order of Melchizedek, that is, according to the dignity and rite of ordination of Melchizedek's priesthood, which was not in time: for scripture is silent as to the beginning and end of his life; and this prefigures Christ, Who has no beginning and no end. And just as the former once offered bread and wine,[35] so Christ gave His body and blood to His disciples under the aspect of bread and wine. And it is added in the Gloss: "But Christ was a priest not inasmuch as He is God, but inasmuch as He took flesh as the victim which He then offered for us."[36] And, as to what this priest and pontiff did, the Apostle adds: "Who in the days of His flesh," that is, of His mortality, "when He had offered up prayers and supplications,"[37] and so on - when, that is, His Passion being nigh, He prayed more earnestly, or [poured out] prayers and supplications. This is the work and life of Christ, Whose every act is a lesson to the faithful and a prayer to God. For in all that Christ did He made prayers and supplications for men. Even in the pouring out of His blood He "made a strong crying";[38] and now, in Heaven, He assists the will of God as an advocate for us, interceding with the Father.[39]

It must be known, however, that Christ is called both priest and pontiff,[40] and that He is as much pontiff as priest and as much priest as pontiff. For the priest is a mediator between God and the people, because he teaches the people divine things and leads the people back to God by offering, praying and teaching; and that is also the meaning of the name 'pontiff'. Hence the Gloss on *Hebrews* III, where the Apostle calls Christ an apostle and pontiff,[41] says: "He is the pontiff by Whom we are brought to God."[42] For 'pontiff' means 'mediator'; and so it is said at *Hebrews* V: "For any pontiff

---

33. *Heb.* V,6, quoting *Psalm.* CIX,4.
34. *Glossa interlinearis* on *Heb.* V,6.
35. *Gen.* XIV,18.
36. *Glossa ordinaria,* PL 114,652.
37. *Heb.* V,7.
38. Ibid.
39. Cf. I *Joan.* II,1.
40. In English versions of the Bible, the original Greek word *archiereus*, translated in the Vulgate as *pontifex*, is usually rendered as 'high priest'. But the point of James's arguments will be somewhat obscured unless we consistently translate *pontifex* as 'pontiff'.
41. *Heb.* III,1.
42. *Glossa interlinearis* on *Heb.* III,1.

taken from among men is ordained for men",[43] that is, so that he may help them, and so that through him they may obtain mercy from God. Is ordained, I say, "in those things pertaining to God": that is, for the offering of the gifts and sacrifices and entreaties which are brought to God; "that he may offer gifts", that is, first fruits and sacrifices and other such things to God for the forgiveness of sins.[44] And the blessed Bernard says that a pontiff is so called because he as it were makes himself a bridge [*pontem*] between God and his neighbour.[45] In this respect, however, the pontiff differs from the priest: because the former has a certain excellence above that of the priest. For, as Isidore says at *Etymologiae* VII: "The pontiff is the prince of priests and, as it were, a path for those who follow, and he is himself the supreme priest."[46] Hence, the name 'pontiff' is explained at *Leviticus* XXI, where it is said: "The pontiff, that is, the high priest."[47] And so the bishops, who are set over the other priests, are properly called pontiffs; and the others, who are beneath them, are called by the general name of priests [*sacerdotes*] from the fact that they offer sacrifice [*sacrificando*].[48] And because Christ is the Supreme Priest, He is therefore most properly and especially called a pontiff; and so the Apostle says of Him at *Hebrews* III: "We have a great pontiff";[49] who, as the Gloss[50] notes, is above all pontiffs because "no man taketh this honour unto himself, but he that is called of God, as was Aaron", as the Apostle says in *Hebrews*.[51] And so, in the same place, he adds: "Christ glorified not Himself to be made a pontiff". Rather, He has appointed Him a pontiff Who in the psalm says to Him: "Thou art my son";[52] in which psalm it is shown that Christ is both priest and king.

But the priesthood of Christ differs from the priesthood of the Law; for the priesthood of the Law had need to make offerings not only for others, but also for itself, because it was itself surrounded by the infirmity of sin. Christ, however, had no need to make an offering on His own behalf, but only for others; for He is immune from every sin. Again, the priesthood of the Law was fleshly; but the priesthood of Christ is spiritual. Moreover, the priesthood of the Law was temporal, and had an end; but the priesthood of Christ is eternal. Hence, priesthood under the Law was translated to Christ, and this was prefigured in the translation of the priesthood from Eli, who was of the priestly tribe - that is, of Levi - to Samuel, who was not of

---

43. *Heb.* V,1.
44. Ibid.
45. *De moribus et officio episcoporum* III,1O (PL 182,817).
46. *Etym.* VII,XII,13 (PL 82,291).
47. *Levit.* XXI,10.
48. Cf. n.12, above.
49. The correct reference is to *Heb.* IV,14.
50. *Glossa interlinearis* on *Heb.* IV,14.
51. *Heb.* V,4.
52. *Psalm.* II,7.

the tribe of Levi, but of Ephraim.[53] And, similarly, in the translation of the priesthood to Christ, the royal tribe became the priestly (for the Lord was born into the tribe of Judah, which was the royal tribe[54]) so that the priestly and royal tribes should be the same, and so that Christ should be at one and the same time priest and king, and so that, moreover, the Israelite kingdom, which was temporal, should be transformed into the kingdom of Christ, which is eternal. This translation had already been prefigured when Saul was deposed and David took his place in the kingdom.[55] And wherever that kingdom and priesthood [of the Old Testament] is called eternal, we are to understand that by this is meant the kingdom and priesthood of Christ, which was prefigured by it.

Of the priesthood and kingship of Christ the Apostle speaks in the epistle cited above - that is, *Hebrews* - adducing the analogy of Melchizedek, who was both king and priest. "This Melchizedek", he says, was "king of Salem and priest of the most high God";[56] for, as the Gloss says: "He was appointed not by man, but by God."[57] And [the name Melchizedek] is interpreted "king of justice"; and he is called "king of Salem", that is, "of peace".[58] Also, he is without father or mother or offspring, for the scriptures make no reference to these.[59] And all these things apply also to the Son of God, Who is the King of Justice because He makes His people just and reigns through justice in this world; and the King of Peace because those whom He rules in justice here he will not fail to rule in eternal peace hereafter; and He is the Priest of the most high God because He has offered Himself upon the altar of the Cross; and He is without a father according to the flesh, and without a mother according to divinity, and without offspring because He begat no son of the flesh; and He has neither beginning nor end of days, because He is coeternal with the Father. And, as the Gloss[60] adds, if all the patriarchs and prophets were forerunners of Christ, Melchizedek was nonetheless especially so, who, not being, as some say, of the nation of the Jews,[61] was in many ways the precursor or type of Christ's priesthood, Who is called a priest according to the order of Mechizedek.

Again, on that passage of the Apostle in *Hebrews* - "He entered once into the holy place"[62] - a Gloss of the blessed Augustine says: "For Christ is both king and priest: a king Who has fought for us, and a priest Who has offered Himself for us."[63] And that same blessed Augustine, in the book

---

53. Cf. I *Reg.* I,1; II,27ff; III,11ff.
54. Cf. e.g. *Matt.* II,1ff; *Mich.* V,2.
55. Cf. I *Reg.* XV,26; XVI,1ff.
56. *Heb.* VII,1.
57. *Glossa interlinearis* on *Heb.* VII,1.
58. *Heb.* VII,2.
59. *Heb.* VII,3.
60. Peter Lombard, *Collectanea*, PL 192,448.
61. *Heb.* VII,6.
62. *Heb.* IX,12.
63. Cf. Peter Lombard, *Collectanea*, PL 192,471.

[*De diversis*] *LXXXIII quaestionibus*, where he expounds Christ's miracle of the five loaves and two fishes, says, among other things, that the five barley loaves signify either the Law of Moses or the Israelite people themselves. "The two fishes, however, which gave a pleasant flavour to the bread, seem to signify those two persons by whom the people were ruled so that they might receive the guidance of their counsels: that is, the royal and the priestly persons, to whom also belonged the holy anointing, and whose duty it was never to be subdued and weakened by the storms and floods of the populace, and often to burst asunder the contradictions of the mob like opposing waves. These two persons, however, prefigured our Lord, for He alone sustained both tasks; and not figuratively, for He alone fulfilled them. For Jesus Christ is indeed our king, Who has shown us an example of striving and conquering in His mortal flesh by taking our sins upon Himself; by not yielding to the blandishments and dark temptations of the enemy; by afterwards divesting Himself of flesh; and by resolutely despoiling principalities and powers and triumphing over them in Himself. He is indeed a priest according to the order of Melchizedek; for He made of Himself an offering for our sins";[64] and to the priestly office indeed belongs the cleansing and abolition of sins.

Of these two powers of Christ the Apostle speaks in *I Corinthians*, where he says of Christ: "He of God is made unto us wisdom and righteousness and sanctification and redemption."[65] For wisdom in ordering and righteousness in the giving of judgment are proper to His royal dignity, from which the power of judgment flows; and sanctification and redemption belong to his priestly power. But Christ is called the king, not only of the heavenly and eternal, but also of a temporal and earthly kingdom, because He dispenses and judges both heavenly and earthly things together. The sword which goes forth from His mouth is sharp on both edges;[66] for this one sword is His one royal power, which nonetheless has two edges, to rule heavenly and earthly things. He did not, however, wish to administer a temporal kingdom while he was sojourning with men in this mortal life, for the reasons which will be discussed below. These remarks, therefore, concerning the power of Christ, are sufficient for our present purpose.

---

64. *De div. quaest. LXXXIII* LXI,1f (CC XLIV(A),120ff).
65. *I Cor.* I,30.
66. Cf. *Apoc.* I,16; II,12.

II

That Christ's power has been communicated to men; and why and in what way

Next, then, we must treat of the communication of this power; and first, indeed, we must show that Christ's power has been communicated to men, and why and in what way. As to this, it must be known that creative power, which belongs to Christ only inasmuch as He is God, is not communicable to anyone. For if it was not communicated, or communicable, to His humanity, which was personally united with His divinity, still less can it be communicated to other men. And this is not because of any defect on God's part, as if He could not communicate it, but because of the deficiency of the creature, which is not in the least capable of such power, as catholic authors show by valid arguments which it is not here necessary to review.[1] Priestly power, however, which belongs to Christ as man, and the power to perform miracles, and royal power, both of which belong to Him both as God and as man: these are communicable, and are communicated, to men. For each of the powers of which we have just spoken pertains to governing power, and this is communicable. And in order that the communication of these powers may appear more clearly, we must carefully say something of the communication of governing power which is made by God to His creatures.

Governing power is indeed communicated to creatures by God; for He governs and rules certain created things through the mediation of others; and this does not come about because of a defect and weakness on the part of God, as if He Who created all things by Himself were not able to to govern all things by Himself. On the contrary, He can do by Himself whatever he does through the mediation of a creature, for a creature has no virtue or efficacy whatsoever save from God. But this communication pertains to the manifestation of His goodness and wisdom. For in the fact that governing power is communicated to creatures there shines forth the goodness of God, Whose pleasure it is to communicate Himself to His creatures not only so that they may exist and have being in themselves, but also so that they may influence other things and have causality in relation to other things. From

---

1. See, e.g., Aquinas, *Summa theol.* I,q.45,a.5.

54

such a communication of governing power, order is brought about in other things; and in this is made manifest the wisdom of Him Whose nature it is to bring order to things. And of this communication, and the reason for this communication, Hugh of Saint Victor speaks in the prologue to his commentary on *De angelica hierarchia*,[2] where he says: "God Himself, the maker of all things, Whose ineffable majesty and limitless power was able to govern alone what it had created alone, desired nonetheless to have sharers and co-workers in the government of the things made by Him: not so that He might be assisted by their ministry, but so that they might themselves be made more sublime by sharing in His power. The Lord alone, therefore, is indeed the prince of all things; but dominations and principalities are appointed to be under Him in the ministry of perfecting what the order of the universe requires, so that His works may be completed by their orderings and dispositions."[3]

So, therefore, the good and wise God governs the creatures which He alone has made in a certain order, according to their degree of perfection: that is, the lower through the mediation of the higher. For, in this fashion, he governs bodies through spirits, and the more gross bodies through the more subtle: that is, the generable and corporeal through the incorruptible or heavenly; and the lower spirits through the higher.[4] But although the dignity and power of government may be communicated to the different creatures, they are nonetheless communicated in a special way to rational creatures; for, just as these are governed by God in a special way by reason of their dignity, as we have said above, so in a special and superior way is communicated to them the power to govern other things. For because they have free will, they are therefore governed as free creatures, and they also govern others as free creatures insofar as the others are of this kind. Hence, the lordship which pertains to government is properly said to be in them, even though, in a certain sense, it may also be said to belong to non-rational creatures, inasmuch as an active body is said to have lordship over a passive one.

Government is, however, communicated to the rational or intellectual creature firstly with respect to itself: that is, in order that it may rule and direct its own activity itself; and secondly with respect to other rational creatures. Thus, some angels are governed by other angels, and some men by other men, and men by angels.[5] For although each rational creature is intended to govern itself by the power of its own intellect, nonetheless, when some rational creatures are governed by other rational creatures, this is either because the order of the universe requires it, or because, in some respects, the government of reason alone is not sufficient. Hence, it is

---

2. That is, on the Ps.-Dionysius's *De coelesti hierarchia*.
3. *Commentariorum in hierarchiam coelestem sancti Dionysii areopagitae* I,II (PL 175,927).
4. Cf. Augustine, *De Trinitate* III,IV (CC L,135f).
5. Cf. Ps.-Dionysius, *De coel. hier.* VIff (PG 3,199/200ff); Aquinas, *Summa theol.* I,q.110,a.1.

fitting that they should be directed in their actions by the government of others; and this is clear in the case of men, some of whom, when others are not sufficient, are themselves appointed as kings, and preside over the direction and rule of others because they are deemed to be more outstanding in intellect and more righteous in what they desire than are the others over whom they are appointed. So also amongst the angels, those who rule are the stronger in intellectual light.

Third, government is communicated to rational creatures with respect to non-rational ones; for, by divine institution, rational creatures have lordship over the non-rational in the order of nature. But man governs non-rational creatures in one way, whereas rational beings are subject to him in another. For he rules over non-rational beings, not for their advantage, but for his own; for he uses them for his own purposes, and so man is said to be the end of these things, because they are appointed for his sake and for his service. But he rules over other rational creatures for their own good, even though there also arises from this a good proper to the governor himself, because, by this means, he ministers to God and so approaches the likeness of God. Hence, such is the government appropriate to rational creatures inasmuch as they are rational: such, that is, that they are to be governed for their own good. And those who, when they rule over any persons, intend to secure, not the good of their subjects, but their own advantage: these fall away from the true nature of the government which is appropriate to rational creatures. For those who are governed in this way are not ruled as free men, but as slaves, and they are as it were conducted in a manner appropriate to non-rational beings.[6] For this reason, those who rule in such a way are called, not kings, but tyrants. But it is our intention now to examine only that kind of government which is appropriate to rational creatures, and, specifically, to men, who are properly called rational. And we shall speak especially of the government, or of the governing power, which has been communicated to the Church by Christ and through Christ.

The governing power of Christ has indeed been communicated to men, first, because it is consistent with His goodness that He should make men the sharers of His power, and, second, because it completes His dignity. For it pertains to the dignity of one who governs and rules that he should have ministers through whom his power may be exercised. And the ministers themselves, to whom Christ has communicated power, are rendered worthy and honourable by the fact that they govern others on Christ's behalf. Hence, by the same token, in the psalm it is said of the apostles: "Thy friends, O God, are made exceedingly honourable; their principality is exceedingly strengthened."[7] Third, [Christ's governing power has been communicated to men] because it is expedient to human advantage. For man makes use of knowledge which he acquires through the senses; and, for this reason, just as it is appropriate for him to be led by perceptible signs

---

6. Cf. Aquinas, *De regimine principum* I,1.
7. *Psalm.* CXXXVIII,17.

to grasp intellectual truth, and by perceptible sacraments to receive invisible grace, so also is it appropriate for him to have as governor one who is visible and present to the senses.

Inasmuch as He is God, however, Christ, although present in all things and everywhere, governing and ruling all things, is nonetheless not visible to bodily sight. According to His human nature, of course, He was indeed visible; for He was seen on earth and had converse with men. It was not, however, consistent with His dignity and blessedness that He should remain always on earth in converse with us, Who was worthy to be exalted above all the heavens and lifted up in body. Hence, after the ascension, although He is always present to us in spirit - according to what He Himself said in the final chapter of *Matthew*: "Behold, I am with you all days, even to the consummation of the world"[8] - He ceased, however, to be present to us in body according to its own aspect; although, under another aspect - that is, in the sacrament of bread and wine - He is with us even in body. It was, therefore, for the sake of human advantage that Christ's governing power over men should by communication be handed over and relinquished to some men by Whom His Church should be ruled and directed towards her end, for the sake of the obtaining of which by men Jesus Christ deigned to come into the world. For Christ does not leave the Church in want of the things necessary to salvation.

But this governing power of Christ, as can be inferred from what we have said above, is of three kinds. One, indeed, is priestly, another royal, and the third is the power to bring about miraculous transformations. And Christ communicated each of these to men because each was of benefit to the Church. For by the working of miracles the teaching of the faith was confirmed and man moved to praise the divine power; by the priestly office man is sanctified and reconciled to God; and by royal acts man is directed and rightly ordered in his converse with both God and neighbour.

And in order to see something of the manner of this communication, we must consider that the priestly power is communicated as a ministry to some persons who are indeed called ministers of grace because they are called to minister by dispensing those perceptible sacraments in which grace is conferred, and which are the vessels and instruments of grace. Hence, some say that no power is communicated [by ordination to the priesthood], but that only a ministry is imparted. And it is undoubtedly true that the power which is communicated is not such as Christ has, Who, inasmuch as He is God, has the power to bring into existence [rather than merely administer] the effects of the sacraments. Inasmuch as He is man, however, he has only the power of a minister: although not in any fashion whatsoever, but in a pre-eminent way, because He brings about the effects of the sacraments by His merit and as their efficient cause. For His Passion, which belongs to Him according to His human nature, is the cause of our justification both by its merit and as an efficient cause, in the manner of an instrument; for the

---

8. *Matt.* XXVIII,20.

humanity of Christ is the instrument of divinity itself. And because it is an instrument united [with the Word of God], it therefore has a certain ruling power and causality in relation to those instruments not so united: that is, the ministers of the Church and the sacraments themselves.

Hence, the power of ministry which belongs to Christ as man, because it is pre-eminent, is called an excellent power; and, as catholic doctors teach, it consists in four things: first, in the fact that His merit and virtue operate in the sacraments; second, in the fact that the sacraments are consecrated in His name; third, in the fact that He was able to institute the sacraments Himself; and, fourth, in the fact that He can confer the effect of a sacrament without the sacrament.[9] And this pre-eminent power of ministry Christ could communicate, but He has not communicated it, lest hope be reposed in man, and lest divisions arise in the Church.

Nonetheless, Christ has communicated the power of ministry in a secondary sense, and He has bestowed it upon certain persons who are called, and who are, the priests and mediators of the New Testament because they are the ministers of the Supreme Priest and of Christ, the true mediator, acting on His behalf and displaying the saving power of the sacraments to men. And royal power also has been communicated to certain persons who are the rulers of others and who are for this reason called the heads of the peoples, although they are under the one principal head, Christ, to Whom royal power belongs pre-eminently. For although some may be called heads with respect to priestly power, the name of head more properly belongs to those who hold royal power, because by priestly power one is made a mediator between God and man. The title 'head', however, implies something that is first in some order; and so it more properly belongs to the holder of royal power, through which he is appointed to be the first, and to be above others.

But the holders of priestly and royal power alike are called vicars of Christ and ministers of Christ and co-workers of Christ. For Christ communicates His power to others in such a way as not to diminish His own but to retain it; and because it is He Who works in all things principally, those who share in His power and who work by means of His virtue are therefore rightly called the co-workers of Christ. Moreover, the power to work miracles can be communicated, and has in the past been communicated, to men by Christ: not, however, in the way that Christ has it, because, as with the sacraments, so with miracles, Christ, inasmuch as He is God, has the power to bring them into existence but, inasmuch as He is man, only an instrumental power. He has the latter with a certain pre-eminence and excellence, however; for not only can He perform miracles Himself, but He can also extend this power and grace to others, as is said at *Luke* IX: "He gave the apostles power over all devils, and to cure diseases."[10] But others have from Christ a secondary, instrumental power. For, universally, in the

---

9. Cf. Aquinas, *Summa theol.* III,q.64,a.3.
10. *Luc.* IX,1.

case of every power communicated by Christ to men, Christ Himself has it principally and pre-eminently, whereas the mere man has a secondary ministry and co-workership. It is clear, then, from what we have said, that the power of Christ has been communicated, and how it has been communicated, to men.

To what men the power of Christ which could be communicated has been communicated. Priesthood and royal power distinguished

After what has been said above, it is appropriate now to consider to what men the power of Christ which could be communicated has been communicated, and what advantage has come about from that communication. And we must speak first of the power to bring about miraculous transformations. Now this power has not been communicated to all men, but only to some. For this power pertains to government, which has not been communicated to all, but only to some. Nor is this power communicated only to the good, but sometimes to the wicked: "For many will say, Lord, in Thy name have we not cast out devils and done many wonderful works? And I will say to them, I do not know you."[1] Hence, just as other gifts, such as prophecy and grace of speech and other such things, are freely given to good and evil men alike, so also is the working of miracles.

Nor again does this power belong to all good men. For there were and are many saints who are not workers of miracles. Also, this power has no connexion with royal and priestly power, for it is frequently found without them and they without it. Therefore, Christ communicates this power to whom He wills, and when, and to what degree, and as He wishes, in such manner as He knows will be conducive to the advantage of the Church and the salvation of men. And it was communicated more abundantly in the primitive Church, because it was then more necessary to the dissemination and confirmation of the faith and the increase of the Church. And so the apostles, as the propagators of the Church and the fathers of the faithful, possessed this power in great fulness. Now, however, that the Church is enlarged and the faith confirmed, this power is not as necessary as it was in the beginning. Even now, however, miracles are performed by some persons in the Church for the edification of the faithful, although more rarely than in former times. But a discussion of this power does not much pertain to the matter before us. From now on, then, it must be left to one side, and the two other kinds of power discussed: that is, the priestly and

---

1. *Matt.* VII,22f.

the royal; for it is with these, and especially the royal, that this treatise is more concerned to deal.

Now it may seem to some that these two kinds of power should not be communicated, and have not been communicated, to the same person. Rather, because they are distinct powers, they should be communicated to different and distinct persons;[2] and this appears to be the state of things in the Old Testament, where royal and priestly power were distributed to different persons. So also in the New Testament, they seem to belong to different persons. For the priestly power belongs to those in the Church who are called priests or pontiffs, who preside over spiritual things; whereas the royal power belongs to earthly princes and temporal lords, who are also called kings, under whom exist the various degrees of power. And, according to this, we must, it would seem, say that, although Christ is both king and priest, his vicars - that is, the apostles and their successors - are nonetheless not priests and kings: that, on the contrary, only priestly or pontifical power belongs to them, by Christ's grant. And if royal power belongs to any of them, this is by the grant of earthly princes, as in the case of the Donation of Constantine, from which the Roman Pontiff holds imperial power. Although this may at first sight seem a reasonable and true saying, however, it nonetheless behoves those who wish to arrive at the truth to consider the matter more deeply and to speak of it more fully and in another way.

First of all, then, we must make a distinction as between priesthood and kingship or royal power. And it seems that these are to be distinguished in the same way as the sciences. For some of the sciences, such as the science of physics, are discovered by human effort, but some by divine revelation, as in the case of holy scripture; and both come from God, Who is the lord and principal author of the sciences, from Whom, as is said in *Ecclesiasticus*, is all wisdom.[3] Nonetheless, each comes from God in a different way. For the first - that is, physics - comes from God through the medium of the natural intellect of man by which this kind of science is discovered, and through the medium of the objects which are the subject-matter of this science. And because both the human intellect in which this science resides and the objects themselves with which this science is concerned are the works of God, the science itself is therefore said to be from Him, because the work of nature is the work of God. Hence also, God Himself is said to be the principal teacher of mankind, as Augustine shows in the book *De magistro*.[4] And the second science - that is, holy scripture - comes from God, but not through the medium of the discovery of the human intellect. Rather, it has come from Him in a special way, by revelation and inspiration, to those men by whom it has been handed down to us: to the saints of God - that is, the prophets, the apostles, and the other authors of

---

2. Cf. *Decretum*, dist. XCVI,10 (*Duo sunt*) (CIC I, 340).

3. *Eccli*. I,1.

4. *De mag*. XIV,46 (CC XXIX,202).

holy scripture - who have spoken to men by the inspiration of the Holy Spirit.

In the same way, then, we must draw a distinction in the case of priesthood. For a certain kind of priesthood came into being by human institution; and this was under the law of nature, before the time of the written Law, and also, after the Law was given, amongst those who lived only by natural law. For, in those days, firstborn sons were appointed as priests; or, again, others discharged the office of priest by making offerings of their own free will, even though they perhaps did not have the title of priest. Priesthood of another kind, however, came about by divine institution; and this began in Aaron. For that which came about by human institution began at the very foundation of the human race. Hence, Isidore says, in his book concerning the servants of the Church: "Priesthood began with Aaron, although Melchizedek offered sacrifice before him and, after him [i.e. after Mechizedek], so did Abraham, Isaac and Jacob. These, however, did so by spontaneous act of will, and not by priestly authority. But Aaron was the first of them all to receive the priestly title under the Law, and the first to be robed with the pontifical vestments and to offer sacrificial victims at the command of God, Who said to Moses: 'And thou shalt bring Aaron and his sons', and so on",[5] as is written in *Exodus*, where the rite of priestly investiture and priestly unction and consecration is described.[6] There was no such rite in the priesthood of the law of nature, however, although some persons then had an inward anointing, as can be gathered from the Gloss on that verse in *Hebrews* where Melchizedek is described,[7] of whom the Gloss says that "he was not of the race of the Jews, and he discharged the priestly office before the circumcision, so that the Jews might receive priesthood from the gentiles and not the gentiles from the Jews, and he was anointed, not with the visible oil which Moses used, but with the oil of exultation and purity of faith. Nor did he sacrifice animals, but foretold the priesthood of Christ with bread and wine."[8]

So far, then, we have said that there are two kinds of priesthood. And both come from God, but in different ways. For the first comes from God through the medium of nature, because the natural law prescribes that God is to be worshipped and that sacrifices and offerings are to be made to Him;[9] and to make offerings and sacrifices is the task of priests. Hence, under the promptings of the law of nature, some persons exercised the priestly function either spontaneously or by human institution, and by making offerings and sacrifices to God. For this reason, amongst the virtues which exist in us as aptitudes bestowed by nature and perfected by human effort, the prophets include a certain virtue called religion, to which it pertains to exhibit due

5. *De eccl. offic.* II,V (PL 83,780f).
6. *Exod.* XXIX,4ff.
7. *Heb.* VII,1.
8. Peter Lombard, *Collectanea*, PL 192,448.
9. Cf. Aquinas, *Summa theol.* IIaIIae,q.85,a.1.

worship to God, and which is called a species of justice.[10] Priesthood of this kind, then, is said to be from God because it arises from an inclination of nature placed within man by God, Who is the author of nature. But the other kind of priesthood arises spiritually, by God's instituting and intending it; and it is of this second kind that we now propose to treat, and which we shall now call priesthood. This kind began, indeed, with Aaron, but it was translated to Christ, Who was appointed by God to be a priest according to the order of Melchizedek. And His priesthood, because it has been communicated, now exists in the Church, where it is more excellent and more perfect than the priesthood of the Law.

And so three kinds of priesthood can be distinguished. One, indeed, arises from human institution by the prompting of natural reason; but this is imperfect and, as it were, unformed. Another arises from divine institution, and this came about by God's ordinance through Moses the lawgiver. This is called the priesthood of the Law, and it is also imperfect. But it prefigures the third kind, which is also by divine institution; and this was given by God to mankind through Christ, not by the ministry of any man or according to a visible rite of anointing, but without any intermediary and by the invisible anointing of the fulness of grace. In this way, He appointed Him to be a priest; and this is the priesthood of the gospel and of grace, which is true and perfect. And there are persons in the Church who, according to their participation in this priesthood, are made and are and are called priests: upon whom, in the image of the priesthood of the Law, a visible anointing is bestowed as a sign of invisible grace. The priesthood of nature is therefore not destroyed by that of the gospel, but perfected and formed by it; because grace does not abolish nature, but forms and perfects it.[11] The priesthood of the Law, however, has ceased, because it was a forerunner, and the forerunner has ceased with the coming of the truth. But the priesthood of the gospel, because true and perfect, now remains, containing the priesthood of nature within itself and fulfilling that of the Law, which was translated to it.

Moreover, another distinction can be drawn with respect to priesthood; for it is in one way private and in another public. It is private in the sense that every one of the faithful is called a priest when he offers on his own behalf spiritual sacrifices to God, whether of a contrite heart or the afflictions of the flesh or any good work whatsoever. Mention is made of this priesthood at *Revelation* I, where John, speaking of Christ, says: "He hath made us kings and priests unto God and His father";[12] and the Gloss[13] on this passage says that He has made us priests so that we who formerly sacrificed to demons might now sacrifice to God, and so that we who once offered to the Devil the sacrifice of our sins might henceforth offer to God the sacrifice

---

10. Cf. Aquinas, *Summa theol.* IaIIae,q.60,a.3.
11. Cf. Aquinas, *Summa theol.* I,q.1,a.8.
12. *Apoc.* I,6.
13. See Pt.I,Ch.I,n.20(ii).

of good works. But priesthood is public in that it is given to some for the salvation of many, because certain persons are ordained as priests in the Church to sacrifice to God for the salvation of the people, and to offer to God the people's prayers and supplications. And it is with priesthood in this second sense that we now intend to deal. (There is, however, a certain other kind of priesthood which is neither of nature nor of the Law nor of the gospel, but of the Devil, which is contrary to nature and the Law and the gospel; and this is the priesthood of abominable idols and false gods, which must be called not so much priesthood as a perversion of priesthood.)

We must also draw a distinction with respect to kingship or royal power. For one kind arises from human institution, because nature inclines us to it. For even amongst the beasts, some of which are gregarious and sociable by instinct of nature, a kind of government is found. So much the more, therefore, amongst men, to whom it is more natural to live in society than it is to any animal, is there a natural inclination towards the institution of government;[14] and such government is said to exist by human law, which arises from nature. But another kind of royal power arises from divine institution or from divine law, which proceeds from grace. And both kinds of royal power are from God, but in different ways. For the first comes from God through the medium of the nature of man, which is inclined towards it, and through the medium of human institution, which perfects the inclination of nature; and so it is called a human and natural power. But the second is from God in a special way, by His own institution and transmission; and so it is called a divine and supernatural power. And the first power, indeed, is concerned with the government of temporal and earthly things, and it is therefore called earthly and temporal or secular. The second, however, is concerned with the government of spiritual and heavenly things, and so it is called, and is, spiritual and heavenly, as will be shown more clearly below.

Moreover, royal power of the first kind is found amongst all men and at all times: that is, at the time of the law of nature and the written Law and the Gospel; and amongst men of all kinds, of whatever custom and condition: that is, amongst believers and unbelievers, Jews and gentiles; for that which is natural is common to all who have a share in nature. In one respect, however, such government and power existed differently as between the Jews and the gentiles. For, amongst the gentiles, it came about only by human institution; but amongst the Jews it did not in any sense come about by human institution, but through the intervention of a special divine ordinance, according to which both judges and kings were instituted for that people; and so there was much better government amongst the Jews than amongst the gentiles. Royal power of the second kind, however, was and is found only amongst the worshippers of the one true God; and, in the Old Testament, such power was granted to certain persons by God, but partially

---

14. Cf. Aquinas, *De reg. princ.* I,1.

and imperfectly and as to forerunners, as will become clear. In the New Testament, however, it was transmitted more fully, through Christ.

Furthermore, it will be shown below that both kinds of royal power are distinct from priesthood because of the difference of their offices and actions. Royal power of the first kind, however, was made distinct from priesthood, and in such a way that it might be distributed to many different persons, because of the great difference in the action of the two powers, so that the one might not be impeded in its operation by the other. Nonetheless, both powers are found to reside simultaneously in some persons in every age. For in the time of the law of nature, Melchizedek was a king and a priest. So too, Job was a priest, for he offered burnt offerings, and he was also a king, as he himself says: "When I sat as a king with his army standing about him".[15] Also, the firstborn sons of kings were priests and kings, as certain persons have shown; and Isidore says at *Etymologiae* VII: "The custom of the men of old was that the king should also be a priest or pontiff. Hence, the Roman emperors were also called pontiffs."[16] In the time of the Mosaic law also, Samuel was a priest and simultaneously performed the office of a judge, as we gather from *I Kings*.[17] At another time again, the people were ruled by the priests of God. And, in the time of grace, the Supreme Pontiff exercises both imperial and pontifical power; and we shall discuss whence he receives these below.

Royal power of the second kind is also thus distinct from priesthood, although both are nonetheless found in one and the same person. For both reside in all bishops; and, here, it is customary to distinguish these two as the power of orders and the power of jurisdiction.[18] For the power of orders is priestly, whereas the power of jurisdiction is royal. Sometimes, however, one of these is found in some persons without the other. For some have the power of orders but not of jurisdiction, and, on the other hand, some have the power of jurisdiction but not of orders. Having set out these distinctions, then, we must now see, in the case of both priestly and royal power, to whom they belong and to whom they have been communicated.

If by priesthood is meant that which is called natural and which arises from human institution, this was communicated to some persons simply according to the will of men. The priesthood of the Law, however, was communicated to some persons spiritually, by divine precept, as to Aaron and his posterity. This, however, was altered at the time of Eli and translated to Samuel, in whom, as we said above, was designated the change from the priesthood of the Law to the priesthood of Christ, Whom Samuel, who was prophet, priest

---

15. *Job* XXIX,25.

16. *Etym.* VII,XII,17 (PL 82,291).

17. *I Reg.* III,20; VII,9,15.

18. Traditionally, the power of the Church (*potestas ecclesiae*) is distinguished into the power of orders (*potestas ordinis*), according to which the Church teaches the faith and administers the sacraments, and the power of jurisdiction (*potestas jurisdictionis*), according to which she forgives sin through absolution or withholds forgiveness through excommunication.

and judge, prefigured. And the priesthood of the Gospel was communicated by Christ to the apostles and their successors, and by these latter to others again. For as regards the act of sacrificing, Christ transmitted priestly power at the Last Supper where, after He had consecrated His own body and blood and given them to the disciples to consume, He conveyed to them the power to do likewise, and the form [in which they were to do so,] when He said: "Do this in remembrance of me."[19] As regards the act of teaching and of administering the other sacraments, He gave them the power of priesthood and granted them the office when He said: "Go ye, therefore, and teach all nations, baptizing them in the name of the Father, and of the Son, and of the Holy Spirit";[20] and when He said: "Whose sins you shall forgive, they are forgiven them", and so on.[21]

Now royal power over temporal things, which arises from human law, is communicated to certain men, who are appointed to be rulers of others, either simply by the appointment and common consent of some community of men, as with the people of the gentiles, or by the intervention of a special divine ordinance or grant in addition to this, as with the people of Israel. And we must believe that some men were instituted in this way for the governance of others after the human race began to be multiplied.[22] Such rulers were not always called kings, however (although, even where they were not kings in name, they were so in fact). Hence, amongst the Jews they were sometimes called judges, and only subsequently were they called kings; and sometimes also they were called captains. But the name of king is said to have begun after the Flood, with Nimrod;[23] and, amongst the Jews, it began with Saul, who was the first to be called king, this being granted by God at the insistence of the people.[24]

But royal power over spiritual things was indeed communicated, to some degree and partially, to the priests of the Old Testament, to whose office it pertained to judge certain spiritual matters, or matters which were spiritual in their import, such as between leprosy and leprosy, clean and unclean, and other such things.[25] And, in the New Testament, this was communicated and delivered by Christ to the apostles and their successors; that is, when it was said to them: "Whatsoever ye shall bind on earth shall be bound in Heaven",[26] and so on. For the power to bind and release is a judicial power which certainly belongs to kings. In a singular and pre-eminent way, however, this royal power was given to the blessed Peter and, in him, to each of his successors; and, indeed, to the whole Church, when it was said

---

19. *Luke* XXII,19.
20. *Matt.* XXVIII,19.
21. *Joan.* XX,23.
22. Cf. *Gen.* VI,1
23. *Gen.* X,8f.
24. *I Reg.* VIII,5ff.
25. Cf. *Deut.* XVII,8.
26. *Matt.* XVIII,18.

to him: "I will give unto thee the keys of the kingdom of Heaven."[27] For the keys, as the term is here used, signify the spiritual power to grant admission to the kingdom of Heaven or to exclude from it. And such power is judicial and, for this reason, royal; for the act of judging properly belongs to the office of a king. Hence, those who have this power in the Church are called kings no less truly and properly, but more so, than those who have temporal jurisdiction: more so, indeed, because the government of spiritual things is more excellent and more worthy than the government of temporal things; and just as they are truly and properly called judges, so can they truly and properly be called kings. Also, they are called shepherds, because it belongs to the power of a king to feed his flock. The kings of old were therefore called shepherds, and so to Peter also it was said by Christ: "Feed my sheep."[28] By this, He entrusted to him the government of the Church, and appointed him to be the king and prelate of the Church.

Moreover, what we have said - that is, that those who have spiritual jurisdiction may truly and properly be called, and are, kings - can be proved. For, according to Isidore, kings [*reges*] are so called from 'ruling' [*regendo*];[29] and it belongs to those whose power is so called to rule the faithful people, according to what is said at *Acts* XX: "Take heed to yourselves, and to the whole flock, wherein the Holy Spirit hath placed you bishops, to rule the Church of God, which He hath purchased with His own blood."[30] And these bishops are said to have been placed by the Holy Spirit either because they were appointed by the apostles under the inspiration of the Holy Spirit, or because the ordination of bishops is confirmed by the grace of the Holy Spirit which is represented by that oil which is applied at their consecration. Again, the apostles and their successors are called princes according to that passage in the psalm: "Instead of thy fathers, sons are born to thee: thou shalt make them princes over all the earth."[31] And again: "But to me Thy friends, O God, are made exceedingly honourable: their principality is exceedingly strengthened"[32] - because, the Gloss says, they are made leaders and shepherds of the Church.[33] For this reason, they must by the same token be called kings; and of these kings it is said in the psalm: "When He that is in Heaven scattered kings in her."[34] And the Gloss here says: "'He that is in Heaven', that is Christ, Who is raised up above all the heavens, has scattered, that is, has apportioned or distributed, kings, that is, rulers, in her, that is, in the Church."[35] Again, it is said in

---

27. *Matt.* XVI,19.
28. *Joan.* XXI,15ff.
29. *Etym.* IX,III,1 (PL 82,341).
30. *Act.* XX,28.
31. *Psalm.* XLIV,17.
32. *Psalm.* CXXXVIII,17.
33. *Glossa interlinearis* on *Psalm.* CXXXVIII,17.
34. *Psalm.* LXVII,15.
35. *Glossa interlinearis* on *Psalm.* LXVII,15.

another psalm: "The daughters of kings have delighted thee."[36] And upon this the Gloss says: "He calls the apostles kings, who govern themselves and others in the virtues, and whose daughters are all those begotten by them into the faith."[37] And the blessed Dionysius, at *De divinis nominibus* XII, says that, in sacred eloquence, those who are the more highly distinguished, that is, those who are placed in the first rank and who are above all others, are called saints and kings and lords and gods.[38]

Moreover, the Gloss on that verse of *Revelation* I - "the first begotten of the dead, and the prince of the kings of the earth"[39] - makes a distinction concerning kings, saying that some are kings because they rule their subjects by divine disposition; others are kings because they rule over the faithful people entrusted to them; and others are kings simply because, with God's help, they rule over themselves. The first of these are secular princes; the second are the shepherds of the Church; and the third are the individual believers.[40] Christ, however, is the prince of them all, because from Him comes secular power and pastoral care and every single talent of each one of the faithful. And just as all things derive their origin from Him, so do they owe to Him the capacity by which they act: the princes by secular power, so that they may maintain justice as between those men subject to them; the shepherds by pastoral care, so that they may offer doctrine to the faithful entrusted to them; and each individual believer by his own particular talent, so that he may preserve himself in holiness. It is clear from this distinction, then, that the shepherds of the Church are truly kings, amongst whom he who is supreme - that is, the successor of Peter - is the king of kings, be they secular, spiritual, or individual believers. Just as Christ Himself, Whose vicar he is on earth, is called the prince of the kings of the earth - of those, that is, who are on the earth - so, from the fact that these are kings, the prelates also are so called: because they rule, and this task belongs to kings. Hence, in the *Book of Wisdom*, after it says: "O ye kings of the people, love wisdom", it adds further, "Love the light of wisdom, all ye that bear rule over peoples"[41] - as though it were the same thing to be a king and to bear rule over peoples.

Although, however, everyone who bears rule may be called a king, nonetheless, because royal power is the supreme form of human power, as Hugh says in the book *De sacramentis*,[42] only those who have the highest power are usually called kings, whereas those who have power under them of a limited kind are indeed not ordinarily called kings, but are allotted another title of their own. For this reason he who is supreme amongst the

---

36. *Psalm.* XLIV,10.

37. *Glossa interlinearis* on *Psalm.* XLIV,10.

38. *De div. nom.* XII; but James is here paraphrasing the translation of *De div. nom.* made by Johannes Scotus Eriugena: See PL 122,1169.

39. *Apoc.* I,5.

40. See Pt.I,Ch.I,n.20(ii).

41. *Sap.* VI,22f

42. Hugh of Saint Victor, *De sacramentis fidei christianae* II,II,IV (PL 176,418).

prelates of the Church is called a king according to royal power over spiritual things (and the manner in which he is a king according to the temporal sense will appear below); but the other prelates, although they may be called, and are, kings, are nonetheless not so in the simple and unlimited sense that the Supreme Prelate - that is, the pope - is; and the same thing may be said of royal power over temporal things.

But there now arises a doubt over what we have said. For if, as has been shown, the prelates of the Church are truly and properly kings, why are they not commonly called kings by the faithful, and why did Christ not distinguish them with a royal title? To this, we must reply that there are two reasons why the prelates of the Church are not called kings. The first reason has to do with the avoidance of pride. For Christ, the master of humility, desired that His disciples and vicars should exhibit and preserve humility in all things. And so at *Luke* XXII He said to them: "He that is greater among you, let him become as the younger; and he that is the leader, as he that serveth."[43] For this reason, not only pride, but even the name and title of pride, must be avoided and shunned by them. But the name of king seems to imply pride because of the malice of those who have so often abused royal power, ruling over their subjects as tyrants and not holding fast to the true meaning of their title. For although kings are so called because they rule, these do not rule their subjects, but oppress them; for they do not intend and seek the welfare of their subjects, but their own advantage and glory. And so the blessed Augustine says at *De civitate Dei* V: "'Kingdom' is derived from 'kings', and 'kings' from 'ruling'; but kingly ambition was not deemed [by the Romans] to betoken a ruler or a benevolent counsellor, but rather the pride of a tyrant."[44] And so it is that, because of the wickedness of kings, royal dignity has been rendered odious and burdensome to many even though, for the good of the multitude, God has willed it to exist amongst men. For this reason, the blessed Augustine says of the Romans in the same place that: "Because they could not bear the proud mastery of kings, they appointed for themselves two consuls, so called because they were counsellors, for an annual term of office."[45]

And what we have said of the name of king can also be said of the name 'lord' when used as a title. For this name does indeed rightly belong to the prelates of the Church so far as what is chiefly implied by the name is concerned, for it signifies governing power. But because many have abused their lordship, the name of lord now sometimes smacks of pride and, for this reason, the blessed Peter said to the shepherds of the Church that they were not to lord it over the clergy.[46] And Christ said to His disciples: "The kings of the gentiles lord it over them; but you shall not do so."[47]

---

43. *Luc.* XXII,26.
44. *De civ. Dei* V,12 (CC XLVII,143).
45. Ibid.
46. *I Pet.* V,3.
47. *Luc.* XXII,25f.

And the second reason [why the prelates of the Church are not called kings] is in order to indicate a difference. For just as there is a difference in power as between spiritual and temporal kings, so must there also be in their names. For secular princes properly retain to themselves the name of king which is [strictly speaking] common [to both prelates and princes]; and they do so specifically because, as we read, many men had held the office and name of king before kings in the spiritual sense were instituted. Spiritual princes, however, are called by other names which imply, not pride, but action and power, and by which their difference from secular princes is indicated. For they are called shepherds, priors and bishops, pontiffs and abbots; but they are not customarily called kings and, similarly, they are not usually called princes and dukes, unless the title belongs to them in their own right. They are, however, called rulers and judges.

And for this reason it must be known that, strictly speaking and in the proper sense of the terms, the power of spiritual and secular princes should not be differentiated in such a way that the one is called royal and the other priestly [as if the distinction between them were absolute]. For, in addition to that kind of priestly power which does not involve jurisdiction and prelacy, but only a power of orders, a royal power does truly belong to the prelates of the Church. Both powers [i.e. that of the prince and that of the prelate insofar as the latter is not simply a power of orders] are indeed truly called royal; but the one is divine and the other human, the one is heavenly and the other earthly, the one spiritual and the other secular, as will be seen more clearly below. But because the name of king is not usually given to the prelates of the Church, both to avoid pride and for the sake of differentiation, the royal jurisdiction and power over spiritual things which is conjoined with the priestly power in one and the same person is therefore [only] implied in the term priestly or pontifical power [and not made explicit]. In this way, pontifical or priestly power is distinguished from royal to the extent that [in ordinary speech] the latter belongs only to those earthly princes to whom the name of kings has been granted. [In truth, however, the prelates of the Church also have royal power.] Hence, it is said in the *Decretum*, dist. XCVI: "There are two agencies by which this world is principally ruled: the consecrated authority of the bishops and the power of kings."[48] Moreover, it must be noted in the case of each power that it can be righteous and perverse, legitimate and illegitimate. For priesthood is rightly attained by some, as in the case of Aaron, who was called by God; but others assume it by usurpation, as we read in *Numbers* of Dathan and Abiram.[49] Moreover, some achieve royal power over earthly things rightly, whether by election and the common consent of the multitude or by divine ordinance; and some do so improperly, by violence. So also, many acquire royal power over spiritual things rightly, according to the ordination of the Church; but some do so perversely, as in the case of

---

48. *Decretum*, dist. XCVI,10 (*Duo sunt*) (CIC I,340).
49. *Num.* XVI.

certain heretics, who usurp it and award it to themselves. Moreover, not a few persons who call themselves Christians arrogate spiritual power to themselves unworthily in certain respects.

It is clear, then, from what we have said, to whom priestly power and to whom royal power, whether over spiritual or secular things, have been communicated; and that both powers belong simultaneously to the prelates of the Church: that is, the priestly or pontifical, and a royal power over spiritual things. But whether a royal power over temporal things may belong to them, and in what way it may and in what way it may not, will appear below.

IV

On the differences between priestly and royal power in the prelates of the Church; and of the actions of each; and certain other comparisons of the one with the other

Given, then, that the prelates of the Church have two kinds of power, we must consider the differences between the two powers that are in them so that we may see from this what it is proper for them to do by virtue of priestly power, and what by virtue of royal. And although these things may be inferred from what has been said above concerning the power of Christ, we must nonetheless discuss them more fully in this chapter, where we must carefully consider what may pertain to priestly and what to royal power.

In general, it can be said that it pertains to priestly power to sanctify and to royal to rule. For as Isidore says at *Etymologiae* IX, 'priest' [*sacerdos*] is derived from 'sanctifying' [*sanctificando*] and 'king' [*rex*] from 'ruling' [*regendo*].[1] Indeed, every act of the priest can be called a sanctification because by every priestly act it is intended to sanctify something [by releasing it] from either guilt or unknowing or ignorance. So also, every royal act can be called an act of ruling. In order that something more specific may be said of the actions of each power, however, we must note that the priest is an intermediary between God and the people, and therefore that those things are proper to the priest by which he is equipped for mediation between God and man: which is nothing other than the uniting of man with God, for an intermediary has the task of uniting those who are far apart. Now man is united with God when he is released from the sins which separate him from God. And, in one way, this is done through sacrifice; and so it pertains to the priest to offer sacrifices for the sins of the people - and, indeed, for his own also, insofar as he is subject to sin. Also, man is united with God when he is lifted up to Him in mind, and when he strives to obtain blessings from Him; and this is done through prayer which, as is said, is the ascent of the mind to God, and the petitioning of God for what is fitting.[2] But this requires the approach to Him of a kind of trusted servant; and so it pertains to the priest to pray for the people and to offer to God the

---

1. The correct reference is to *Etym.* VII,XII,17 (PL 82,291f).
2. Cf. Aquinas, *Summa theol.* III,q.21,a.1.

72

people's prayers, supplications and entreaties. Again, man is united with God when he comes to have knowledge of Him and also of the other things by which he is led to Him, and when he is subject to His will by fulfilling it; and so it pertains to the priest to teach the knowledge of salvation, through which both the mysteries of God and what is pleasing to His will are made known to us. Hence a knowledge of the law must be conjoined with the priest's office, as is said at *Malachi* I: "For the priest's lips should keep knowledge, and they should seek the law at his mouth."[3] Also, man is united with God when he is a sharer in divine grace, through which he is made in the image of God and becomes a son of God by adoption.[4] And so it pertains to the priest to administer the sacraments through which grace is conferred. (It does not, however, pertain to all priests to administer all the sacraments, for some are specially reserved to those greater priests who are called pontiffs.) Again, man is united with God by the fact that he serves and worships Him by doing Him honour; and so it pertains to the priests to minister in those things which belong to the worship of God, and it pertains to them to consecrate and bless those things which are used in the worship of God.

Moreover, it must be known that every ecclesiastical order is comprehended under the term 'priestly power', because each such order is either itself priestly or is related to priesthood as to an end for the sake of which it exists, and is subservient to it just as a lower art serves a higher. But how this is, and in what ways the other orders serve the priestly, we are not now to discuss. For the present, it is enough to have examined in brief those things which pertain to priestly power.

Next, we must examine those things which belong to royal power. Now the principal and special action of royal power is to judge. Hence, it is said of Solomon at *III Kings* X: "He made thee king to do judgment and justice"[5] - that is, to judge according to justice; and in the psalm: "The honour of the king loveth judgment."[6] Also, at *Wisdom* VI it is said: "Hear, ye kings, and understand: learn, ye who judge the ends of the earth."[7] Now judgment is the right determination of what is just [*iustum*]; and so to judge [*iudicare*] is to declare the law [*ius dicere*]. Moreover, the word 'just' is derived from 'law' [*ius*]; and so the power of judging [*iudicandi*] is called jurisdiction [*iurisdictio*]. And because judgment is the right determination of the law or of what is just, a determination and decision in these matters is therefore called a judgment, according to that verse of *Proverbs* XXVI: "Judgment determines causes";[8] and to pass sentence in a legal case is to judge. Moreover, because investigation is a necessary path to judgment, there is therefore contained in the act of judging

---

3. The correct reference is to *Mal.* II,7.
4. *Gen.* I,27; *Eph.* I,5.
5. *III Reg.* X,9.
6. *Psalm.* XCVIII,4.
7. *Sap.* VI,2.
8. *Prov.* XXVI,10.

the investigation and examination of those things around which the case revolves and on which a judgment is required. Again, because the determination of what is just is often accomplished by means of correction and punishment, the punishment and correction of the wicked therefore pertains to judgment, as, on the other hand, does the rewarding of the good. Hence, Augustine says at *Confessiones* XIII: "Someone is said to judge in those matters over which he has a power of correction."[9] And because it is a punishment to be excluded from the fellowship of the kingdom, it therefore pertains to judgment to exclude from the kingdom or to admit to the kingdom. And because judgment must be given according to determinate laws, it therefore pertains to kings, whose office it is to judge, to make laws or to receive and promulgate those established by others, and to secure their observance by the admonition of words and by the fear of punishment and the promise of reward. And so kings are called lawgivers, as is said in *Isaiah* of our Supreme King: "For the Lord is our judge, the Lord is our lawgiver, the Lord is our king."[10] Established laws, however, ought to be such that men are made good and virtuous by them; otherwise they are not laws, but corruptions of laws.[11] And so the intention of the king, as judge and lawgiver, ought to be that his subjects should live according to virtue. To this end, teaching and instruction are of great value; and so it pertains to kings to teach, as is said concerning Solomon in the final chapter of *Ecclesiastes*: "Because the preacher was wise, he taught the people."[12] And because a teacher teaches to good effect only when he carries out what he teaches in his own actions, kings must therefore observe the laws, so that they may with good effect lead their subjects to observe them also: as is said of Christ, the King of Kings, that "He began both to do and to teach."[13]

But because external goods serve the virtuous life as instruments, it therefore pertains to the king to procure and provide for the people a sufficiency of such goods as are necessary to life. Hence, it is the act of a king to feed and nourish, as is said of David in the psalm: "He chose David also His servant, to feed Jacob His people, and Israel His inheritance. So he fed them according to the integrity of his heart, and guided them by the skilfulness of his hands."[14] Also, it pertains to the king to dispense such goods prudently and with justice, and to distribute them in due proportion, according to each person's condition. Hence, in the psalm it is said: "Distribute her houses."[15] And, in the proper sense, distribution pertains to those things, whether external goods such as riches and honours, or tasks and burdens or duties, which are required for the order and perfection of the

---

9. *Confess.* XIII,23 (CC XXVII,262).
10. *Isa.* XXXIII,22.
11. Cf. Aquinas, *Summa theol.* IaIIae,q.96,a.4.
12. *Eccles.* XII,9.
13. *Act.* I,1.
14. *Psalm.* LXXVII,70ff.
15. *Psalm.* XLVII,14.

commonwealth. It is, then, the king's task to dispose and ordain in all respects the multitude over which he is set.

Moreover, because every community is preserved through unity and peace, it therefore pertains to the king to secure and foster the unity of peace in the multitude subject to him. But the peace of a multitude is indeed sometimes disturbed from within, by mutual injury and unjust hurt, and sometimes from without, by violent assault; and so it pertains to the king both to abolish the domestic injuries of his subjects and to protect and defend the community of the kingdom against external adversaries.

And because wisdom or prudence is required for all the foregoing tasks, kings are especially urged in sacred scripture to love and strive after wisdom. Hence it is that Solomon asked of the Lord, not riches or any external goods, but wisdom to rule the people.[16] Hence also, Boethius, speaking to Philosophy in the first book of *De consolatione*, says: "Thou hast confirmed the saying of Plato, that commonwealths would be blessed if those eager for wisdom were to rule them, or if those who rule them were to become eager for wisdom."[17] In sum, then, these are the things which pertain to royal power.

And from what we have said it can be inferred that both priestly and royal power truly belong to the prelates of the Church. For they are priests in that they offer sacrifices, intercede for the people, instruct the common folk, administer the sacraments, minister in the divine worship, and bless and consecrate those things which are used in the worship of God. But they are indeed also kings, because they are spiritual judges in matters of sin and in spiritual causes. They determine and pass judgment in such cases; they correct and punish; they bind and release; they close and open Heaven (for the kingdom of Heaven is closed to anyone who is subject to sin, but it is opened when he is cleansed from sin); and they remit sins. Hence, the Gloss on that verse of *Mark* II - "Who can forgive sin but God only?"[18] - says that only the Judge of all things has power to forgive sins, but He also forgives them through those upon whom He has bestowed the power of forgiveness.[19] These mitigate and compute penance. They excommunicate and restore to communion, or absolve from excommunication. By their judgment, men are expelled from the kingdom of Heaven or admitted to it, because they are vicars of Christ, to whose judicial power it pertains to do this; and so they are said to hold the keys of the kingdom of Heaven. For the power of the keys is the power of binding and releasing by means of which the ecclesiastical judge must receive the worthy into, and exclude the unworthy from, the kingdom: whether the kingdom of the Church Militant or the kingdom of the Church Triumphant. For what they bind on earth will be bound in Heaven and what they release on earth will be released in

---

16. *III Reg.* III,5ff.
17. *De cons. phil.* I, pr.IV (PL 63,615f).
18. *Marc.* II,7.
19. *Glossa ordinaria,* PL 114,186.

Heaven.[20] They are establishers of law; they are teachers; they are stewards, as the Apostle says: "Let a man so account of us, as of the ministers and stewards of the mysteries of God."[21] They dispose and ordain the ministers of divine worship and the other things which relate to the worship of God. They distribute ecclesiastical benefices. They are shepherds, because they feed Christ's sheep by word and example and temporal aid.

Truly, therefore, are they priests and kings, and it behoves them to do what is proper to each power. Hence, at the consecration of a bishop it is said that a bishop must judge and interpret (that is, teach or interpret) what is doubtfully determined, consecrate, confirm, ordain, make offerings, and baptize; and so they have both pontifical and royal power, and they have the power both of jurisdiction and of orders. For to judge belongs to the power of jurisdiction, and to consecrate, confirm and so forth to the power of orders. There are, then, two powers in them, after the pattern of the angelic spirits, in whom there is a twofold power: one like that of orders, according to which it is their task to illuminate, purify and make perfect; and the other like that of jurisdiction, according to which it is their task to govern peoples and provinces. It is for this reason that the prelates of the Church are sometimes called angels, as Isidore says in the book *De angelica hierarchia*.[22]

From what has been said, however, we must note that a certain distinction can be drawn as between the actions of each power. For there are some acts which are purely priestly: for instance, to offer sacrifice and to intercede or pray for the people. Hence, these acts can be done by those who have no jurisdiction, provided only that they have priestly orders. Again, there are some acts which are purely royal, because they can be done by those who have spiritual jurisdiction but who are without priestly orders: for instance, to judge in spiritual cases of an external character, and to impose spiritual penalties, and to correct and punish. But some acts are common to both powers - that is, to the priestly and the royal - because they belong to each in a different way. For this reason, neither he who has orders without jurisdiction nor he who has jurisdiction without orders can do these acts. And such an act is the absolution or remission of sins. For, as learned men teach, this act pertains to the power of priestly orders for the following reason: because to bestow some perfection and to prepare the material which is to receive that perfection pertains to the same power. Now the power of priestly orders is concerned to effect the sacrament of the body of Christ and to bestow it upon the faithful for their spiritual perfection; and it is fitting that the same power should concern itself with that which renders the faithful apt and fit to receive such a sacrament: and this is done by cleansing them from their sins. For the effect of that sacrament is to unite

---

20. *Matt.* XVI,19; XVIII,18.
21. *I Cor.* IV,1.
22. The correct reference is to Ps.-Dionysius, *De coel. hier.* XII (PG 3 297/298).

men with Christ, and no one can be so united other than through freedom from the sin which separates him from God. It is fitting, therefore, for the priestly power to concern itself with the remission of sins by administering those sacraments which are ordained for the remission of sins, of which kind are baptism and penance. But this act pertains to the power of jurisdiction because of the material in relation to which it is performed; and this material is the faithful themselves. For this act cannot be performed in relation to anyone unless they have been made subject to him by whom the act is done; and this is not achieved other than through the power of jurisdiction. And so it is customarily said that the power of the keys is bestowed along with holy orders, but that its execution needs proper material: that is, a people subject to it by jurisdiction. Hence, anyone who has priestly orders before he has jurisdiction has the power of the keys indeed, but he does not have the use of the keys or the capacity to act with them. And so it is that not every priest can use the keys which he has in relation to everyone, but only in relation to those who belong to his jurisdiction either ordinarily or by special commission or for some other reason. Only for the Supreme Pontiff is it possible to use the keys in every case whatsoever, because all the faithful belong to his ordinary jurisdiction.

For the same reason again, the administration of all the sacraments requires a power of jurisdiction in relation to the faithful to whom they are dispensed. But it is also possible to state in another fashion how the remission and absolution of sins specifically in the court of penance belongs to both powers but in different ways. For inasmuch as such absolution is directed towards the sanctification of men and towards reconciliation with God, it pertains to priestly power; for it is the task of the priest to sanctify and reconcile with God. But inasmuch as there must be a certain kind of judgment in such absolution, it pertains to royal power, or to jurisdiction. For, as we said above, to judge is an act of royal power, and the priest, when hearing confessions and absolving from sin and imposing penance for sin, exercises the power of judgment on behalf of Christ, Who is judge of the living and dead. Moreover, such judicial power requires both the authority of one who understands fault and the power to absolve or condemn; and these are the two keys which Christ entrusted to Peter: namely, the wisdom to discern, and the power to bind and release.[23] But He entrusted them to him in such a way that, through him, they might descend to others; and so it is said that, in Peter, they were given to the whole Church, and that they were given for the salvation of the faithful. Hence, no one can be saved unless he subjects himself to the keys of the Church which, in all their fulness, are in the hands of Peter's successor: the Roman Pontiff, who is also the shepherd of the whole Church.

So also, the act of teaching pertains to both powers, but in different ways. For inasmuch as teaching is directed towards the purification of the mind from ignorance or unknowing and towards an orderly inward judgment, it

---

23. Cf. Aquinas, *Catena aurea* on *Matt.* XVI,19.

pertains to priestly power (in the sense that the minor orders are also comprehended within it; for deacons also can teach, and for this reason the deacons are called an illuminating order[24]). Inasmuch as it is directed towards the guidance of outward acts, on the other hand, it pertains to royal power. Again, such guidance belongs to it because of the material [which is to receive such guidance]; for one who is taught is in some sense made subject to the one who teaches; and it is by the power of jurisdiction that one person is made subject to another (although what we have said concerning the act of teaching is to be understood as applying to public teaching undertaken in the Church for the salvation and edification of the faithful. Private teaching directed towards one or a few by means of informal conversation does not require either orders or jurisdiction).

Similarly again, it requires both the power of orders and of jurisdiction to confer ecclesiastical orders and to do many other tasks. It must be noted, however, that of those things which belong to both powers, some belong to all priests, whether greater or lesser, such as to baptize, to preach, and to release and bind; but certain others, such as to ordain clerics, and to do many other things, belong only to the greater priests: that is, to the bishops, who have a more special kind of consecration.

From these considerations, then, it appears that priestly power and royal power over spiritual things are linked with respect to their holders (for both powers are found within the same person; although not always, because it happens in some instances that the one is found without the other) and with respect to their action, because, as we have said, there are certain actions which require both powers. They are also linked with respect to their end, because each is immediately directed towards the same end, which is the salvation of the faithful; and so each is called a spiritual and saving power. And because of the way in which these powers are linked, sometimes a thing is attributed to priestly power which in fact belongs to the royal power with which the priestly is linked.

Now the two powers began to be linked in this way even in the Old Testament. For the priests of the Law, and especially the High Priest, had something of a royal power over spiritual things; for not only did he offer sacrifice and pray for the people: also, he judged certain causes which, in a symbolic sense, were spiritual. For he judged concerning leprosy, by which is signified sin. He also judged between the sacred and the profane, the clean and the unclean; and although this judgment concerned bodily uncleanness, such uncleanness was nonetheless a symbol and a sign of spiritual uncleanness: that is, of sin. And so, although they did not have the keys of the kingdom of Heaven, because their power did not extend to heavenly things, the symbol of the keys was nonetheless foreshadowed in them because their power lay in those things which were symbols of

---

24. Presumably a misremembering of Ps.-Dionysius, *De ecclesiastica hierarchia* VI,V: "The deacons are a purifying order, the priests an illuminating, and the bishops a perfecting order." (PG 3,549/55O).

heavenly things. Indeed, the priest of the Law judged some men worthy and others unworthy to enter the material tabernacle which prefigured the heavenly tabernacle, not made with hands, whose keys are now in the Church.[25] Also, by the judgment of the priest, certain persons were excluded from the society of others and separated from their fellowship and common life; and in this was prefigured the separation which is now effected in the Church by excommunication.

From what we have now said, therefore, it is clear what matters belong to priesthood and to royal power over spiritual things; that both are found in the prelates of the Church, and even in the lesser priests to whom they are entrusted by their superiors; and what may be done by these by virtue of each power.

But it remains to say something briefly concerning the comparison of the one with the other, with respect to both priority in time and priority in dignity. The priesthood which existed under the law of nature indeed preceded royal power not only over spiritual, but also over temporal, things. For Abel, in making offerings, exercised the office of a priest,[26] whereas, at that time, there was amongst men no royal power over either spiritual or temporal things; for the multitude of men was not yet so great as to require the communal living for the sake of which royal power was appointed (unless, in a broad sense, the father of a family might be called a king, just as, conversely, kings are sometimes said to be the fathers of their people). Also, the priesthood of the Law preceded royal power over spiritual things in time (although it was similar to it, because it was the forerunner of such power); but it came after royal power over earthly things insofar as the latter had its being in the human race at large, for kings were instituted and called before Aaron, from whom the priesthood of the Law derived its origin, was. As regards the Israelite people, however, and as to their divine spiritual institution, there were priests before kings were appointed amongst that people under the name of kings; for Aaron preceded Saul, who was the first king of the Israelites, by many years.

Moses, however, who, though he was not called a king, exercised the office of king amongst that people, lived at the same time as Aaron; although Moses himself was also a priest, according to the psalm: "Moses and Aaron among His priests."[27] The Gloss here says that Moses is called a priest because, although he did not offer sacrificial victims, he nonetheless offered the prayers of the people to God and made supplication for the people.[28] Hence, he was called an intercessor and mediator, prefiguring Christ as mediator between God and men; and so Isidore, in his book on the servants of the Church, asks the following question: "Of whom was Moses made the forerunner? For if the sons of Aaron were made forerunners of the

---

25. Cf. *Heb.* IX,11; see also *Deut.* XVII,8f.
26. *Gen.* IV,4f.
27. *Psalm.* XCVIII,6.
28. *Glossa ordinaria,* PL 113,1009.

clergy, then Aaron prefigured the Supreme Priest, that is, Christ. Of whom, then, was Moses made the forerunner?" And he replies: "Of Christ, beyond all doubt; for in him was the similitude of the mediator between God and man Who is the true captain of His people, the true prince of priests and the lord of pontiffs."[29]

But the priesthood of the gospel came into being at the same time as royal power over spiritual things. For Christ was appointed both king and priest; moreover, both powers were communicated to the apostles by Christ. Royal power over earthly things, however, preceded the priesthood of the gospel; although, according to the perfection of their institution, it could be said that such royal power came after the priesthood of the gospel and after the royal power over spiritual things by which, as will appear below, it was instituted. These, then, are our remarks concerning the comparison of these powers with respect to priority in time.

Now as to a comparison of them with respect to priority in dignity, we must consider that royal power over spiritual things is superior to and greater in dignity than priestly power. For the word 'priesthood' does not imply rule and prelacy as the name of king does; rather, it implies mediation and ministry. For the priest has mediation as his office, whereas the king has as his office government and action and purpose. Hence also, Christ is greater in dignity and superior as king than as priest; for He is a priest inasmuch as He is man, and He is a king inasmuch as He is both God and man. The task of the priest is to make offerings and to reconcile, whereas that of the king is to judge and to admit to the kingdom; and so the greater dignity belongs to one who is called a king than to one who is a priest. So also in the prelates of the Church, royal power, which is called the power of jurisdiction, is superior to priestly power, which is called the power of orders. By reason of jurisdiction, therefore, an archdeacon is superior to an archpriest, for the latter [though not inferior in terms of holy orders] does not have a full jurisdiction.

It may, however, be objected to this that the power of priestly orders has to do with the true body of Christ, whereas that of jurisdiction has to do only with Christ's mystical body - that is, with the faithful; and that priestly power is therefore the greater in dignity. We must reply that the priest is said to have power in relation to the true body of Christ inasmuch as he has a certain power of ministry to transform the substance of bread and wine into the true body and blood of Christ by uttering the words by virtue of which this blessed transformation is effected. He does not, however, have a judicial power over the true body of Christ, as those persons to whom the power of jurisdiction is entrusted do over the faithful; and so it does not follow that priestly power is superior. Rather, it can be said that priestly power is greater in dignity in one specific respect than is the power of jurisdiction; but, in a wide sense, the power of jurisdiction has the greater dignity. For although both are directed towards the same end, royal power

---

29. *De eccl. offic.* II,V (PL 83,781).

[over spiritual things] nonetheless acts towards that end in a higher and more dignified fashion. Royal power over temporal things, however, inasmuch as it is temporal, is inferior to and lesser in dignity than the priestly, which is spiritual; but it can be superior to it either insofar as such royal power [over temporal things] is the instrument of royal power over spiritual things, which is superior to priestly power; or to the extent that the priestly power in some person, which he uses in respect of certain temporal things, is derived from an earthly king. Of this, however, we shall speak more fully below. And this, in sum, is a comparison of priestly and royal power with respect to superiority and dignity.

V

On the degrees and inequalities of priestly and royal power in the different persons who hold them. Here also is discussed the primacy of the Supreme Pontiff over all churches and rulers of churches

We must speak now of the degrees and inequalities of each power in the different persons who hold them. For in both powers there is found higher and lower, greater and lesser, and, for this reason, degree and inequality. In one respect, indeed, priestly power is equal in all priests. In another, however, it is unequal. For with respect to the act of consecration which it is the task of the priest to perform in relation to the true body of Christ, priestly power is the same in all who have it. But with respect to the acts which it is the priest's task to perform in relation to the mystical body of Christ - that is, in relation to the faithful - of which kind are the acts of baptizing and releasing and binding, there is found inequality in priestly power: for certain persons are the superiors of others, as are the bishops, who are also called pontiffs. For the performance of the foregoing acts requires not only priestly orders, but also jurisdiction, as we have said above; which jurisdiction the lower priests do not have other than by the commission of their superiors: namely, the bishops. Also, there is another way in which the degrees of priestly power can be understood; for in the bishop the priestly order exists according to a certain perfection. For something is said to be perfect when it can produce another and communicate its own goodness to others; and the bishops do not only have priestly orders in themselves: they can indeed also transmit the power of orders to others, for they themselves can confer the sacrament of holy orders upon others. And although such transmission requires a power of jurisdiction, it nonetheless pertains to the power of priestly orders in its perfect form; and, by reason of the perfection of their priesthood, the bishops are said to be superior priests because certain things are especially reserved to them as more perfect and superior. For it is their task to do whatever is lofty in relation to the faithful, and it is by their authority that lesser priests can do that which is entrusted to them. Hence also, in those acts which the latter perform, they make use of things consecrated by the bishops.

And as a sign of their more perfect power, a special form of episcopal consecration is used, in which there is indeed conferred upon them a special power with respect to certain sacred acts. Hence also, although it is not an order which is a sacrament in its own right, the episcopate is in a manner of speaking an order set above the priesthood in the sense that it is an order whose duties include certain sacred acts [which priests who are not also bishops cannot do]. The bishop, therefore, is not only superior by reason of jurisdiction, but also by reason of the priestly orders which he has in a more perfect form. And so it pertains to all priests in common to catechize, baptize, preach, and release and bind the penitent. But it belongs specifically to the pontiffs to ordain clerics, to bless nuns, to consecrate pontiffs, to lay on hands or to confirm, to participate in councils, to dedicate church buildings, to depose the unworthy, to prepare holy oils, and to consecrate vestments and sacred vessels.

There is, then, degree and inequality within the priesthood, inasmuch as some priests are called greater and others lesser; and, as we read, there has at all times been such inequality in the priesthood. For before the Law was given, as Innocent notes, "there were many lesser priests, who were commonly called Nazarites. And there was one chief priest whom they specifically called Arabarcus."[1] After the Law was given, Aaron was the chief priest, and his sons were lesser priests, ministering under him.[2] Again, there were amongst the gentiles lesser priests called *flamines* and greater priests who were called *archiflamines*.[3] In the New Testament also, Christ Himself appointed greater and lesser priests: that is, the twelve apostles, whose places in the Church the bishops now occupy, and the seventy-two disciples to whom have succeeded the presbyters or lesser priests whose task it is to assist the greater in their work, so that the multitude of the faithful may be more easily and beneficially governed.[4] And just as, in the Old Testament, certain things were proper to the high priest with regard equally to his actions, vestments and adornment, so also, in the New, the bishops have spiritual tasks above those of the lesser priests, as we have said, and they have special adornments also, which are the signs of their special power.

Although there is degree and inequality within the priesthood, however, there are no degrees of pontifical power with regard to those things which

---

1. Innocent III, *De sacro altaris mysterio* I,VI (PL 217,777). For 'Nazarites', see *Num.* VI, passim. There is no 'Arabarchus' in the Bible. ('Arabarches' is an Egyptian tax-officer, according to Juvenal (I,130) and Cicero (*Ad Att.* II,17,3)). The same word appears in the text as given at PL. It is palaeographically not impossible that *arabarchus* is a copyist's hash of *archiereus* (see Ch.I,n.40, above), or perhaps of the rare papal title *archierarchus* or *archiierarchus*. See Frithegode of Canterbury, *Breviloquium vitae beati Wilfridi* (ed. A. Campbell, *Thesaurus Mundi* (1950), 1-62), 773.

2. *Exod.* XXVIII,1.

3. Cf., e.g., Augustine, *De civ. Dei* II,15 (CC XLVII,47); Geoffrey of Monmouth, *Historia regum Britanniae*, IV,19.

4. *Luc.* X,1; and see Pt.I,Ch.VI,n.17.

belong to the episcopal order; for all bishops are equal in respect of those things which belong to the episcopal order. With regard to those things which belong to jurisdiction, however, they are not all equal: rather, there is degree amongst them. Next, then, we must consider such degree.

Now royal power, which is called jurisdiction, is not equal in all who have it, but is found in them according to certain degrees; and this is true of each kind of royal power: that is, over temporal and spiritual things alike. For there are degrees of royal power over temporal things because some kings are superior to other kings, and kings are superior to dukes and to the other orders of power which share in royal power to some extent even though they are not called kings. Moreover, there is one who is over all these: namely, the emperor. And of these degrees it is said at *Ecclesiastes* V: "For he that is high hath another higher, and there are others still higher than these. Moreover, there is the king that reigneth over all the land subject to him."[5] Also, the blessed Peter refers to these degrees when he says: "Whether it be to the king, as supreme; or unto governors, as unto them that are sent by him."[6]

Moreover, there are degrees of royal power over spiritual things. For the need of the Church requires a plurality of rulers, because one man does not by himself suffice to govern the whole ecclesiastical multitude: for a great harvest requires many labourers. And so it is fitting that royal power should be communicated to many persons. But "the powers that be are ordained of God",[7] and just as there is an order in things, so is there amongst the powers. Order, however, requires inequality and degree; and so royal power over spiritual things is not held equally by all, but according to certain degrees. For above the bishops are the archbishops, and above the latter are the primates or patriarchs. For just as one community or congregation encompasses and includes another, as does the community of a province the community of a city and the community of a kingdom the community of a single province, and the community of the whole world the community of a kingdom: so also does one power encompass and include another. Also, there is degree in such power in another sense: in that, within the same community, certain persons, such as bishops, have a complete power, and others, such as archdeacons, have only a partial one.

But we must consider in addition that, where degree exists according to greater and lesser and higher and lower, it must be that there is one which is supreme; for 'greater' and 'lesser' arise from comparison with a 'greatest', and it belongs to one thing only to be so called, by reason of its excellence. For this reason, then, every degree relates to something which is primary and supreme. It is fitting, therefore, that there should be one person to whom royal power over spiritual things belongs in the highest degree and pre-eminently and according to its fulness; and, as a symbol of this, David

5. *Eccles*. V,7f.
6. *I Pet*. II,13f.
7. *Rom*. XIII,1.

instituted twenty-four chief priests, all of whom, however, were subject to the one.[8] And because that which is what it is pre-eminently and in the greatest degree is the cause of other things being of the same kind - as, for instance, the greatest degree of heat is the cause of other things being hot - so also, from him to whom royal power over spiritual things belongs primarily and in the greatest degree, this power is devolved to others as sharers and according to such degrees as the Church requires for her benefit and adornment alike; and from the one source - that is, from Him Who is above all churches and rulers of churches - descend all who are in any way sharers in spiritual government. Here, then, the one ruler is Christ. But because Christ's bodily presence was to be withdrawn from the Church, it was fitting that the whole government of the Church should be entrusted to some one person, who should rule the Church in His place and on His behalf.

And this one person was Peter, to whom alone Christ said: "Feed my sheep."[9] And He willed that others should succeed Peter in equal and similar power when he was sundered from the faithful by death, so that this supreme power in the Church should always be embodied in one man for the benefit of the Church herself, until the end of the world. And it is in this way that we are to understand the words of Christ: "Behold, I am with you all days, even to the consummation of the world."[10] For because he who acts through another is understood to act by himself, therefore, because of the fact that there is always amongst the faithful some one person ruling the Church on Christ's behalf, not by fleshly but by spiritual succession, Christ Himself is said to be with us all days, even to the end of the world - after which the Church will have no use for such rule, because she will be ruled and fed, illuminated and blessed, immediately by Christ Himself. Just as, therefore, in the kingdom of the Jews, king succeeded king after David, so also in the Church has pontiff succeeded pontiff in Christ's place. Hence, what David says in the psalm - "Of the fruit of thy body will I set upon thy throne. If thy children shall keep my testimony, their children shall also sit upon thy throne for evermore"[11] - is fulfilled in Him Whom David prefigured, that is, in Christ, in Whose place upon the throne of the ecclesiastical kingdom, even to the day of judgment, sits one king: not always the same in person, but always the same in power. And of this one king it is said in *I Kings*: "The Lord shall judge the ends of the earth; and He shall give empire to His king, and exalt the horn of His anointed."[12]

This one king, then, with whom rests the highest power of spiritual government, is the successor of Peter: that is, the Roman Pontiff, the Vicar of Jesus Christ. For although the other rulers of the Church who have succeeded to the rest of the apostles may be called, and are, vicars of Christ,

---

8. *I Para*. XXIV, passim.
9. *Joan*. XXI,17.
10. *Matt*. XXVIII,20.
11. *Psalm*. CXXXI,11f.
12. *I Reg*. II,10.

this one person nonetheless acts principally, absolutely and universally on Christ's behalf on earth. And he is called the Vicar of Christ both inasmuch as Christ is simply man, because he is a priest, and inasmuch as He is both God and man, because he is also a king; and so he is indeed truly called God's vicar. He is the king of all spiritual kings, the shepherd of shepherds, the father of fathers, the head of all the faithful and of all who rule the faithful. Hence also, the church over which he presides - that is, the Roman - is the mother and head of all the churches. Although he is appropriately called the Roman Pontiff, he is nonetheless most truly called, and is, the pontiff of all Christians and the ruler of all churches, and the Bishop of the City and of the World. Although he governs the different individual churches through the agency of other shepherds, he can nonetheless exercise direct kingship over any church whatsoever. He is the one Supreme Priest, to whom all the faithful owe obedience as to the lord Jesus Christ.

He is the universal judge who judges all the faithful of whatever condition, dignity and station, and who can himself be judged by no one;[13]   rather, as the voice of the Apostle declares: "He that judgeth me is the Lord."[14] It is to him that the keys of the Church have been most fully delivered by Christ; and with them he binds and releases, closes and opens, excludes and admits, exacts and relieves, sentences and judges. He is the supreme ordainer of divine worship and of all the things which are applied and pertain to the worship of God. He is the supreme and universal dispenser of the ministers of God and the treasures of Christ, and the distributor of the dignities of the Church and of all ecclesiastical offices and benefices, in the conferment and distribution of which he exhibits his pre-eminent and supreme power.

He is the supreme and universal establisher of the canons; he is the approver of laws and the ordainer of all decrees; he disposes all the orders of the Church; he confirms appointments and elections; he determines doubtful cases; he reveals to all men what each must know, and he discerns all the things which are in the Church. He it is who, according to Bernard, "has no peer upon earth";[15]   rather, all men are subject to him by divine law. According to the words of that same Bernard, he is "the chief priest, the Supreme Pontiff, the prince of bishops, the heir of the apostles: an Abel in primacy;   a Noah in government;   an Abraham in patriarchate;   a Melchizedek in orders;   an Aaron in dignity;   a Moses in authority;   a Samuel in judgment;   a Peter in power;   a Christ in unction, to whom the keys have been given and to whom the sheep are entrusted. For there are indeed others, who are both doorkeepers of Heaven and shepherds of the flock; but his glory is as great as is his difference from them, for he, before all others, has inherited both titles. For other men have had assigned to them this flock or that. To him, however, is entrusted the whole flock, and he himself is the one shepherd of them all: not only of the sheep, but of

---

13. Cf. *Dist*. XL, c.6 (*Si Papa*) (CIC I,146).

14. *I Cor*. IV,4.

15. *De consideratione* II,I,4 (PL 182,744).

their shepherds also."[16] He it is, then, to whom belongs the task of feeding all the sheep and lambs of Christ: upon whom rests the care of the all the churches. For others are called to take some part in this care; but in him is vested fulness of power, and the others who take some part in this care do so in a manner which does not in any way detract from this fulness of power.

He is the primate and patriarch, supreme hierarch and monarch of the whole Church Militant, to whom every soul must be subject as of right, as to the most pre-eminent power. He who is not so subject cannot attain salvation, for he is not part of the unity of the Church; nor does anyone belong to the flock of Christ who refuses to have Peter's successor as his shepherd. Four titles, and the things which those titles denote, belong to him, according to the four conditions of the Church which we have described above, in the first part.

For, first, the Church is one, and so her head is one and her shepherd is one; and hence there is one man who is foremost and supreme, of whom it was foretold by Ezekiel: "They shall all have one shepherd, and there shall be one king to rule them all."[17] And the reason why the king is one is so that he may strive and seek after the common good of the multitude. Just as, therefore, in the case of the one specific people of one particular church, one bishop who is the head of the whole people is required, so in the case of the whole Christian people, which is one, it is required that there be one head of the whole Church.

Second, the Church is catholic, that is, universal, and we must in the same way say that she has a universal shepherd, the Roman Pontiff, concerning whom it is said at his consecration or enthronement: "Bestow upon him, O Lord, a pontifical throne, that he may rule Thy Church and Thy chosen people throughout all the world."[18] Indeed, in every multitude directed towards one end, there must, above particular ruling powers, be one general power which seeks the common good and which, for this reason, is more divine than the particular ones. For a good is more divine in proportion as it is more common, as with the First Good, in Whom is contained the foundation of every good. There is, therefore, one universal shepherd and ruler of the whole Church; and so the Roman church, of whom he is the pontiff, is called universal. We must, however, carefully note the distinct senses of the term 'universal' which Innocent specifies in a certain letter.[19] He says that, in one sense, the Church is called universal because she consists of all the particular churches; and, according to this meaning of the term, the Roman church is not the universal Church, but only a part of the universal Church - albeit the primary and principal part, as the head is of the body, because, in her, there is fulness of power, and this fulness is distributed to the other parts. In another sense, the Church is called

---

16. *De consid.* II,VIII,15 (PL 182,751).

17. Cf. *Ezek.* XXXVII,24.

18. *Ordo Romanus XIV vel ordinarius s[anctae] r[omanae] e[cclesiae], auctore, ut videtur, Iacobo Caietano cardinale* XLIV (PL 78,1141).

19. Possibly *Serm.* XXII (PL 217,556ff).

universal because she contains all the particular churches under herself; and, on this understanding of the term, the Roman church is indeed called universal because she is above all the others in having been granted a matchless eminence: just as God Himself is called the Universal Lord because all things are contained under His lordship. For there is the one general Church, concerning which the Truth said to Peter: "Thou art Peter, and upon this Rock I will build my Church."[20] And there are the many particular churches, of which the Apostle says: "That which cometh upon me daily, the care of all the churches."[21] But the one is made up of all, just as the general is made up of particulars; and the one surpasses them all because, since there is the one body of the Church, of which the Apostle says "we are one body in Christ",[22] the head therefore excels the other members. But as to those who pertinaciously deny the primacy of the one head with respect to the one ecclesiastical body: these divide Christ, they sunder the Church, they take away her unity, and, consequently, they sin against the Holy Spirit by Whom the Church is made one; and so they are worthily deemed heretics and schismatics.

Third, the Church is holy, and so the universal shepherd of the Church must be called holy. For although it may be that the person who rules is not holy, his rank and office is holy nonetheless: indeed, it is supremely holy in this life, and supremely perfect, and the foundation of all sanctification in the Church. And so the Roman Pontiff is called Most Holy Father, because he acts on behalf of the Holy of Holies and holds His place.

Fourth, the Church is called apostolic, and so the supreme ruler of the Church is rightly named apostolic, and his See is called apostolic. For he is the vicar of the Great Apostle, Christ, and he is the successor of the prince of the apostles, Peter, in whom the whole apostolic authority is vested in all its fulness.

Now certain things may be adduced in confirmation of what we have said. First, indeed, by way of showing that there must be one head and one king in the whole Church, certain reasons can be cited which are derived from the writings of the great doctors. The chief of these is this: that the kingdom of the Church is ordered in the best way and according to the best mode of government insofar as it is founded and disposed according to the best principle. Now the best principle for the government of a multitude is that it be ruled by one.[23] The government of the Church, therefore, is disposed in such a way that one man presides over the whole Church. And that the best form of government is that of one man may be shown by the following argument. Now rule or government is nothing other than the direction of what is governed to its end, which is some good. But unity belongs to the nature of the good, as Boethius proves in Book III of *De consolatione*, by

---

20. *Matt* XVI,18.
21. *II Cor.* XI,28.
22. *Rom.* XII,5.
23. Cf. Aquinas, *De reg. princ.* I,II.

the fact that, just as all things desire a good, so do they desire that unity without which it is not possible to exist.[24] For anything whatsoever exists only insofar as it is one. Hence, he to whom belongs the task of governing a multitude rightly seeks the unity and peace of the multitude, in which unity the good and health of every society consists. The cause of unity, however, is in itself one in nature, and several things cannot make many things into one unless the several things have themselves somehow been made one. Hence it is that that which is one in itself is a more efficacious and better cause of unity than several things which have been made one; and from this it follows that a multitude may be better ruled by one man than by several, provided that there exists in that one the goodness which is required in a ruler.

This is also shown in another way. Now those things are best which are according to nature. For in each case nature brings about what is best according to the particular circumstances of each; because the work of nature is the work of God, Whose works are perfect and best. And all natural government is by one.[25] For in the multitude of the body's members there is one member that principally moves them: namely, the heart. And amongst the faculties of the parts of the soul there is one faculty which governs the others: namely, the reason, inasmuch as it comprehends the intellect and will. Also, amongst the bees there is one king; and the cranes follow one leader; and in the whole universe there is one First Principle Who produces and moves all things. So it is that, in the human multitude, if it is to be ruled in the best way, it is appropriate that there should be one ruler. And if unity of government is required for the best rule of the human multitude, which is united by inclination of nature, so much the more is it required for the rule of that community which is united rather by the gift of grace, of which kind is the ecclesiastical community. For that which is according to grace does not run counter to that which is according to nature, but perfects it.[26] It follows, therefore, that there is one ruler in the kingdom of the Church.

And this same conclusion can be shown by another argument, which arises from the previous one. For Christ does not fail in those things necessary to His Church, whom He has loved even unto death. But it is necessary to the Church that her unity be preserved; and it can be preserved most effectively when she is governed by one man. For it is required for the Church's unity that all the faithful agree in matters of faith; and when it happens that questions of faith arise and are settled by the judgment of one man, the unity of the faith is preserved in the Church and the divisions which could arise from diverse judgments are avoided. We must therefore hold firmly to the belief that, by Christ's ordinance, one man rules the whole of the Church.

---

24. *De cons. phil.* III, pr.XI (PL 63,771).
25. Cf. Aquinas, *De reg. princ.* I,II; *Summa theol.* I,q.103,a.3.
26. Cf. Aquinas, *Summa theol.* I,q.1,a.8.

And this view is confirmed by what Hugh of Saint Victor says near the beginning of his commentary on *De angelica hierarchia*, where he shows that the universe is preserved by the relation of all powers to one First Principle. He speaks as follows: "For the sake of the grace and beauty of those things which they adorn with the wisdom of their works, many virtues are distributed, and many powers formed, by the one Virtue and the one Power. On the other hand, however, lest multitude produce discord and division, and strive against itself in opposition for mastery of the world, there is one First Principle and one Moderator of them all, from Whom they derive their being and under Whom they are directed, so that they may have efficacy, and led back to Him in all that they do, so that unity may endure in all things and peace prevail throughout the kingdom of God, Who is the creator and ruler of all."[27] And what Hugh says of the whole world in general can be adapted to the ecclesiastical kingdom in particular, whose unity is best preserved by the fact that all the faithful, and the rulers of the faithful everywhere, depend upon the one ruler. It is clear, therefore, that there is one king and shepherd of the whole Church. For just as the one God, by Whom, indeed, the universe is governed, presides over the Church Triumphant, so also, in the Church Militant, which is derived from the Church Triumphant by analogy, there is one man who presides over the whole of the faithful.

And that this one person is the Roman Pontiff, the successor of Peter, by virtue of the primacy and prerogative of the blessed Peter himself, may be confirmed with the greatest of ease. For a predecessor and his successor are equal in office and power, even though they may differ in merit and goodness of life. Since, therefore, the blessed Peter was appointed by Christ as prince over the whole Church, it is proper to say that his successor is also the universal ruler of the Church. And, by way of showing how matchless power was granted to Peter, this first occurred when, as we find in *John*, the Lord said to him: "Thou shalt be called Cephas",[28] which, although translated as 'rock' [*petrus*] according to one language, nonetheless means 'head' according to another. Thus, just as the head holds the chief place amongst the other members of the body because of the fulness of sensation which flourishes in it, so Peter amongst the apostles and, consequently, his successors amongst all the prelates of the churches, is foremost and pre-eminent in power and dignity.

We must next note what is recorded in St Matthew's gospel. For when Peter had confessed Christ to be the Son of the living God, Christ replied: "And I say also unto thee, That thou art Peter, and upon this Rock I will build my Church", and so on. Here, we must first note that it is not without sacred significance that, when Christ asked all the apostles, "Whom say ye that I am?" Peter alone, as their leader, answered for all of them: "Thou

---

27. *Commentariorum in hierarchiam coelestem S. Dionysii Areopagitae* I,II (PL 175,930).
28. *Joan.* I,42.

art the Christ, the Son of the living God."[29] Next, we must consider
carefully the words which Christ spoke to Peter. "Thou art Peter," He said.
(Although, as Augustine remarks,[30] it was not at this time that Peter first
received this name, but when it was said to him: "Thou shalt be called
Cephas, which is by interpretation, A rock", as we have said.) Hence, as
Chrysostom says: "Here, one honour was conferred upon Peter by Christ,
in that He bestowed a name upon him."[31] And, in that which follows -
"upon this Rock I will build my Church" - He makes Peter the shepherd, as
Chrysostom says in the same place; for "upon this Rock" can, in one way,
be understood to mean "upon thee and thy successors". (Alternatively,
"upon this Rock" means "upon Him Whom thou hast confessed", because
the Rock was Christ.[32])

Christ next conferred another honour on Peter, saying: "And I will give
unto thee the keys of the kingdom of Heaven; and whatsoever thou shalt
bind on earth shall be bound in the Heavens, and whatsoever thou shalt
release on earth",[33] and so on. As to this, the Gloss says that by the keys of
the kingdom of Heaven He means discernment and power: power, to bind
and release, and discernment, to tell the worthy from the unworthy.[34] Also,
He speaks in the future tense: "I *will* give unto thee" - as if to suggest that
He is not giving them only to Peter, but that He is to give them also to his
successors; or that He will later give them in a more perfect fashion when,
after the Resurrection, he says to the others also: "Receive ye the Holy
Spirit: whose soever sins ye remit, they are remitted unto them",[35] and so
on. And they later received the Holy Spirit more fully, on the day of
Pentecost.[36] Alternatively, he said "I *will* give" because this power draws its
efficacy from the Passion of Christ which, when He spoke, was yet to come.
Hence, according to Chrysostom, that which He promised before the Passion
He gave after the Resurrection by way of confirmation, when He said to
Peter: "Feed my sheep."[37] And Christ next showed the use of those keys,
saying: "Whatsoever thou shalt bind on earth", and so on; that is,
according to the Gloss: "Whomsoever thou shalt judge unworthy of
forgiveness while he lives shall be judged unworthy with God; and for
whosomever thou shalt judge worthy to be released while he lives,
forgiveness will follow."[38] And it is added in the Gloss: "See how great a
power has the Rock upon whom the Church is built, that his judgments may

---

29. *Matt.* XVI,15f.
30. *Serm.* LXXVI,I,1 (PL 38,479); Cf. Aquinas, *Catena aurea* on *Matt.* XVI,18.
31. *In inscriptionem actorum* II,6 (PG 51,86).
32. *I Cor.* X,4; and see Pt.I, Ch.VI,n.27, above.
33. *Matt.* XVI,19.
34. Aquinas, *Catena aurea* on *Matt.* XVI,19; Cf. Innocent III, *Serm.* XXI (PL 217,554).
35. *Joan.* XX,22f.
36. *Act.* II,1ff.
37. *In Joannem homilia* LXXXVIII,1 (PG 59,479).
38. *Glossa interlinearis* on *Matt.* XVI,19; Aquinas, *Catena aurea*, ad loc..

indeed stand as firmly as though God were judging through him."[39] We must also note what comes next in the Gloss, where it says that although this releasing and binding power seems to have been given by the Lord to Peter alone, it is nonetheless given to the other apostles also, and now, indeed, to the bishops and priests of the whole Church. "But Peter especially has received the keys of the kingdom of Heaven and the supremacy of judicial power, so that all believers throughout the world may understand that all those cut off from the unity or fellowship of the faith in any way whatsoever cannot be absolved from the bonds of sin, nor can they enter the gates of the heavenly kingdom."[40] He granted this power especially to Peter so that he might invite us to unity. For He therefore appointed him prince of the apostles so that the Church should have one principal vicar of Christ, to whom the different members of the Church might have recourse should there happen to be dissension amongst them.

If, however, there were several different heads of the Church, the bond of unity would be ruptured. So, therefore, although it was said to all the apostles together: "Whatsoever you shall bind [*alligaveritis*] on earth shall be bound in Heaven", and so on, as is recorded at *Matthew* XVIII,[41] this was nonetheless first said in the singular, to Peter alone: "Whatsoever thou shalt bind [*ligaveris*] on earth shall be bound also in the Heavens." We are to understand by this that there is an order in such power, because it belongs first and principally to Peter, and it descends through him to others. Therefore, this was said to Peter without the others, but not to the others without him. This was done so that it might be understood that such power was conferred upon him in such a way that he can do without others what others cannot do without him, because of the fulness of power conferred upon and granted to him, by which he can bind others, but cannot be bound by others. Also, Chrysostom notes that, in giving the keys to Peter, Christ said "in the Heavens", whereas, in giving power to the apostles in general, he did not say "in the Heavens", but "in Heaven" in the singular, because the others are not so great in perfection as Peter.[42] Moreover, by this power of releasing and binding we are given to understand a judicial power: not only with respect to the remission of sins, but also with respect to the resolution and determination of causes, excommunication and the infliction of other penalties, indulgences, and any relaxation of what is commanded and of any institution or observance whatsoever.

In addition, as is recorded in St Matthew's gospel, the Lord commanded Peter to pay the tribute for himself and Him.[43] In the same way, as the Gloss says, when the disciples saw the same tribute paid for Peter and the

---

39. *Catena aurea*, ad loc..
40. Ibid.
41. *Matt.* XVIII,18.
42. Cf. *Homiliae in Matthaeum* LIV,2f (PG 58,534f); but Chrysostom does not attach any Petrine significance to the grammatical facts here noted. Cf., however, Origen at Aquinas, *Catena aurea* on *Matt.* XVIII,18.
43. *Matt.* XVII,26.

Lord equally out of the same sum of money, all the apostles gathered from this that Peter was to be their leader.[44] Again, as we learn in the same gospel, Peter alone asked Christ: "How often shall my brother sin against me, and I forgive him? Till seven times?" And only to him did Jesus reply: "I say not unto thee, Until seven times: but, until seventy times seven."[45] Now seven is the number which signifies wholeness.[46] In this place, therefore, seven multiplied by itself signifies all the sins of the whole world; for only Peter can remit, not only all things, but also all offences.

Moreover, as we find in St Luke's gospel, Peter spoke to Christ, saying: "Lord, speakest thou [this parable] unto us, [or even to all]?"[47] The Gloss on this verse says that Peter, to whom the Church had by now been entrusted as to the one having the care of all men, asked whether the Lord intended the parable for all men.[48] And again, on that passage in *John* where Peter says: "Lord, dost thou wash my feet?"[49] the blessed Augustine says: "We ought not to suppose here that Peter was one amongst others who had expressed fear and reluctance and that others before him had undergone it gladly and with composure. For we are not to understand these words to mean that Christ had already washed the others and had come to Peter after them. For who does not know that the most blessed Peter was the first of all the apostles? Rather, we must understand that He began with Peter. When, therefore, He began to wash [the disciples' feet], He came to him with whom He began: that is, to Peter."[50]

Again, at the time of the Passion, when Christ said to all the apostles collectively: "Simon, behold, Satan hath desired to have you [*vos*], that he may sift you as wheat", He nonetheless also said to Peter in the singular: "I have prayed for thee [*te*], that thy faith fail not"; and straightway He added: "And when thou art converted, confirm thy brethren."[51] For it pertains to Peter, as master and leader, to confirm the others. Hence, the Gloss[52] says that, having dismissed the others, Christ came to Peter, the leader, saying: "And when thou art converted, confirm thy brethren." In other words: "Afterwards, when thou hast denied me and wept and repented, fortify the others, because I have deputed thee to be the prince of the apostles. This befits thee because thou art my chosen one and the rock of the Church." And it is clearly implied by these things that the See of Peter was never at any time to deviate from the catholic faith but, rather, was to rescue others

---

44. Cf. *Glossa ordinaria*, PL 114,146; Aquinas, *Catena aurea* on *Matt.* XVII,26. Again, the Petrine significance which James finds in *Matt.* XVII,26 is not, in fact, warranted by the glosses.

45. *Matt.* XVIII,21f.

46. See Pt.I,Ch.III,n.27, above; Cf. Aquinas, *Catena aurea* on *Matt.* XVIII,21f.

47. *Luc.* XII,41.

48. *Glossa ordinaria*, PL 114,299.

49. *Joan.* XIII,6.

50. *In Joannis evangelium tractatus* LVI,1 (CC XXXVI,467).

51. *Luc.* XXII,31f.

52. Aquinas, *Catena aurea* on *Luc.* XXII,31f.

from error and confirm the doubters. Also, by the fact that power to strengthen the others was given to Peter and his successors, there is imposed upon those others the necessity of obedience. Moreover, immediately before Christ's Passion it was Peter alone who, drawing a sword, struck the high priest's servant and cut off his right ear.[53]

Again, when Christ had risen, the angel who declared the Resurrection to the women said that they were to "tell His disciples and Peter" that He had risen.[54] And on the day of the Resurrection itself, Christ appeared to Peter, as is said in St Luke's gospel: "The Lord is risen indeed, and hath appeared to Simon."[55] And Paul declares in [I] Corinthians that He was first made manifest to Peter alone, and only then to the other disciples who were Peter's fellow apostles; for he says that the Lord rose on the third day, according to the scriptures, and that he was seen by Cephas and then by the eleven.[56]

Furthermore, after the Resurrection itself, when the time of the Ascension drew nigh, Peter was three times asked by Christ if he loved Him; and, confessing his love for Christ three times, he three times heard Christ say: "Feed my lambs" and "my sheep".[57] Now Christ did not say: "Feed these sheep or those", but "sheep", simply and indefinitely; and so it is understood that all the sheep everywhere were entrusted to Peter. And, as the Gloss says, expounding the words "Feed my sheep", the Lord spoke these words to Peter, passing over the others; for Peter was singled out from the apostles as the disciples' spokesman and the head of their fellowship. Hence also, overlooking his denial, Christ entrusted to him the leadership of his brethren. For to feed the sheep is, as the Gloss says, "to comfort those who believe in Christ, that they may not lack faith; to provide temporal aid, if necessary, to those who are cast down, and to furnish examples of virtue when preaching the word; to oppose enemies, and to correct erring charges."[58] Chrysostom also, expounding the foregoing words, says: "'Feed my sheep', that is, Be the chief and head of the brethren in my place, and employ the love that you have declared yourself to have for me, so fervent that you would lay down your life for me, for the sheep. For what I once promised you I now affirm before the brethren, so that they also, receiving you in my place, may everywhere on earth proclaim and confirm you and those who sit upon your throne in such a way that, just as they have received me from the Father, so may the nations of the world receive you in my place in the order of obedience and by the authority of the gospel."[59]

---

53. *Joan.* XVIII,10.
54. *Marc.* XVI,7.
55. *Luc.* XXIV,34.
56. I *Cor.* XV,4f.
57. *Joan.* XXI,15ff.
58. *Glossa ordinaria*, PL 114,425.
59. See n.37, above. But the quotation is very inaccurate, and, once more, the original is without the Petrine significance here attributed to it.

Then, after Christ had entrusted to Peter the feeding of the sheep, He added, on the same occasion: "Follow me";[60] and, as Innocent says, this must be taken to mean not only in the company of martyrs, but also in the order of teachers.[61] For Andrew and certain others followed Christ before Peter in being crucified; but Peter alone did the Lord set in His own place, both in the office of vicar and also as His successor as a teacher. Hence also, the Gloss[62] on this says that when the Lord said to Peter: "Follow me", He appointed him leader of all the faithful; and you are also to understand 'follow' here as simultaneously embracing in meaning all things, both words and deeds.

Again, the blessed Bernard, in Book Two of *De consideratione*, treating of the primacy and universal power and prelacy of Peter and his successors, derives his demonstration from other written sources, and speaks to Pope Eugenius as follows: "What has been granted to you, therefore - both the giving of the keys and the entrusting of the sheep - stands unshaken. Notice, however, how your prerogative was nonetheless confirmed for you when the disciples put out to sea and the Lord appeared on the shore. Peter, knowing that it was the Lord, cast himself into the sea, and so came to Him, while the others came in a little ship. What does this mean? Undoubtedly it was a special sign of Peter's pontificate, whereby he received, not one boat to govern, as each of the others did, but the whole world itself. For the sea is this world, and the boats are the churches. Hence it is that, in another place, by the image of our Lord walking on the waters, Peter alone was designated as the Vicar of Christ, who should rule not one people, but all; for the many waters indeed signify the many peoples. While each of the others has his own [little ship], then, to you alone has been entrusted the greatest of ships: the universal Church, composed of all men spread throughout the whole world."[63]

Further, after the ascension of Christ into Heaven, Peter began to rule the Church as His successor. For in order to fill the place of the traitor Judas and make the number of the apostles up to twelve, according to the words of the prophecy, he caused another to be appointed and chosen in Judas's stead.[64] Also, after the reception of the Holy Spirit, he stoutly cited the words of Joel to show that the disciples were not "full of new wine" but enlightened by the grace of the Holy Spirit, instructing the ignorant and confounding the unbelievers.[65] He commanded believers to do penance and be baptised. By curing the cripple, he was the first to perform a miracle;[66] and, as the first and chief of the apostles, he pronounced sentence of death

---

60. *Joan* XXI,19.
61. The reference is perhaps to Innocent III, *Serm.* XXI (PL 217,551); but the correspondence is not close.
62. Cf. *Glossa ordinaria*, PL 114,425.
63. *De consid.* II,VIII,16 (PL 182,752).
64. *Act.* I,15ff.
65. *Act.* II, passim; Cf *Joel* II,28.
66. *Act.* III,1ff.

upon Ananias and his wife Sapphira, because they lied to the Holy Spirit.[67] He alone pronounced the sentence of condemnation against Simon Magus, even though the latter had offered money not to Peter only, but to all the apostles together.[68] He himself, in a trance, "saw Heaven opened, and a certain vessel descending unto him" containing all manner of creatures; and to him it was said: "Rise, Peter; kill and eat."[69] By this, it was shown that Peter was the leader of all peoples; for the vessel signifies this world, and all the things contained in it signify all the nations, Jews and gentiles alike. For, after the ascension of Christ, he converted first Jews and then gentiles to the faith, so that he might show himself to have primacy over the faithful of both nations. For on the day of Pentecost, about three thousand of the Jews received the sacrament of baptism through the word of his preaching; and, next, Cornelius the centurion and his family were baptized, as the first fruits of the revelation of the gospel to the gentiles.[70]

Now there are many other things by which the primacy of Peter, and therefore of his successor, can be shown; but those arguments which we have already adduced are enough for our present purpose. To them, however, we can also add that Peter is called, and is, the head and prince of the apostles, and consequently of the whole Church, not only by the institution of Christ but also by the general approval of the apostles, as holy doctors have demonstrated from some of the authorities already cited and from others also. Moreover, we must not omit to mention that the Roman Pontiff, the successor of Peter, has primacy over all churches and rulers of churches not only by divine law, which comes from Christ, but also by human law, which comes from earthly princes. This is clear from the grant made by Constantine to the Roman church and her ruler.

And if it be objected that an earthly prince could not confer spiritual primacy, [we shall reply that,] although he does not have authority to act in spiritual matters, it must be said that, where spiritual power is concerned, he may nonetheless make such a grant, not according to authority, but according to confirmation and declaration. That is, the human law by which Peter's successor is said to have primacy over the churches and rulers of churches is a confirmation and promulgation of the divine law: a kind of co-operation, to the end that the pope may possess in fact what he already possesses as of right. We shall, however, speak of this grant of earthly power below.

---

67. *Act.* V,1ff.
68. *Act.* VIII,18ff.
69. *Act.* X,11ff.
70. *Act.* X, passim

VI

On the differences and similarities of the two kinds of royal power: that is, the spiritual and secular

Having determined these things, then, we must now consider the differences and similarities of the two kinds of royal power: that is, the spiritual and secular. Now the difference between these powers can be inferred from the names themselves; for the one is called spiritual and the other secular or temporal. And to understand this difference, it must be known that the word 'spiritual' is used in two ways.

For, in one way, 'spiritual' means 'that which pertains to the soul', which is spiritual in nature, and especially to its rational part; and, in this sense, the sciences and the virtues are said to be in a manner spiritual. In this sense, 'spiritual' is the opposite of 'corporeal', that is, of that which pertains to the body, or to the soul insofar as it is the form of the body, corresponding as such to the souls of the beasts. And thus certain persons say that the power of the prelates of the Church is called spiritual because it is over souls and over those things which pertain to the soul's perfection; and that the power of secular princes is called corporeal because it is over corporeal things and over those things which pertain to the body. This, however, is a doubtful saying. For secular power, if it is rightful and well-ordered, intends as its principal and final purpose to direct and lead its subjects to a virtuous life, and this pertains principally to the soul. For all rightful power amongst men ought to strive after that purpose for which man is ultimately ordained. But the end of man, considered as man, is felicity; and so every rightful power ought to seek the felicity of the multitude subject to it. Moreover, the felicity of man consists primarily in the achievement of virtue; and so it pertains to the duty of this power to direct men towards this end. But because the external goods which subserve bodily life are required for felicity, and especially for political felicity, the government of the external and corporeal things without which the tasks of the soul are not performed in this state of life therefore properly belongs to this duty. On this account, therefore, it seems that secular power ought principally to be called spiritual, taking 'spiritual' in the sense just stated, since a virtuous life pertains to the soul, which is spiritual.

97

For the following reasons, however, it can be called corporeal. For, in another sense, 'spiritual' denotes that which belongs to the soul not according to nature, but according to grace; and, in this sense, those things are called spiritual which concern grace and which are related to grace in the following ways: either in the manner of an opposite, such as guilt; or in the manner of a sign; or through their effects; or in some other fashion. And because grace elevates man above temporal things and causes him to share in eternity, since, through it, man is made in the image of God, that which is spiritual in this sense is therefore placed over against the temporal, inasmuch as 'temporal' denotes that which concerns nature as such, and that which is related to nature. For nature, as such, is temporal, since even the intellect of our soul, which, by reason of its abstraction from matter, seems to be withdrawn from time, depends upon time for its operation. Taking the word 'spiritual' in this sense, therefore, secular power is not called spiritual but temporal, because, as such, it concerns nature, whereas spiritual power concerns grace. And, for the same reason, it is called secular and temporal because the word *saeculum*, properly understood, implies temporal duration.

There is, therefore, a clear difference between the two kinds of royal power discussed above, one of which is said to be over spiritual things and the other over temporal. From this consideration, it also follows that the one is called natural and the other supernatural; because that which is over temporal things as such is concerned with nature, whereas that which is over spiritual things is concerned with grace, which is above nature [*super naturam*]. It follows from this moreover that the one is called heavenly and the other earthly. For because grace makes us heavenly and directs us towards heavenly things as to an end, spiritual power, which is concerned with grace, is therefore called heavenly. Temporal power, however, is called earthly because it has earthly things as its end: not merely in the sense that external goods are called earthly, but in the sense that all things which are adapted to the purposes of earthly life - by which is meant that earthly life which belongs to man according to his nature - can be called earthly. Again, it follows from this that the one is called divine and the other human. For spiritual power is called divine because it relates to grace, which makes man in the image of God, whereas temporal power, which relates to the nature of man itself, considered simply as man, may be called human.

Having dealt with the foregoing differences, then, we can now consider the many similarities of these two kinds of power, and we can consider certain differences in relation to each similarity.

For, first, these two kinds of royal power are similar with respect to their efficient cause; for each of them comes from God. They do so in different ways, however, as we have said above, in the third chapter of this second part; and so, within this resemblance, there is a difference to be noted.

Second, they are similar with respect to their final cause; for, in each case, blessedness is sought as an end, but in different ways. For temporal power, as such, seeks the blessedness which can come to man through the resources implanted in him by nature, whereas spiritual power seeks the blessedness which is prepared for man supernaturally, by the providence of God. Hence, it pertains to the latter's office both to procure those things which are serviceable to this end and to remove those which are incompatible with this end.

Third, these two powers are similar with respect to those in whom they are vested, because each kind of power is vested in a man, and this is so specifically with regard to the rational part of the soul. For we are now speaking of power insofar as it is communicated to men. Some say, however, that these powers differ with respect to the disposition of those in whom they are vested, because in the man to whom temporal power has been communicated there is required a perfection of prudence, by which he may be guided in what he does; whereas in the man to whom spiritual power has been communicated there is required a perfection of wisdom, by means of which he may contemplate the divine. Hence, temporal power requires an active life, and spiritual a contemplative. Moreover, they say that to temporal power there is to be attributed only a perfection of nature and of those things which can come about through the resources of nature, whereas there is to be attributed to spiritual power a certain supernatural perfection, and that this attribute is conferred in holy orders.

These distinctions do not, however, seem to be correct. For the first such distinction is defective in two ways: first, because certain persons have temporal or spiritual power who are without the perfection of prudence or of wisdom. For we see many secular princes who are imprudent, and many spiritual prelates who are not wise in their understanding of divine things; yet these no less truly have power, even though they are unworthy of that power because they are not able to use it in a proper fashion. Perfection of prudence or wisdom, therefore, is not a necessary disposition without which there can be no power. Rather, it is a desirable disposition, by which the use of power is rendered worthy and made good. And, second, the first distinction is defective because spiritual power does not require only a perfection of wisdom, but of prudence also, and not only the contemplative life, but also the active. Both prudence and training in the active life are required for the government of every community; but spiritual and temporal government differ in this respect: because spiritual government requires a prudence which is supported by the principles of divine teaching, whereas temporal government requires a prudence which is supported by the principles of human reason. Also, the second distinction is defective; for even those who do not have the attribute of holy orders can have a power of government and jurisdiction [over spiritual things] in respect of certain specific acts. (There is, however, another way in which it can be said that faith is a precondition of spiritual power; because this power, which is ordained and communicated for the salvation of the faithful, is not communicated to unbelievers.)

Fourth, these powers are similar with respect to their object, because both powers are exercised in relation to men (for we are here speaking of power relative to men). Each, however, has its existence in relation to men in a different way. For temporal power has its existence in relation to men considered according to their nature; but spiritual power has its existence in relation to men inasmuch as they are capable of receiving grace. For this latter power, because it arises from grace, concerns grace and those things which are related to grace either in the manner of their disposition or in the manner of an opposite or in some other way.

Fifth, these powers are similar with respect to action, because the actions of both powers resemble one another. They differ, however, in their mode of action. For it belongs to both to judge, but the one judges corporeally and the other spiritually: the one determines spiritual causes and the other temporal; the one inflicts temporal or corporeal penalties, and the other spiritual penalties. Hence it is said that a material sword is suitable for the one and a spiritual sword for the other.[1] It pertains to both of them to feed; but the temporal power feeds in the bodily sense and the spiritual in the spiritual, although the latter should also feed in the bodily sense when it can. It pertains to both of them to fight; but the spiritual does so by preaching and the word, whereas the temporal does so with arms and the material sword. It pertains to both of them to dispense; but the spiritual dispenses those things which relate to spiritual life, and the temporal dispenses those which have to do with earthly life. And we must say the same thing of all the other actions of royal power: that they belong to the temporal and spiritual powers in different ways; that the actions of each power therefore have certain mutual resemblances, not only according to species, but according to a certain likeness; and that, associated with resemblances of this kind, there are many and great differences, as is clear from those things which have been discussed in this chapter and other preceding chapters, and as will also appear from those which are to be discussed more fully below.

---

1. Cf. *Luc.* XXII,38; Bernard of Clairvaux, *De consid.* IV,III,7 (PL 182,776).

VII

On certain other comparisons between these two kinds of royal power: that is, the spiritual and the temporal

Having assigned, therefore, the similarities and differences of the powers discussed above, it remains to consider certain other comparisons between them. And first, indeed, we must see how they compare with one another with respect to priority in time. Now just as the law of nature preceded the written Law in time, so, it seems, we must say that royal power over temporal things, which arises from nature, preceded royal power over spiritual things in time; for the latter derives its origin from grace. For the spiritual power, in truth and in fact, had its beginning in Christ, Who revealed a heavenly kingdom to us, as a consequence of which the spiritual power was ordained. In a symbolic and figurative way, indeed, this power began to exist in the Old Testament also; but we read that temporal power existed before the Law itself was given, even though it may be said that such temporal power was instituted in its perfect form only after the law of the gospel.

Second, we must see how the powers compare with one another with respect to dignity. For we must say that, in a simple and absolute sense, spiritual power is the greater in dignity and in many respects the higher:

1. By reason of its cause; for although both powers come from God, the spiritual nonetheless comes from God in a manner which is greater in dignity because more special.

2. By reason of its end; for the spiritual power is directed towards a higher end than is the temporal, that is, towards supernatural blessedness, as we have said above.

3. By reason of its object; for although man is the object of both powers, he is nonetheless the object of the spiritual power in a higher way than he is of the temporal. This is clear from the fact that the object of the temporal power is man considered according to his own nature, whereas the object of the spiritual power is man considered as perfectible by grace and as capable of becoming a member of Christ and a child of God by adoption.[1]

---

1. Cf. *Rom.* VIII,15; 23.

4. By reason of its action. For the operations of the spiritual power are higher and greater in dignity than are those of the temporal, for just as one end is related to another, so is the operation which leads to that end related to another.

5. By reason of its mode of action; because the spiritual power operates more rightly than does the temporal, in which there often occurs uncertainty and defect. For although the persons who hold spiritual power may be deficient in what they do, spiritual power in itself always has rightness.

6. By reason of its utility; for the spiritual power can do many more things and has many more modes of action than the temporal. Moreover, more people are subject to the spiritual than to the temporal power. For both laymen and clerics are subject to the spiritual power, and no one who in any way belongs to the Church is exempted from subjection to him to whom spiritual power fully belongs: that is, to the Roman Pontiff. Only laymen, however, are subject to the temporal power, and not even these in all respects; whereas clerics are not directly subject to it, unless perhaps in respect of some temporal thing. And there are many other ways in which the spiritual power is the greater in dignity, as will appear from what we shall say.

Third, we must see how these powers compare with one another with respect to causality. For the spiritual power indeed has a higher causality than does the temporal, and a mode of causality which is many times greater. For the spiritual power is related to the temporal in the manner of a final cause; for the end of the temporal power, which is natural felicity, is subordinated to the end of the spiritual power, which is supernatural blessedness. The temporal power, therefore, exists for the sake of spiritual ends, and there is no doubt that those persons act wickedly who hold temporal power which they do not direct towards spiritual ends. Just as amongst the arts, therefore, the end of one exists for the sake of the end of a higher - for example, the end of harness-making is to serve military ends - so is it also amongst the powers. And just as, in the arts, the higher end is that to which the lower end is directed as an end, so also is it amongst the powers.

Moreover, the spiritual power is related to the temporal in the manner of an active cause; and this is so in three ways. For, first, the spiritual power is an active cause in relation to the temporal in respect of the latter's institution, since, as Hugh of Saint Victor says, the spiritual power has the task of instituting the temporal.[2] We must, however, at this point note that there seem to be contrary opinions as to the institution of temporal kingship. For certain persons say that temporal power comes from God alone and that, so far as its institution is concerned, it does not depend upon the spiritual power in any way. Others, however, say that temporal power, if it is to be legitimate and just, is either united with spiritual power in the same person or is instituted by the spiritual power: otherwise, it is unjust and

---

2. *De sacramentis* II,II,4 (PL 176,418).

illegitimate. Between these two opinions, however, we can discover a middle way which seems to be more reasonable. Hence, it may be said that the institution of the temporal power takes its origin, in a material and incomplete sense, from the natural inclination of men and, for this reason, from God, inasmuch as the work of nature is the work of God. As perfected and fully formed, however, it takes its origin from the spiritual power, which is derived from God in a special way. For grace does not abolish nature, but perfects and forms it; and, similarly, that which is of grace does not abolish that which is of nature, but forms and perfects it. Hence, because the spiritual power is related to grace and the temporal to nature, the spiritual power therefore does not exclude the temporal, but forms and perfects it. All human power is, indeed, imperfect and unformed unless formed and perfected by the spiritual power; and this formation consists in approval and ratification. The human power which exists amongst unbelievers, therefore, however much it may be due to an inclination of nature and, to that extent, legitimate, is nonetheless unformed because it is not approved and ratified by the spiritual power. And, as further evidence of this, it must be known that human or temporal power needs a twofold formation in order that it may be perfected according to the nature of what it can do. For it needs the formation of faith, because, just as there is no true virtue without faith, as Augustine says - that "where knowledge of the highest and unchangeable truth is lacking, there is false virtue in even the best morals"[3] - so no power is entirely valid without faith. This is not to say that it is entirely null and illegitimate, but that it is not true nor perfect, just as the marriage of unbelievers is neither perfected nor confirmed, yet still has a kind of validity and legitimacy.

The temporal power also needs the formation of ratification and approval by the spiritual power. For however much it may have faith, the temporal power is nonetheless not formed and perfected unless it is ratified, approved and confirmed by the spiritual. Hence, anointing is bestowed upon kings not only as a sign of the holiness which is required in them, but also as a sign of approval and formation; and kings are anointed by pontiffs because that power which is called temporal is perfected and formed by the spiritual. In a sense, therefore, the spiritual power can be called the form of the temporal in the way that light is called the form of colour. For colour has something of the form of light, but it has such a feeble light that, unless there is present a more excellent light by which it may be formed, it can move the vision, not inherently, but virtually. Similarly, temporal power has something of the validity of power, since it comes from human law, which arises from nature; but it is nonetheless imperfect and unformed unless it is formed by the spiritual power; and, in this sense, it is said to be instituted by the spiritual power. Hence also, Hugh of Saint Victor says that, in the Church of God, the priestly dignity consecrates and sanctifies the royal dignity by

---

3. Prosper Aquitanicus, *Sententiae ex Augustino delibatae* CVI (PL 45,1868).

benediction and forms it by institution:[4] in other words, the former sanctifies the latter by its blessing and institutes it by its formation.

And this is also shown by the following argument. For that a man should be placed over men arises from human law, which is perfected by nature; but that a believer should be placed over believers arises from divine law, which springs from grace. For it is grace, and not nature, which makes men believers. And because the divine law is vested in the Vicar of Christ, it therefore pertains to him to institute Christian kings and temporal power over the faithful inasmuch as they are believers. Hence, the temporal prince has power over men within the Church by human law, but over the faithful by divine law. Because, therefore, faith gives form to nature, the temporal power is instituted through its formation and formed through its institution by the spiritual power, and is approved and ratified by it. Hence, the temporal power ought not to make use of laws unless they have been approved by the spiritual power.

It is clear, therefore, in what way the spiritual power has the nature of an active cause in relation to the temporal with respect to the latter's institution.

Second, it has the nature of an active cause in relation to the temporal power with respect to judgment. For, since it institutes the temporal power, it also pertains to the spiritual power to judge it. Again, since those things which are means to an end are judged in relation to that end, the spiritual power, which seeks the ultimate and supreme end of man, has the task of judging the temporal, which seeks a lower end, subordinated to the end of the spiritual power. For just as the science of sacred scripture judges any physical science, so the spiritual power judges any temporal power whatsoever. And just as the judgment of the senses, when it is deficient, is corrected by the judgment of the intellect, which is its superior in the degrees of cognitive power, so the action of the temporal power, when it is found to deviate from what is right, is corrected by the spiritual power as by a superior. Hence, Hugh of Saint Victor says that it is the task of the spiritual power to institute the earthly power, so that it may exist, and also to judge it if it is not good.[5]

For the spiritual power has the task of judging the temporal power because it can and must correct and guide it, punish it, and impose on it a penalty not only spiritual, but temporal also, in the event of its sin and transgression, and proceed even to the point of deposing it if the quality of its fault so requires. Such deposition is not a deposition of the power itself, because, in that case, the order of powers would be abolished, but of the man who uses the power given to him ill. Thus, when it is said that the power is deposed, [what is meant is that] power is taken away from him who has the power. For the Gloss on that verse of Romans - "let every soul be subject to the higher powers"[6] - says that the word 'power' sometimes means the power

---

4. See n.2, above.
5. Ibid..
6. *Glossa ordinaria* on *Rom.* XIII,1.

given to someone by God, and sometimes the man who has the power. The power itself, therefore, which is good and ordained for the sake of the good, is not abolished or condemned: rather, he who has the power is deposed because he has used it unworthily. For just as temporal power over the faithful is conferred on someone through the spiritual power, so can he be deprived of that power through the same agency. And no temporal prince whatsoever is exempt from the judgment which belongs to the spiritual power over the temporal power, because temporal power in general, in whomever it is found, is subject to spiritual judgment, and especially to the judgment of him in whom there is fulness of spiritual power: that is, the Roman Pontiff. For although it may belong to other pontiffs to judge matters involving a temporal power - for a bishop can excommunicate a king as a member of his diocese - the Supreme Pontiff nonetheless has full judgment over all princes and according to every mode of judgment which has been communicated to the spiritual power.

Third, the spiritual power has the nature of an active cause in relation to the temporal power with respect to command. For just as, in the arts, the art to which belongs the ultimate and principal end commands the art to which belongs a secondary end which is subordinated to the principal one, so also is it amongst the powers. Hence, the spiritual power, to which belongs the chief end, which is supernatural blessedness, is so related to the temporal power, to which belongs natural blessedness - which is a secondary end, subordinated to the supernatural one - that the former commands the latter, and uses in its own service both it and all the things which are subject to it and which pertain to it; because natural things ought to serve those things which pertain to grace and to be moved and guided by them: the temporal by the spiritual, the human by the divine, the earthly by the heavenly. Hence, the spiritual power has command over all temporal things whatsoever, inasmuch as the latter were created to serve and be directed towards spiritual ends. And the temporal power, by divine law, is in all respects subject to the spiritual, inasmuch as it is ordained to and for the sake of the spiritual power. So, therefore, the spiritual power is related to the temporal just as the art of architecture is related to a subordinate art [such as that of the stonemason or carpenter], and just as sacred scripture is to the sciences discovered by mankind, of which it makes use in its service so that its truth may be made manifest. The temporal power, then, is called upon to aid the spiritual and, when so called, should bring aid and render service. The comparison of these two powers with respect to dignity and causality is therefore clear.

Now from what has been said we can pass to a comparison of them with respect to their content. For because lower powers are contained within higher, and because what is caused is contained within what causes, the temporal power, which stands in comparison to the spiritual as inferior to superior and as caused to cause, is therefore contained by the spiritual power; and, for this reason, it is said that the laws of both the earthly and heavenly empires were given by Christ to the blessed Peter,[7] because Peter and each of his successors, in whom the fulness of spiritual power resides, simultaneously has temporal power also: not, indeed, in the same way as the temporal prince has it, but in a superior and more worthy and excellent fashion. For [the pope] does not have it in such a way that he carries out the functions of the temporal power directly, except in certain cases. Rather, he carries out its functions in a more noble fashion, by commanding and guiding it and thereby directing its use to its proper end. Temporal power is therefore said to pre-exist in the spiritual by reason of the latter's primary and supreme authority, even though the spiritual power does not directly execute temporal functions in a general and regular way. For this reason, all temporal princes must obey the pope, in whom spiritual power resides in its highest form, as they would our Lord Jesus Christ; and they must acknowledge him as their superior and head, and they must revere and honour and be subject to him. Hence, as the blessed Bernard says in a letter to the Emperor Conrad, we read: "'let every soul be subject unto the higher powers', and 'Whosoever resisteth the power resisteth the ordinance of God.' I desire and urge you to cherish this commandment in all things, and to show reverence to the Supreme and Apostolic See and to the blessed vicar Peter just as you would wish it to be shown to you by the whole empire."[8] And in the psalm it is said: "Be wise now, therefore, O ye kings; be instructed, ye judges of the earth: serve the Lord with fear."[9] The Gloss[10] on this verse says that Christ is here speaking to the kings of the earth, saying: And now that I am appointed to be your king, as it was foretold - "But I am appointed king by Him" - be not cast down, you kings who judge the earth; rather be wise and instructed. For it is expedient for you to be under Him from Whom wisdom and instruction come, and it is expedient for you to fear Him, and not lord it as do those who do not acknowledge themselves to be subjects, and for you to serve the Lord of all: that is, Christ, and, if Christ, then His vicar also, Whom He has set in His place in the Church. And if kings must obey the Vicar of Christ, so therefore must all other men of whatever kind who are under kings: indeed, far more readily than they do kings, because he is in all things and always higher [than kings], and because he holds the summit of spiritual and temporal power.

Hence, if the Supreme Pontiff commands one thing and some temporal prince another, obedience must be given rather to the Supreme Pontiff than to the prince. This is not true of other pontiffs, because they do not have fulness of power. Hence, in those matters which pertain to the health of the soul, obedience is to be given rather to them than to the prince, but in those

---

7. Cf. *Dist.* XXII,c.1 (*Omnis*) (CIC I,73).

8. *Epistola CLXXXIII ad Conradum regem Romanorum,* quoting *Rom.* XIII,1f (PL 182,345).

9. *Psalm.* II,10.

10. *Glossa ordinaria,* PL 113,847, quoting *Psalm.* II,6; but the gloss is here paraphrased very freely, and with an imported Petrine bias.

things which pertain to the civil good, it is the prince who is to be the more readily obeyed. The temporal power, therefore, stands in comparison with the spiritual in the following ways: it is subject to it; it serves it; it is instituted by it; it is judged by it; it is led and ordered by it; and it is contained and reserved in it. This is always and especially true of the fulness of spiritual power which is in the Supreme Pontiff; and it is true in certain respects and partially of the partial spiritual power which is in the other prelates.

Certain reasons can be adduced in confirmation of what we have said. And first, indeed, it can be shown by the following arguments that one of these powers is superior to the other and greater in dignity. For it is proper that many things should be reduced to one according to a certain order. This is clear in the case of efficient causes, which are reduced to the one First Efficient Cause according to a certain order; and in the case of final causes, which are referred to the one Ultimate End in a certain order. Also, opposites themselves are reduced to a certain order in one genus, because one of them is always more powerful and noble than the other; and so the powers discussed above are also reduced to the one Primary Power in a certain order. For these powers have the nature of an efficient cause and of a final cause, and so they are reduced to order under the one principal Efficient and Final Cause: that is, God, by Whom and for Whom they are made one. The Apostle says that "there is no power but of God: the powers that be are ordained of God."[11] Also, in some circumstances the powers have a certain mutual opposition; and so they are brought together under one kind of Power, according to a certain order. Such an order is not without degrees, however. Rather, there is a higher and a lower within it, and so it must be that one of the stated powers is superior to the other.

Now it can be shown from certain arguments that the spiritual power is the greater in dignity and higher.

1. From the payment of tithes, which temporal powers give to the prelates of the Church in recognition of their subjection to God, from Whom they have temporal things and power over them, in the same way that certain men are tributaries to a certain lord by reason of those things which they hold of him.

2. From sanctification and blessing; for the spiritual power consecrates and blesses the temporal, and he who blesses is the greater, as the Apostle says in *Hebrews*.[12]

3. From the government of things; for just as, in the order of things, corporeal things are ruled by spiritual and the grosser bodies by the more subtle, so in the Church, which is ordered in the best fashion, the temporal power is ruled by the spiritual;[13] and just as, in the universe, one body is governed by another, and body by spirit, and the lower spirits by the higher,

---

11. *Rom.* XIII,1.
12. Cf. *Heb.* VI,16.
13. Cf. Augustine, *De Trin.* III,4 (CC L,135f).

and all spirits by God, so, in the Church, one temporal power is governed by another temporal power, and the temporal by the spiritual, and one spiritual power by another, and every spiritual power by the one primary one, the Supreme Pontiff.

Moreover, this can also be shown by arguments derived from the origin of both powers. For temporal power originates from nature, whereas spiritual power is derived from grace. Now grace is superior to nature, and so spiritual power is superior to and greater in dignity than temporal. Furthermore, other reasons for this conclusion can be derived from what has been said above concerning the comparison of these powers with respect to dignity. For there are many arguments in support of the view that the spiritual power simultaneously has temporal power also, so that it rules over temporal things, and secular princes are under it, and, consequently, so are those things which are under princes, not only with regard to spiritual, but also with regard to temporal, matters.

First, he who has been entrusted with a principal power is understood also to be entrusted with those powers which are ancillary to it. But spiritual power is a principal power, and temporal power is ancillary to it, because it is under it and exists for its sake. Therefore, he to whom spiritual power has been entrusted is understood also to be entrusted with temporal. Now Peter and his successors have been entrusted with spiritual power, and fully so, as we have said above. And so it is understood from this fact that temporal power also has been entrusted to them. Just as Christ possessed both powers, therefore, so does His vicar.

Again, it must be that he whose task it is to seek an end also has charge of those things which tend towards that end. But the task of the spiritual power is to seek the end of man, which is the salvation and blessedness of his soul. And so it has authority over all those things which can contribute to the achievement of that end, and of those things which impede its pursuit. And temporal things are amongst these, because by making good use of them we merit an eternal reward, and, by abusing them, an eternal punishment. The spiritual power, therefore, rules even over temporal things insofar as these are directed towards the end of salvation. And because they are given to us by God to the end that we may use them well in the order of salvation; nor are they to be desired or possessed and dispensed other than for the sake of blessedness: the spiritual power therefore extends itself to these things with respect to that end for which they are given to us. Hence, it pertains to the spiritual power to command the good use of them and to prohibit their abuse.

Moreover, just as Christ is the head of the faithful with regard to both souls and bodies, so also is His vicar; and so the latter has power over bodies and over those things which are subservient to bodily life: of which kind are external and temporal goods insofar as these things support bodily life and are instrumental to the achievement of salvation. For the soul makes use of the body's members in spiritual actions. For this reason, the Apostle says that our bodies themselves are temples of the Holy Spirit, Who dwells in us.[14] The soul makes use of external goods also; and so the spiritual power also extends itself to temporal things.

Again, the spiritual power can judge the temporal by reason of fault, and call upon it for the defence of the Church. Also, it can require of the temporal power, and of those subject to it, assistance and monetary and material subvention for the common good of the Church. And it follows from these things that the temporal power is subject to the spiritual; because the temporal power itself, it seems, can do no more than this in relation to its subjects. For it can chastise them by reason of fault, and make exactions, not merely as it wishes, but for the good estate of the commonwealth or in certain other circumstances, according to approved customs.

Moreover, the secular prince and those who are subject to him in temporal matters pay tax to the spiritual power: that is, tithes; and so again the spiritual power rules over princes and the subjects of princes with respect to temporal things.

Again, the spiritual power can exclude from the community of the faithful. But the possession of temporal goods and property and office is founded upon community; and so the spiritual power extends itself to temporal things.

Again, according to divine law, no one justly and legitimately holds any temporal possession if he does not freely submit himself to the lordship of God, from Whom he holds it, and if he does not use it rightly. For this reason, unbelievers and sinners, who withdraw themselves from the lordship of God and use temporal goods ill, possess those temporal goods unworthily and unjustly according to the divine law, whatever human law may prescribe. And it is according to this principle that the saying of Augustine is shown to be true: that "by divine law, all things belong to the just."[15] But he is not subject to God who is not subject to the ecclesiastical power. Moreover, the right use of temporal goods is according to order: towards the end which the spiritual power seeks and to which it guides. No one, therefore, justly possesses any temporal thing unless, in his possession of it, he subjects himself to the spiritual power. And this would not be so if the spiritual power did not extend itself even to temporal things.

We must, however, consider what certain learned persons say: that the spiritual power extends itself to temporal things in two ways. One way is with respect to the necessary use of them; for it is fitting that he who sows spiritual seed should reap a temporal harvest. The other way is with respect to judgment; because, since it may judge spiritual matters, which are superior to and weightier than temporal, the spiritual power can also judge temporal matters, either immediately or through an intermediary, as we have said above.

But although, as we have also said above, the temporal power is instituted by the spiritual, we also encounter the following argument. The Israelite

---

14. *I Cor.* VI,19.
15. *Epist.* CLIII,26 (CSEL XLIV,427).

people prefigured the Christian people, and those things which occurred amongst that people prefigured those which exist amongst the Christian people. Amongst the former people, however, God did not entrust the choice of the supreme prince and king to the people, but reserved it to Himself, as is said in *Deuteronomy*: "Thou shalt appoint him king over thee, whom the Lord thy God shall choose."[16] Hence, by the special ordinance of God, judges were instituted amongst that people, and subsequently kings. Amongst the Christian people, then, [it would seem to follow that] kings must be instituted by the special ordinance of God [and therefore that they are responsible directly to God, and not to the spiritual power]. In the Old Testament, however, this ordinance of God was declared through prophets and priests, by whom certain kings were anointed. In the New Testament, therefore, it must again be declared by the priests, who have spiritual power; and, according to this reasoning, the spiritual power is said to institute the temporal inasmuch as the former acts on God's behalf. And what the spiritual power does, God is said to do, just as those whom it absolves from sin are absolved by God. But such institution of the prince by the Church, which is done under divine law, does not remove what is done under human law. Rather, as we have said above, it forms and perfects it. For in the case of the institution of a bishop also, which is done by a superior bishop, there first takes place a kind of imperfect institution under the law of elections, which is done in order to preserve the unity and peace of the churches.

Moreover, that the temporal power may be judged by the spiritual can be shown by the following arguments in addition to what we have already said on this subject above. For temporal princes and kings easily degenerate from good government and become tyrants, as is clear from many examples both amongst the gentiles and the Israelite people, and subsequently amongst the Christian people, amongst whom many princes have been tyrants and only a few of them truly kings. The reason for this is that great power is granted to kings, and only the virtuous man is able to bear good fortune well; and so perfect virtue is required in him to whom great power is granted. Perfect virtue, however, is found only in few men. Few kings, therefore, rule royally, and many decline into tyranny; and this is especially so because of covetousness, which, according to the Apostle, "is the root of all evil."[17] It is for this reason that the Lord did not at first institute a prince with full power over the people of Israel, but appointed judges and governors to have custody of them. Subsequently, indeed, he granted them a king at the petition of the people, but as it were in anger, as is clear from what He said to Samuel: "They have not rejected thee, but they have rejected me, that I should not reign over them."[18] But the easy decline of princes into tyranny occurs at the expense of the salvation of both the unjust

---

16. *Deut.* XVII,15.
17. *I Tim.* VI,10.
18. *I Reg.* VIII,7.

rulers themselves and of their subjects also, who, when they are oppressed by tyranny, fall away into those things which are contrary to salvation. But God wills that His Church should be disposed and governed in such a way as to secure the salvation of His people most readily. The people's salvation, however, will be better served if secular princes are quickly turned from tyranny; and so the latter may in many respects be judged by some superior power in the Church, the fear of which restrains them from the exercise of tyranny, which would not be so if they were subject to the judgment of no human power. By divine law, therefore, the temporal power must be judged by the spiritual. It is clearly enough shown, then, by the foregoing remarks, that the spiritual power directs the temporal in its sway and that the latter must submit to the former.

VIII

On certain aspects of the powers discussed above which are especially worthy of note

Now from what we have said, and having regard to what we have said, we can bring forward certain aspects of these powers and take special note of them. For, first, we must consider that, because temporal power pre-exists in the spiritual power as an inferior capacity does in a superior, and as that which is caused does in its cause, as we have said, whoever is subject to the temporal power is therefore also under the spiritual. As we have said above, however, the opposite is not true. For laymen and clerics alike are under the spiritual power (although clerics are so in a more special way, in that their condition is more spiritual because they are numbered amongst those specially chosen of the Lord); whereas only laymen are under the temporal power, and they are not so in all things, but only in respect of temporal matters. Clerics, however, because they are placed in charge of spiritual things, are exempt from temporal power, even though, in some cases and for some temporal reason, they are from time to time subject to the secular prince according to a certain manner.

Moreover, all temporal goods which are subject to the temporal power are also subject to the spiritual, although not in the same way. For they are subject to the temporal power directly [*immediate*], but to the spiritual through an intermediary [*mediate*]: they are subject to the temporal power with respect to their immediate administration and dispensation, and to the spiritual power with respect to their general oversight. Moreover, certain temporal things are subject to the spiritual power which are not under the temporal, as in the case of those temporal things which have a spiritual connexion, such as ecclesiastical property, whether this consists of tithes, first-fruits and the offerings of the faithful, or in those things which are given to the Church in fealty, or in the other things of whatever kind which are allotted to or acquired by churches.

Moreover, every act which is appropriate to the temporal power is appropriate also to the spiritual: not in the same way, however, but in a more excellent fashion. For [every such act] is appropriate to the spiritual power according to authority, according to command, according to direction, and through an intermediary [*mediate*]; whereas it is appropriate

112

to the temporal power according to use, according to ministry and service, and directly [*immediate*]. Certain acts, however, belong to the spiritual power which do not belong to the temporal, and in which the temporal power neither should, nor without wrongdoing can, involve itself: of which kind are spiritual acts or acts in respect of spiritual matters. The reason for this arises from the order of the powers; for a lower power may not usurp to itself that which pertains to a higher. Hence also, many of those who have perverted this order and extended themselves to things which do not belong to their proper station and office have been punished. This is clear from what we read in the case of Uzziah the king, who offered incense,[1] and in many other instances, as the blessed Dionysius excellently shows in his letter to Demophilus, where, after many examples which point to the conclusion that a man should do nothing whch does not belong to his proper office, he concludes that "it is not lawful, as the holy scriptures say, nor are those things rightly done which are not done according to what is fitting. Rather, it is right for each to attend to what is proper to him, without seeking what is higher or lower, and to consider only those things subordinated to him according to his rank."[2]

Nonetheless, because not a few temporal princes involve themselves in certain spiritual matters, such as the collation of ecclesiastical benefices or the custody of ecclesiastical property, therefore, in order to see how such matters can or cannot belong to them, it must be known that certain things are spiritual in their very nature and absolutely, and that the temporal power does not extend to things of this kind in any way. Such things are absolution from sin in the court of penance, the consecration of the eucharist, and other such things. On the other hand, certain things, such as ecclesiastical benefices, are spiritual, not in their very nature, but by reason of the connexion that they have with spiritual things; and to things of this kind the temporal power does extend in one sense and does not in another. For it does not extend to these things by virtue of its own power; but it can extend itself to them by virtue of the spiritual power which is its superior: not, however, in such a way that the right to confer ecclesiastical benefices or the right to dispose of ecclesiastical goods may belong to it, for it is not possible for a lay person to have such power. For if a lay person cannot receive an ecclesiastical benefice, still less can the right to confer it upon others belong to him (although he can play some instrumental part as a minister in the collation [of an ecclesiastical benefice] by presenting or nominating someone to it or by some similar act). Hence, when a temporal prince is said to confer ecclesiastical benefices with the consent of the spiritual power, such a collation comes from the spiritual power as having the authority to confer it, and it comes from the prince as having the part of a minister in such a collation by presenting or recommending someone to the benefice as fit or worthy. If, however, such a collation is made by the prince without the tacit

---

1. *II Para.* XXVI,16ff.
2. *Epist. VIII, ad Demophilum* III (PG 3,1091/2).

or express consent of the spiritual power which has authority in the matter, the collation is as of right null, and the prince who has made such a collation in point of fact, believing himself to have authority to do so, has usurped to himself that which is not his. Nor can this be done lawfully from custom, no matter how long established and ancient. Indeed, the more ancient such a custom is the more deplorable it is; for it cannot be made lawful by any custom for one who holds a lower power to extend himself beyond his proper bounds and perform those tasks which properly belong to a higher power. From the order of the powers, therefore, we may conclude generally that whatever pertains to the temporal power also belongs to the spiritual, but in a more excellent fashion, whereas it is not true that whatever pertains to the spiritual power can belong to the temporal.

Second, we must notice that, when it is said that temporal power pre-exists in him who has spiritual power, it is not to be supposed that he has the two powers in a distinct and separate manner, but, rather, that he has a single power over both temporal and spiritual things. This is so because lower things are contained in higher things and what is distinct in lower things is united in higher. For the sake of distinguishing acts of different kinds, however, it is said that there are two kinds of power in him. For inasmuch as he performs spiritual acts and administers spiritual affairs, he is said to have spiritual power, whereas, when he directs and counsels and rules in temporal matters, he is said to have temporal power. Therefore, just as the one power of reason is differentiated as higher and lower according to its different offices - because, inasmuch as it seeks to contemplate and be mindful of the eternal, it is called higher reason, whereas, when it dwells on temporal things, it is called lower, as the blessed Augustine says:[3] so the one spiritual power is called both temporal and spiritual and is differentiated according to its different offices, and is called higher and lower. Because, however, it is named from its more worthy office, it is therefore simply called spiritual power, even though temporal power pre-exists in it in a pre-eminent fashion.

Third, we must notice that although he who holds spiritual power simultaneously has temporal power also, it is nonetheless not superfluous that there should be in the Church temporal princes who also have such temporal power. [This is so for the following reasons:]

1. Because there are different modes of action; for, as we have said, temporal and spiritual princes do not exercise temporal jurisdiction in the same way, and so it is proper that there should be different agents because there are different ways of acting.

2. By reason of impropriety and unworthiness. For it is unworthy and improper that those persons to whom worthier and weightier matters belong should perform baser tasks. Hence it would be unworthy and improper for the spiritual power, whose task it is to act in spiritual matters, to be occupied

---

3. Cf. *Liber de spiritu et anima* XIII (PL 40,789).

with the discharge of temporal business. It is suitable, therefore, that there should be some lower power to be occupied with such temporal concerns.

3. For the sake of freedom of action: that is, so that the spiritual power may be more at liberty to devote itself to spiritual matters without being impeded by the administration of temporal business. For man is not like God, Who, in governing lower things, is not impeded in His government of higher things and conversely. On the contrary, in man, concern with the one impedes his concern with the other. In order, therefore, that the spiritual power may without impediment occupy itself with things spiritual and divine, it is expedient that there should be another power under it, which concerns itself with things temporal and human. And from this and the preceding consideration can perhaps be inferred the reason why there are not two distinct kinds of priestly power in the Church like the two kinds of royal power. For a priestly act which arises from the law of nature does not impede a priestly act which comes from the divine law, and is not inconsistent with its dignity, even though the former is imperfect in relation to the latter. Hence, the former is perfected by the latter, as we have said above, and a single priesthood is made from both, by the co-operation of both nature and grace.

4. For the sake of necessary help; for the spiritual power is not able to do alone all the things over which it has authority, but has need of help, and, for this reason, it is proper that there should be some lower power to act as the minister of the spiritual power in the government of temporal affairs and to help it in the many things that it cannot manage to do alone, and to defend and protect it. Hence Isidore, in the third book of his work on the Supreme Good, says: "Not seldom within the Church do secular princes attain the summit of power, so that, by that same power, they may protect ecclesiastical discipline. Other powers would not be necessary in the Church, were it not for the fact that the secular power imposes by the discipline of terror what the priest cannot manage to effect by the preaching of doctrine."[4]

5. For the sake of good order; for just as God, Who is good and more than good, even though He could do all things Himself, nonetheless communicates the dignity of rule to the different creatures so that, in His creating as well as in His being, good order may shine forth in the things produced by Him: so also He wills that there should be some lower power in the Church under the spiritual, to which temporal rule should be communicated so that, with respect to ruling power, good order should be found in the Church.

And from these arguments, by which we have shown that the power of temporal princes is not superfluous in the Church even though the spiritual power already has temporal power, it can be concluded that the spiritual power should not directly exercise the temporal jurisdiction which it has in a regular and general way. For the mode of action which the Church's

---

4. *Sentent.* III,LI,4 (PL 83,723).

temporal jurisdiction requires is one of authority and direction, not one of immediate execution; and this requires a dignity which should not concern itself with inferior acts. It also requires a liberty in relation to spiritual acts such that the spiritual power should not be implicated in and impeded by the administration of temporal business. And it requires a freedom of action in respect of which the spiritual power is assisted and protected by the temporal power. Also, this requires an order as between the powers, which would be removed if the spiritual power were to exercise an immediate temporal jurisdiction.

But although the spiritual power should not exercise temporal jurisdiction regularly and generally, it can nonetheless intervene directly in temporal affairs on the investigation of certain causes and in some cases: just as God Himself, although, in the ordinary way, He acts in the world through the mediation of secondary causes, sometimes, in special circumstances, acts outside the order of secondary causes. But although, for good reason and in appropriate cases, the spiritual power can intervene in temporal matters, it ought not to do so regularly and indiscriminately. This can be gathered from the words of the Apostle at *I Corinthians* VI,[5] where, speaking against those who had submitted themselves to the judgment of unbelievers, he says: "Do ye not know that the saints shall judge this world?" - and by 'this world' he means wicked men, whom the good shall judge by both comparison and power, as the Gloss[6] says. The Apostle continues: "And if this world shall be judged in you," (that is, by you) "are ye unworthy to judge the smallest matters?" - as if, the Gloss adds, saying, No: truly indeed can ye judge these things. "Know ye not that we shall judge angels?" (that is, the wicked and apostate angels) "How much more things that pertain to this life?" (that is, secular things) And he goes on: "If then ye have judgments of things pertaining to this life, set them to judge who are least esteemed in the Church." The Apostle here speaks ironically against those who had chosen judges who, though believers, were least esteemed because indiscreet and base; and this interpretation agrees with what follows: "I speak to your shame", and so on. Or, again, according to the Gloss, because the Apostle said that they could judge the smallest matters, he prescribed that the least esteemed in the Church should be appointed to the determination of such matters because the greater men should attend to spiritual matters: therefore, "set them who are least esteemed", that is, those who are wise, but nonetheless lesser in merit, [to judge temporal matters;] for the apostles are so called because they are to travel from place to place preaching. Therefore, let those who are wise in external matters examine earthly causes so that, for as long as those who are endowed with spiritual gifts are not called upon to administer earthly goods, they may be able to devote themselves to spiritual goods. It is, however, very necessary

---

5. *I Cor.* VI,2ff.
6. *Glossa interlinearis* on I Cor. VI,2. For what follows see also *Glossa ordinaria*, PL 114,528 and Peter Lombard, *Collectanea*, PL 191,1576f.

to ensure that those who are great in spiritual gifts do not by any means wholly neglect the business of their weaker neighbours, but either entrust it to others by whom it may be worthily conducted, or attend to it themselves.

Also, the blessed Bernard, in his book *De consideratione,* expounding that saying of the Apostle - "set them to judge who are least esteemed in the Church" - admonishes Pope Eugenius that he should not entangle himself in secular affairs unless for good cause. He speaks as follows: "According to the Apostle, then, you, apostolic man that you are, usurp to yourself a mean and unworthy office [if you undertake to judge temporal things]. Hence it is that, instructing a bishop, the Apostle says: 'No soldier of God entangleth himself in the affairs of this life.'"[7] And, a little later, Bernard adds: "Where at any time did any apostle sit as a judge of men or as a fixer of boundaries or a distributor of lands? Christ said: 'Who made me a judge over you?' Do not, therefore, transgress the bounds which your fathers have set."[8] After this, Bernard also says: "It seems to me that he who thinks it unworthy of apostles, or of apostolic men to whom judgment has been given over great matters, to abstain from judging in these lesser ones, has not properly appraised these things. Why should they not scorn to judge the insignificant earthly possessions of men, who shall judge heavenly things and angels? Your power, therefore, is over cases of sin, not over possessions; for it is with respect to the former, and not for the sake of the latter, that you have received the keys of the kingdom of Heaven, which will shut men out because they are sinners, not because they are owners of property. 'That ye may know', Christ says, 'that the Son of Man hath power on earth to forgive sins.' Which seems to you to be the greater dignity and power: that of forgiving sins, or that of dividing estates? But there is no comparison. These lower and earthly things have their own judges, the kings and princes of the earth. Why invade another man's boundaries? Why put your sickle into another man's harvest? It is not that you are unworthy to do so, but, rather, because it is unworthy for you to concern yourself with such matters when you are occupied with greater things. Finally, where necessity requires, hear the judgment of the Apostle: 'If the world shall be judged by you, are ye unworthy to judge the smallest matters?' It is, however, one thing to turn aside to these matters incidentally, for some urgent reason, and quite another to concern yourself with them as if such things were worthy of the attention of your high office."[9] It is clear from these words, therefore, that the spiritual power should not exercise temporal jurisdiction indiscriminately. In cases of necessary need, however, it can and must involve itself directly with temporal matters; and the contradictions which seem to be present in what we have said above are resolved by this distinction.

---

7. *De consid.* I,VI,7 (PL 182,735), quoting *II Tim.* II,4.
8. *De consid.* I,VI,7 (PL 182,735f), quoting *Luc.* XII,14; see also *Prov.* XXII,28.
9. *De consid.* I,VI,7-VII,8 (PL 182,736), quoting *Matt.* IX,6 and *I Cor.* VI,2.

But as to these temporal matters and the question of when the spiritual power can concern itself with them directly, learned men have concluded as follows.[10] It is the task of the spiritual power to concern itself directly with those temporal things which are in some manner attached to spiritual things. It therefore concerns itself with the collection, receipt and disposal of tithes, because these are attached to a spiritual office. It concerns itself with the dowries which are attached to matrimony, which is a sacrament, and with inheritances, which are annexed to legitimate birth. Because, therefore, the ecclesiastical judge judges concerning matrimony and the legitimacy of the children begotten from matrimony, it pertains to him to judge concerning dowries and inheritances insofar as they are attached to these things; although they may for some other reason pertain to the judgment of the secular power.

Again, because, as is said on the authority of Bernard, the power of the spiritual judge is over cases of sin, which are spiritual evils, he can therefore involve himself in temporal questions which are reported in connexion with the denunciation of sin, since it pertains to him to correct every Christian in matters of sin.

Again, it is his task to intervene in temporal cases where a temporal dispute is contrary to peace, which is a spiritual bond because it is effected by love, and because peace treaties are confirmed by oath; for oath-breaking is a sin concerning which it pertains to the spiritual power to judge.

Again, he concerns himself with temporal matters by reason of some deficiency of temporal lordship, as when the empire is vacant or because of the prince's negligence or malice in not preserving justice and in abusing the power entrusted to him, and in not doing what he is bound to do in the service of the spiritual power and for the common good.

He also intervenes in temporal matters when appeal is made to him; and this is especially true of those things in respect of which appeal is made to him by custom and the custom is tolerated by the secular prince and approved and confirmed by the ecclesiastical judge.

Also, he concerns himself with temporal things which are given to the Church by secular princes or by other believers, simply because they are given.

Also, he intervenes in temporal matters when anything arises which is difficult or ambiguous.

It may be that there are also other cases in which the spiritual power can intervene directly in temporal matters; but it is not the purpose of the

---

10. For this and the following six paragraphs, see especially *Decretales* II,i,13 (*Novit*) (CIC II,243f); II,ii,10 (*Licet*) (CIC II,250f); II,xxviii,7 (*Si duobus*) (CIC II,412); III,xxx,15 (*Ad haec donationem*), 17 (*Quamvis sit grave*), 31 (*Dudum adversus*) (CIC II,561f; 567); IV,xvii,5 (*Lator*), 13 (*Per venerabilem*) (CIC II,711; 714ff); IV,xx,3 (*De prudentia*) (CIC II,725f). The 'learned men' referred to are therefore chiefly Popes Alexander III and Innocent III. Verbal similarities suggest, however, that James is here making use of the treatment of these decretals already undertaken by Aegidius Romanus at *De ecclesiastica potestate* Pt. III, Chs. V-VIII (ed. Dyson, pp. 164ff).

present work to specify such cases more fully and more certainly. We are here concerned in general terms with those things which pertain to the spiritual and temporal power respectively, and certain particular instances are given only by way of example.

Fourth, since it is apparent from what has been said that the power of lower pontiffs and the power of temporal princes is contained under the Vicar of Christ and the successors of Peter as under the power which is their highest cause, we must note that each of these powers stands in relation to the power [of the Vicar of Christ] in a different way. For the power of the [lower] pontiffs is related to it as an effect such that the perfection of the cause is present in it according to the same nature, even though not totally, but in part. For the power which is in the Supreme Pontiff is devolved upon the other pontiffs according to the same nature and with the same mode of action, although not in all its fulness, but partially. The power of secular princes, however, is related to it as an effect such that the perfection of the cause is present in it only defectively and according to a different nature; for, in secular princes, there is only temporal power, and it is in them according to a different nature and with a different mode of action from that which is in the Supreme Pontiff, as we have said above.

Fifth, we must note that the Supreme Pontiff has temporal power not only by divine law but also by human law: that is, by the grant made by Constantine, who held sway over the empire. And if anyone asks how this human law applies to things divine, we can in one way say that this human law is a manifestation of the divine law or a confirmation of the divine law and an imitation of it, and an act of veneration towards it. For the grant of Constantine was a gesture of submission and veneration towards the spiritual power, and, when Constantine granted to the blessed Sylvester and his successors earthly kingship and the imperial insignia and offices, he did not confer authority, but showed reverence: he showed that earthly kingship must be subject to heavenly, and that there is no doubt that the former is made by the providence of God, in Whose hand is the heart of the king,[11] so that the summit of pontifical power should not thereby be demeaned, but should be held in higher honour when seen to be distinguished by such marks of dignity.

In another way, we can say that this grant was an act of co-operation or ministry, to the end that the power which the Vicar of Christ has by divine law might be exercised more freely in point of fact; for the persecution of tyrants was not possible before the time of Constantine. Now, however, secular princes must defend the churches and the ecclesiastical prelates so that they may be able freely to accomplish whatever is expedient to the salvation of the faithful and make use of the law without hindrance.

And there can be yet another explanation: namely, that, because of this grant, the Supreme Pontiff can intervene in temporal matters more directly, as is clear from the fact that he can exercise an immediate temporal

---

11. Cf. *Prov.* XXI,1.

jurisdiction when the empire is vacant;[12] and so, in one way, he exercises temporal power inasmuch as he has it from divine law and, in another, inasmuch as he has it from human law. Hence, in him, temporal and spiritual power are the more clearly differentiated in proportion as temporal power belongs to him by human law, because, insofar as it belongs to him by divine law, he holds it bound together in unity with spiritual power; whereas, insofar as it belongs to him by human law, he holds it separately from spiritual power, divided and discrete from it. Again, however, inasmuch as he has it from human law, he exercises it through the ministry of others, so that he may be more free to perform those spiritual tasks which are more appropriate and proper to him.

Sixth, we must note that, just as the spiritual power already has temporal power pre-eminently, so does the temporal power which is in the Church share to some extent in spiritual power: not in the sense that it is able to perform spiritual acts, but to the extent that it serves and ministers to the spiritual power, and to the extent that the actions which it does perform, if it makes right use of its power, are directed towards a spiritual end; because the temporal things which it has the task of administering themselves exist for the sake of spiritual ends. For he abuses temporal things who does not direct them to spiritual ends. For just as knowledge of what is perceptible is subservient to knowledge of what is intelligible and is subordinated to it, so must the use of temporal possessions be subservient to the spiritual life and be subordinated to it. Hence, although the immediate end of the temporal power may be other than a spiritual end, the ultimate end [of both powers] is the same: namely, supernatural blessedness, of which the spiritual power has the immediate care. Temporal power, therefore, if it is rightly used, is said to be in a certain sense spiritual. It is, however, simply called temporal from its immediate end, just as an effect is named from its immediate cause rather than from a remote one. Thus it is that kings receive an anointing which indicates their spirituality; but the fact that kings are not anointed on the head, as bishops are, but are anointed on the arm, indicates that their power is not spiritual in a principal sense, but is a power of ministry and service which is performed by the arm.

Moreover, there is another sense in which the secular prince in the Church can be called spiritual: namely, in respect of his life. For just as the bishops must be spiritual in respect of their lives, so also must temporal princes in the Church. Nonetheless, greater perfection and spirituality of life is required of the bishops than of princes; and so both are anointed, but the bishops on head and hands, because there must be in them a perfection of both the active and the contemplative life, and princes on the arm, because they must concern themselves especially with the active life. And, indeed, we do not here propose to speak of the perfect life which must be in the bishops; for the blessed Gregory, in his *De pastorali cura*, and in his book *Moralia*, has treated of this more than adequately, and so has the

---

12. See Innocent III at *Decretales* II,ii,10 (*Licet*) (CIC II,250f).

blessed Bernard in his book *De consideratione*; and many other learned men have done so in various places. But as to the perfect life of secular princes, and especially kings, who are the highest and foremost of princes, some few things must be set forth from the teachings of the more distinguished authors, so that the sense in which their power must be spiritual and directed towards a spiritual end may appear more readily from these teachings.

For although we have made certain remarks on this matter above, we must nonetheless now speak more fully on the subject. First, therefore, it is generally held that the holder of secular power, if he is to be worthy to be called a king, must act rightly. For a wicked king is not truly called a king, just as a false penny is not really a penny. Hence, Isidore, at *Etymologiae* IX, says: "the king [*rex*] is so called from 'ruling' [*regendo*]; but he who does not correct does not rule. The name 'king' is therefore retained by acting rightly, but is lost by sinning. Hence, indeed, there was amongst the men of old the following proverb: 'You will be a king if you act rightly, and if you do not do so you will not be.'"[13] And he adds that: "There are two special virtues of a king: justice and godliness; for justice by itself is harsh." To these things should be added prudence, without which justice and godliness cannot be rightly exercised, nor can a subject multitude be governed beneficially. And concerning these three virtues which are necessary to kings, many authorities can be derived from the sacred scriptures which, for the sake of brevity, we shall not now adduce.

Kings, therefore, must be subject to God in faith and devotion, so that they may be able to subject others to themselves worthily. They must cleave to God in mind, so that they may firmly uphold the government of the kingdom. They must not, like tyrants, seek their own advantage or glory, but, like true kings, they must strive after the common good of the multitude subject to them, and procure for their subjects a good - that is, a virtuous - life and those things which sustain it.

They must revere and honour, protect and defend, the churches and the prelates of the churches. For the honour that they show to Christ's ministers and vicars they assuredly show to Christ also; for He has said: "He that receiveth you receiveth me."[14] They must zealously devote themselves to the increase and growth of divine worship. They must repulse the adversaries of Christ and of the Church. They must teach what is just, prohibit what is unlawful, and restrain and punish the wicked, so that the good may live quietly in the midst of the wicked; and they must praise and honour the good themselves. They must inspire love by courtesy and kindness, and fear by justly avenging injury, not to themselves, but to the law. And we must now produce some further testimonies, so that what is consistent with the office of kings and the virtuous life may appear more readily.

---

13. *Etym.* IX,III,4 (PL 82,342).
14. *Matt.* X,40.

First, then, we must consider what the Lord ordains with respect to kings at *Deuteronomy* XVII.[15] For, in the first place, as to the manner of their election, He prescribes that the judgment of God, which is now sought in the Church, should be awaited in the choice of king, and that no one should be made king from another nation: that is, that the judgment of those who hold God's place on earth should be involved in the appointment of the king, and that no king should be chosen other than from a Christian nation; for no one must be received as king who is not a believer and a member of the Christian people.

Second, indeed, He prescribes how those who are appointed as kings ought to behave in themselves: that is, that they should not multiply chariots and horses nor wives nor immense riches, because it is from greed for such things that princes decline into tyranny and forsake justice. And this is not to be taken to mean that the king may not be rich in such splendours and resources at all, but that he must not seek an abundance of such things out of greed and inordinate desire, even though, to such extent as the standing of the king's dignity requires, and for the common good, he can and must procure and possess an ample supply of these external goods.

Third, He teaches how they are to conduct themselves in relation to God: that is, that they must always read and ponder the Law of God, and so always live in the fear and reverence of God. Also, it is expedient that they should be instructed and guided in all their undertakings by the divine law. For it must be known that, because the good life of the multitude, for which the king must strive, must be directed towards that end which is heavenly blessedness, it therefore pertains to the office of the king to procure the good life for the multitude in a way which is consistent with the pursuit of heavenly blessedness: that is, to teach those things which lead to the heavenly fatherland, and, as far as it is possible to do so, to forbid those things which are opposed to it. But those things which form a path to true blessedness and those things which are an impediment to it are known from the divine law, the teaching of which belongs to the office of the priests. And so the Lord teaches that the king should write for himself a copy of the Law and take his copy from the priests, and should read therein all the days of his life, so that he may learn to fear God and keep His commandments. It greatly behoves kings, therefore, often to read or hear the holy scriptures; and it follows from this that the laws which the king institutes must not be at odds with the divine law, but should be in harmony with it. Also, such laws must be examined and approved by the judgment of the spiritual power and made subject to its laws: that is, to the sacred canons. For just as the one power is subject to the other, so must the laws of the one be subject to the laws of the other.

Fourth, He prescribes how the king must stand in relation to his subjects: that is, that he must not proudly despise or oppress them, nor, again, turn aside from justice.

---

15. *Deut.* XVII, 14ff.

And of the good standing of Christian kings the blessed Augustine speaks as follows at *De civitate Dei* V: "We say that Christian emperors and kings are happy if they rule justly; if they are not lifted up by the words of those who accord them sublime honours and pay their respects with an excessive humility, but remember that they are but men; if they make their power the handmaid of God's majesty by using it to spread His worship to the greatest possible extent; if they fear, love and worship God; if they love that kingdom in which they are not afraid to have partners more than their own; if they are slow to punish and swift to pardon; if they resort to punishment only when necessary to the government and defence of the commonwealth, and never to gratify their hatred of their own enemies; if they grant pardon, not so that unjust men may enjoy impunity, but in the hope of bringing about their correction; if they balance whatever severe measures they may be forced to enact with the gentleness of mercy and the generosity of benevolence; if their own luxury is as much restrained as it might have been unchecked; if they prefer to govern wicked desires more than any people whatsoever; and if they do all these things, not out of ardour for empty glory, but from the love of eternal felicity; and if, for their sins, they do not neglect to offer to their true God the sacrifices of humility and contrition and prayer. We say that, for the time being, such Christian emperors are happy in hope and that, in time to come, will be so in possession."[16]

Moreover, Cyprian, in his book *De duodecim abusionibus*, says that: "The ninth kind of evil is the unjust king who, though he should be the ruler of wicked men, does not preserve the dignity of his own title in himself. It is understood that he holds the title of king so that he may discharge the office of ruler for all his subjects; but what kind of correction can he administer to others if he does not correct such faults as there are in his own character? For it is by the king's justice that his throne is exalted, and by truth that the government of the people is strengthened."[17]

And Cyprian proceeds to specify what the king's justice consists in, saying: "It is the duty of the just king to exercise an unjust dominion over no one; to judge justly between men and neighbours without respect for persons; to be the defender of strangers and orphans and widows; to restrain men from robbery; to punish adultery; not to exalt the wicked; not to encourage the unchaste and boastful; to destroy the impious from the earth; not to suffer parricides and perjurers to live; to defend the churches; to sustain the poor with alms; to appoint just men over the affairs of the kingdom; to have as his counsellors men of mature years who are wise and sober; to pay no attention to the superstitions of magicians and fortune-tellers and oracles; to keep his anger in check; to defend the fatherland bravely and justly against its adversaries; to trust in God through all things; not to lift up his soul in prosperity; to endure all misfortunes with patience; to believe in God according to the catholic faith; not to allow his sons to behave with impiety;

---

16. *De civ. Dei* V,24 (CC XLVII,160).
17. Ps.-Cyprian, *Liber de XII abusionibus saeculi* IX (PL 4,956).

to set aside certain hours for prayer; and not to indulge in food before the proper time - 'For woe to the land whose king is a child and whose princes feast in the morning.'[18]" And Cyprian goes on: "These things bring prosperity to the kingdom at the present time and lead the king towards a heavenly kingdom. There is no doubt, however, that he who does not govern his kingdom according to this law is giving shelter to many enemies of his rule. For, by reason of this, the peace of the people is often disrupted and impediments to the kingdom are sustained. The fruits of the earth are also diminished, and the services of the people impeded. Many and various sorrows taint the kingdom's prosperity. The deaths of loved ones and children bring sadness. On every hand, the invasions of enemies lay waste the provinces; the domestic animals and herds of cattle are scattered; storms in spring and winter hinder the fertility of the earth and the employments of the sea; and the standing corn, trees in blossom and the shoots of the vines are sometimes stripped bare by bolts of lightning. But, above all else, injustice on the part of the king not only brings darkness to the present government, but also casts its shadow over his sons and grandsons, lest they inherit the kingdom after him. Because of the wickedness of the reign of Solomon, the Lord scattered the house of Israel by the hands of his sons; but, because of his justice, King David left behind his seed as a light in Jerusalem. And look at the number of ways which reflection so clearly discloses in which the justice of the king may strengthen the world: the peace of the people; the protection of the fatherland; the unity of the people; the defence of the nation; the support of the weak; the joy of men; the mildness of the air; the calmness of the sea; the fertility of the earth; the solace of the poor; the inheritance of his sons; and, for the king himself, the hope of future blessedness."

Also, in the third book of his work on the Supreme Good, Isidore speaks as follows: "He who makes right use of royal power should himself stand out from all men in this: that, the more brightly his honour shines, the more he humbles himself in his own mind, proposing to himself the example of the humility of David, who was not puffed up by his own merits, but, humbly flinging himself down, said, 'Let me walk unworthily, and I shall appear unworthy before the Lord Who hath appointed me.'[19]" And he goes on: "He who makes right use of royal power establishes the image of justice more by deeds than by words. He is not lifted up by any prosperity, he is not disturbed by any adversity, he does not trust in his own powers, nor does his heart withdraw from the Lord." And he continues: "God has given authority to princes to govern the peoples, and He has willed that they should be ruled by those whose lot it is to be born and die like them. The prince must therefore bring good to his people, not harm; he must not oppress them by lording it over them, but graciously ensure that, even in the House of God, he makes use of his great power to protect Christ's members.

---

18. *Eccles.* X,16.
19. Cf. *II Reg.* VI,21f.

Indeed, Christ's members are the faithful people; and when princes rule over them well by the power which they have received, they for their part assuredly return good to God in full measure."[20] And later, in another chapter, Isidore says: "The secular powers are subject to the discipline of religion, and, although those who occupy the summit of the kingdom are subject to no restraint, they are nonetheless bound to keep the faith, so that they may both proclaim the faith of Christ in their laws and observe the preaching of the faith in their own good morals."[21] For it is just for the prince to comply with his own laws, and then his laws will be deemed worthy to be kept by all men, when he himself shows reverence for them. Also, if princes do not allow that which they forbid to the people to be lawful for themselves, the authority of their voice is just.

Again, Hugh of Saint Victor, speaking of earthly power in the book *De sacramentis*, shows what the holder of earthly power must take into account in the performance of justice.[22] He must take account of the persons involved, for it is not lawful for him to lift his hand against clerics or ecclesiastical personages, but only against the laity. He must take account of the nature of the case, for it does not rest with him to examine ecclesiastical matters, but only secular ones. He must take account of limit and measure, and inflict upon the guilty a fitting and suitable punishment. He must take account of place, and not presume to violate sacred places, and not inflict inordinate violence upon those who seek sanctuary there, even though they are guilty and worthy to be condemned for their crimes. He must take account of the season, and show reverence for holy and solemn days. And, when these things are omitted, these are faults for which humble entreaty is due. Hence, in executing justice and in passing sentence, he must take account of proper places and times. In these ways, then, the secular power must execute justice, following the established laws and, in giving judgment, approving nothing which goes beyond justice and truth. Later again, Hugh adds how those things which become a king are indicated by the royal adornments. Hence, he says that "the secular power has certain adornments of its dignity by which the excellence of its station is shown and the sacred obligations of its ministry designated. The ring designates faith; the bracelet, good works; the sceptre, justice; the sword, protection; the purple robe, reverence; and the crown glory."[23]

Also, we must here mention the fact that when the emperor takes his [coronation] oath, he promises to be "the defender and protector of the Supreme Pontiff and the Holy Roman Church in all that is needful and beneficial to her, and to guard and preserve her possessions, honour and laws."[24] It is clear, then, that he is related to the pope just as the hand is to the head in defending it and ministering to it. For this reason also, [during

---

20. *Sentent.* III,XLIX,1ff (PL 83,720f).
21. *Sentent.* III,LI,3 (PL 83,723).
22. *De sacramentis* II,II,VIII (PL 176,420f).
23. *De sacramentis* II,II,IX (PL 176,422).
24. *Ordo Romanus,* PL 78,1239.

the emperor's coronation ceremony, the pope] "takes the unsheathed sword from the altar and hands it to him, signifying by the sword the care of the whole empire, speaking as follows: 'Take thou from on high the sword of the blesssed Peter, received in the flesh at our hands, though unworthy, on God's behalf, consecrated by the authority of the holy apostles, and conferred upon thee imperially by the ceremony of our blessing. Ordained as thou art for the defence of God's holy Church, for the punishment of malefactors and for the praise of good men, be thou mindful of the prophecy of the psalmist: "Gird thy sword upon thy thigh, O most mighty one", that thou mayest by this same power do justice, mightily destroy the foundation of iniquity, and defend and protect the holy Church of God and His faithful people. Do thou no less root out and scatter the false believers who are the enemies of the name of Christian; do thou mercifully help and defend the widows and orphans; restore the desolate; protect those whom thou hast restored; punish the unjust; and strengthen men of good will: that, in so doing, thou mayest deserve to reign as a mighty upholder of justice, glorious in triumph for ever, with the Saviour of the world Whose pattern thou bearest."[25] And these things which are said to the emperor can be applied in the same way to Christian kings.

Next, for the sake of the wicked kings who are now called tyrants (although all kings were once called tyrants, for the Greek word for 'king' is 'tyrant' in Latin), we must add what Richard of Saint Victor says for their correction, commenting on that verse of *Revelation* I: "The prince of the kings of the earth".[26] He says: "There are some kings who scorn to cleave to the Supreme Prince, who refuse to acknowledge that the power by which they act comes from Him, who vent their rage upon their subjects and devour them, and who do not in the least consider that they in their turn have a Prince over them Who will deliver the defenceless from the hand of the mighty and the needy and poor from the robber. For the time being, the Prince of kings allows them to rage, to prove and purify the elect; but in the time of retribution he will judge them harshly for their cruelty." For mighty men shall be mightily tormented and a greater trial shall come upon the stronger.[27] "Let such kings return, then - that is, if they are kings - to their conscience, and acknowledge that they have over them a Prince to whom they will be called upon to render an account of their deeds; and that, just as He can confer power, so also can He take it away. For the Lord will loose the girdle of kings and gird their loins with a cord."[28] And it is written elsewhere: "God hath overturned the throne of proud princes, and hath set up the meek in their stead";[29] as can be gathered from many examples in sacred scripture. But sometimes the sins of the people merit

---

25. *Ordo Romanus,* PL 78,1242, quoting *Psalm.* XLIV,4.
26. *Apoc.* I,5.
27. Cf. *Sap.* VI,7ff.
28. *In Apocalypsim* I,II (PL 196,698); Cf. *Isa.* III,24.
29. *Eccles.* X,17.

such kings (or, rather, tyrants), as sacred eloquence testifies.[30]   Let the people therefore abstain from sin, so that they may be set free from the snares of tyrants.

---

30. Cf. *Job* XXXIV,30; Isidore, *Sentent.* III,XLVIII,11 (PL 83,720).

IX

That in the highest spiritual power there is a fulness of both pontifical and royal power; and in what way

Now because it is manifest from what has already been said that the highest spiritual power, of which kind is the power of the Supreme Pontiff, has primacy over all the pontiffs of all churches, and is also superior in dignity and causality to every temporal power, it can therefore be rightly concluded that in the Supreme Pontiff there pre-exists fulness of pontifical and royal power. And we must now consider of what kind this fulness of power is, and in what ways he is said to have it. For Christ Himself, as man, also has fulness of power, as we have said above; but His fulness is not the same as the fulness which belongs to His vicar. For what is to be said concerning fulness of grace applies also to fulness of power. For Christ is said to be full of grace, and Christ's mother is also said to be full of grace; not equally, however, or in all respects similarly. For Christ is said to be full of grace because He has received grace in the highest degree of excellence with which it can be bestowed, even to all the effects of grace. But the mother of Christ is said to be full of grace because she has received grace in a degree sufficient for the condition for which she was chosen by God: that is, to be the mother of God.[1] And, similarly, we must speak of fulness of power in the same fashion. For fulness of power is in Christ as man, and it is also in His vicar; but there is fulness of power in Christ because He has received full power in a pre-eminent degree, whereas there is fulness of power in the Vicar of Christ because he receives full power in a degree sufficient - that is, to the extent necessary - for the salvation of the faithful.

We must, however, say something more specifically concerning the nature of this fulness and the ways in which it differs from the fulness which belongs to Christ not only as God but also as man. As to this, we must note that the power with which it is now our intention to deal is an active power which can be discussed with reference to two things: namely, that which is subject to it, and the nature of the power itself, considered with respect to its

---

1. Cf. *Luc.* I,28ff. James' comment on the sense in which Mary is 'full of grace' is perhaps an echo of contemporary controversies about the Immaculate Conception. See NCE Vol. 7, s.v. "Immaculate Conception."

mode of action. And in relation to both these things, the power of the Supreme Pontiff is full, but in another way than is the power of Christ. For in relation to those who are subject to it, the power of Christ is full in the sense that every creature - rational and non-rational, heavenly and earthly, and even infernal - is subject to His power. The power of the Supreme Pontiff is not full in this sense, however, for it extends itself only to those creatures who are capable of grace and blessedness. For this power is ordained for the pursuit of the end of blessedness; and not of all creatures, because not of angels, but of men alone; and not of all these, but only of pilgrims.[2] For this reason, the Supreme Pontiff is said to be the head only of men who are pilgrims; whereas Christ is said to be the head of angels and men: both those who have attained their goal and those who are yet pilgrims. But this power of the Supreme Pontiff is nonetheless called full because it extends itself to all pilgrims universally. Properly speaking, however, the word 'pilgrims' [*viatores*] is applied to those who are journeying towards their fatherland; and these are they who walk by faith. For unbelievers ought rather to be called 'wanderers' [*deviatores*], because they wander from the true path of salvation. Hence, the power which extends itself to all believers can be said to extend to unbelievers also, not inasmuch as they are unbelievers, but inasmuch as they are capable of becoming believers and can become members of Christ, brought together into the ecclesiastical unity. Since, therefore, they are potential but not actual believers, so the power of the Supreme Pontiff extends to them potentially, but not actually.

For this reason, the Apostle says in *I Corinthians*: "What have I to do to judge them also that are without? God judgeth them."[3] As the Gloss says, this is as if to say that he does not have the task of judging unbelievers.[4] To all those, then, who are members of Christ through faith, the power of the Vicar of Christ extends precisely because they are members of Christ. And so it was said to Peter, "Feed my sheep"[5] without exception; and, again, "upon this Rock I will build my Church"[6] - not some part of my Church. By divine law, therefore, all men living this mortal life and in any way belonging to the Church Militant must be subject to the power of the Supreme Pontiff; and it is for this reason that his power is called full. Not a few perverse men withold themselves from this full and saving power in point of fact, however; but, for as long as they scorn to obey the vicar of the Author of Salvation, salvation is far removed from these persons.

So far as the nature of power is concerned, however, the fulness of Christ's power differs from that of His vicar [in the following ways]:

---

2. That is, of those of the faithful now alive on earth: the power of the pope does not extend to the souls of the departed.

3. *I Cor.* V,12.

4. Peter Lombard, *Collectanea* PL 191,1575.

5. *Joan.* XXI,17.

6. *Matt.* XVI,18.

1. With respect to the manner in which it is possessed. For it properly belongs to Christ as man through His union with the word of God, and He has also deservedly received a certain power of judgment by reason of His fulness of grace and wisdom. For because He was judged unjustly and fought and conquered for the justice of God, He has therefore deserved to be the judge of all men. To the Vicar of Christ, however, power belongs, not in this way, but as transmitted and communicated to him by Christ's commission.

2. It differs with respect to its mode of action, for inasmuch as He is God Christ has power in such a way that He acts with it by means of His own virtue and authority, and not by the virtue of any superior. Inasmuch as He is man, He acts by means of the virtue of the Godhead, but in a pre-eminent fashion; and so, as we have said above, He is said to have power pre-eminently. The Vicar of Christ, however, acts by the authority of Christ inasmuch as he acts on His behalf, according to what the Apostle says in *II Corinthians*: "For if I gave anything to whom I gave it, for your sakes I gave it in the person of Christ."[7] - that is, as if Christ gave it, as the Gloss says.[8] And, in this same epistle, he says: "Now then we are ambassadors for Christ, as though God did beseech you by us."[9] The Gloss[10] says that 'for Christ' means 'in place of Christ', Who was God's ambassador; and, similarly, the Vicar of Christ can be called Christ's ambassador. Moreover, it must be known that, just as Christ Himself appointed His vicar and ambassador in the Church by His own power, so also can the Vicar of Christ, Peter's successor, appoint his own vicars and ambassadors without consulting any man, where and when he deems it expedient to the salvation of the faithful to do so. But the Vicar of Christ acts, not pre-eminently, as Christ does, but as a minister, as the Apostle says: "Let a man so account of us as of the ministers of Christ."[11]

3. It differs with respect to duration; because Christ has power eternally, whereas the Vicar of Christ has it temporally, for each of Peter's successors has power only while he lives this present life. This power will, however, endure in the Church in his various successors until the end of the world, when, as the apostle says, every principality will be abolished.[12]

4. It differs with respect to the scope of its action; for Christ can do many things which His vicar cannot do. For instance, Christ can subdue all men to Himself, even the unwilling, which His vicar cannot do; and He can judge not only what is manifest, but also the hidden things of the heart, which His vicar cannot do. And the reason for this is that each man judges well concerning those things which he knows well; and Christ, both as God and as man, knows what is hidden because of the overflowing into His soul

---

7. *II Cor.* II,10.
8. *Glossa interlinearis* on II Cor. II,10.
9. *II Cor.* V,20.
10. *Glossa interlinearis* on II Cor. V,20.
11. *I Cor.* IV,1.
12. Cf. *I Cor.* XV,24.

of the divinity with which it is united. The Vicar of Christ, however, since he is only a man, does not have knowledge of things hidden; for a man sees what is visible, whereas God knows the heart. It may, of course, be said that, in a sense, the Vicar of Christ judges hidden things in the court of penance, where he knows hidden things through the secret confession of the penitent. Manifest things, however, he judges in the court of external causes. And many other examples might be adduced of what Christ can do and His vicar cannot, as can be shown from those things said above concerning the communication of Christ's power.

The Vicar of Christ is, however, nonetheless said to have fulness of power, because the whole of the power of government which has been communicated to the Church by Christ - priestly and royal, spiritual and temporal - is in the Supreme Pontiff, the Vicar of Christ. For as much power has been communicated to the Church as was necessary for the salvation of the faithful; and so there is in the Vicar of Christ all the power required to bring about the salvation of men. For what is to be said concerning sacred science also applies to ecclesiastical power. For what God has revealed to us in the scriptures is not everything that a man can know; rather, He has revealed to us those things which avail for our salvation. Hence, the blessed Augustine, speaking of sacred doctrine in his book *De Trinitate*, says: "I assign to that science not everything that can be known to men, but only that by which the most wholesome faith which leads to eternal blessedness is begotten, nourished, defended and strengthened."[13] And, similarly, we must say that not everything that can be done by a man, and not every power that can be communicated to a man, is to be attributed to the power of the Supreme Pontiff; rather, only all that power which is necessary to man's salvation must be said to reside in him, and, through him, to be devolved to others according to participation and a certain order. His power is therefore said to be full.

And in order that the measure of such power may be stated briefly, it must be known that the power of the Supreme Pontiff and Vicar of Christ is called full, first, because no one who in any way belongs to the Church Militant is exempt from it. Rather, every man who exists in the Church of the present time is subject to it. Second, [it is called full] because every power, whether spiritual or temporal, which is ordained and given to man by God for the government of the faithful is contained within that power. Third, [it is called full] because every power within the Church is derived from that power and subordinated to it, as we have declared above, because it is the foundation and end of every power, and every human power is therefore as of right subject to it. Fourth, [it is called full] because no human power exceeds or surpasses it; indeed, it exceeds and surpasses every such power. Fifth, [it is called full] because it is not restrained or subordinated or judged by any other merely human power, but itself restrains and subordinates and judges. Sixth [it is called full] because it is not restricted to the order of

---

13. *De Trin.* XIV,1 (CC L(A), 424).

powers or laws established by itself. For it can act both through the agency of other powers and without their agency when it appears expedient; and, when it judges it appropriate to do so, it can act both according to the laws which it has established, and beyond them.

Properly, therefore, is it said that there is fulness of power in the Supreme Pontiff. Hence, and for this reason, it is said that his power is without number, weight and measure;[14] and this can be understood as follows. It is without number with respect to those who are subject to his power, who, even though their number is known to God, cannot be numbered within our knowledge. Moreover, it is without weight with respect to place; for weight is the inclination of something towards its proper and determinate place, but this power is not limited to one place or to one church, but extends to all churches without exception, in whatever place they are established. And it is without measure with respect to its action and mode of action, because it is in a certain sense boundless in its action and in its mode of action. Hence, just as to Christ, as man, the Spirit is not given by measure,[15] whereas Christ's gift is given to others according to a certain measure, so to the Vicar of Christ, the Supreme Pontiff, power is given not by measure, but as it were boundlessly. To others, however, power is given according to a certain measure of participation in this boundless power, and, while the power of the Vicar of Christ is itself without number, weight and measure, he establishes and determines the number, weight and measure of the other powers. Hence, his power is rightly called full, and it is for this reason greatly worthy to be venerated and feared. And this fulness of power was delivered to Peter and his successors when it was said to him, "upon this Rock I will build my Church; and whatsoever thou shalt bind on earth shall be bound in Heaven", and so on; and when it was said to him, "Feed my sheep." For, truly, it is indicated by these words that all the power which it is fitting for the vicar of Christ to have is given to him; for it was appropriate, now that the time of fulness of grace had arrived, that fulness of power should be placed in the Church.

Now many authorities can be adduced from the holy Fathers concerning this fulness of power; but only a few of the many need here be mentioned, in order to make what we have said more readily believable. Saint Cyril, in his *Thesaurus*,[16] speaks as follows: "Just as He Himself received them from the Father, the guide and rod of the assembly of the tribes who came forth from Israel, so the Son gave to Peter the keys of the kingdom of Heaven fully and perfectly, and fulness of power over every principality and power, so that every knee might bow to him. Thus, He entrusted [the keys of the kingdom of Heaven] to both Peter and his ministers, that is, his successors, not less, but most fully; and He Himself appointed Peter to be head of the

---

14. Cf. *Sap.* XI,21.
15. *Joan.* III,34.
16. The following passage is not found in any extant work of Cyril of Alexandria; it was, however, known to St Thomas Aquinas, who also (*Commentum in quatuor libros sententiarum Magistri Petri Lombardi,* IV, dist. 24, 3) attributes it to 'Cyril in Lib. Thes.'.

Church in the presence of the apostles and evangelists and in the midst of them. This was done so that they themselves, in their gospels and epistles, in preaching to this world and in ordaining churches and prelates, should write what they heard and received from the Lord, and should confirm in all their teaching, in every chapter and synagogue, and in every election and affirmation, that Peter occupies the Lord's place in the Church, and that whatever is to be resolved and established should be approved by his authority, calling him Cephas, which means 'head'. All this is also according to what the divine and most faithful Saint Luke wrote, weaving it into his gospel and the *Acts*, where he narrated the deeds of our forebears and their companions and handed them down indubitably to the Church. And this apostolic Church remains unblemished by all seduction and heretical deceit, above all rulers and bishops, above all the princes of churches and peoples also, with her own pontiffs, in the most abundant faith, and with the authority of Peter. And while other churches must blush at the errors of some of their members, this one Church reigns alone, established immovably, imposing silence and stopping the mouths of all heretics; and we, not deceived by pride in the knowledge of salvation, and not drunk with the wine of pride, confess and proclaim the pattern of truth in union with her and as servants of the apostolic tradition. Therefore, my brethren, if we are to imitate Christ so that, as His sheep, we may hear His voice, remaining in the Church of Peter, let us not be puffed up by the wind of pride, lest perhaps the twisting serpent eject us from the Church of God by reason of our contention, just as, long ago, he ejected Eve from Paradise. Rather, let us remain members of our head, of the apostolic throne of the Roman Pontiff, of whom it is our duty to ask what we are to believe and hold, venerating him and petitioning him for all things, inasmuch as it is for him alone, who has built the Church, to reprehend, correct, establish, dispose, release and bind in her. For to him alone, and to no other, is it given that all men shall by divine law bow their heads to him, and that the prelates of this world shall obey him as they would the Lord Jesus, according to what is written: "We shall go into His tabernacle, and we shall adore the place where His feet have stood."[17] The human race consists of man himself, and his sons; and the whole Trinity has given to a man the fullest power for salvation. One of the three [persons of the Trinity, namely, the Son,] adopted Peter and, in unity of person, displayed him to the Father above every principality and power, so that all the angels of God might adore him. Christ delegated all this, by sacrament and power, to Peter and His Church above every power and principality of this world, so that, just as He is adored by all in Heaven, so the place of His feet might be adored by all in His Church, and they might there adore Christ Himself, receiving the gifts and laws of Christ through the Church's hands."

Here, it is clear from these words of Cyril that the power of the Roman Pontiff is most full, and that every power in this world is subject to him, and

---

17. *Psalm.* CXXXI,7.

that it is necessary to salvation to be subject to him. What he says must be clearly understood, however: that Christ has entrusted what He Himself has, not less, but most fully and wholly, to Peter; for this is true to the extent necessary for the salvation of men.

And Saint John Chrysostom, commenting on that verse of Acts, "Peter rose up in the midst of them",[18] and so on, speaks of the blessed Peter as follows, saying: "He is the most holy head of the blessed company of the apostles, the chamberlain and doorkeeper of Christ Himself, and of the treasures which all desire who come to Christ. As Christ Himself says, 'I am the door';[19] and no one may enter and approach the Father unless Peter opens it. Again, Peter is the good shepherd who has received the keys of Heaven; who is given wisdom of spirit from the Father to know the Son, and who is given power by the Son over all who belong to the Son: not, like Moses, over a single nation, but over the whole world. For just as Christ was sent by the Father for the salvation of all men, so are Peter and the Church sent by Christ for the salvation of all men."[20]

And the same Chrysostom says, on that verse of Matthew, "I will give unto thee the keys of the kingdom of Heaven": "Just as the Son, coming from the Father for the salvation of all men, was sent with full power over all men, so also Peter and his Church are sent by Christ for the salvation of all men with all power over all men, which we believe to be entrusted to no other man." And by saying this - that Peter has been sent for the salvation of all men - he suggests clearly enough that he has fulness of power to the extent that the salvation of men requires it, even if not in the absolute and simple sense that Christ has it.

Again, the blessed Bernard, at *De consideratione* IV, speaks of the Supreme Pontiff by assembling many titles through which we are given to understand his fulness of power and what is due to his office. He speaks to Pope Eugenius as follows: "For the rest, consider that you ought to be a model of justice, a mirror of holiness, an exemplar of piety, a proclaimer of truth, a defender of the faith, the teacher of nations, the captain of Christians, a friend of the Bridegroom, an attendant of the bride, the director of the clergy, the shepherd of the people, the instructor of the foolish, the refuge of the oppressed, the advocate of the poor, the hope of the wretched, the protector of orphans, the judge of widows, the eye of the blind, the tongue of the dumb, the support of the aged, the avenger of crimes, the terror of the wicked, the glory of the good, the rod of the mighty, the hammer of tyrants, the father of kings, the moderator of laws, the dispenser

---

18. *Act.* XV,7.

19. *Joan.* X,9.

20. This passage and the one immediately following it do not, as far as I can discover, occur in the works of Chrysostom (the reference here given by Professor Arquillière - *In actus apostolorum*, PG 60,233 - is incorrect). My impression is that James is here conflating and very loosely paraphrasing several of the passages given by Aquinas in his *Catena aurea* commentary on *Matt.* XVI,18f. As on other occasions, however, James imports a Petrine slant which the originals do not have.

of canons, the salt of the earth, the light of the world, the priest of the Most High, the vicar of Christ, the Lord's anointed, and, finally, the god of Pharoah. Let your countenance be against those who do evil. Let him fear the spirit of your anger, who does not fear man, who does not dread the sword. Let him with whom you are angry think that God, not man, is angry with him. Let him who will not hear you fear that God will hear you when you speak against him."[21]

And the same Bernard, speaking to Eugenius in Book Two of *De consideratione*, says: "Come, therefore, and see that this is the time for pruning, but only if you have already had time for meditation. If you have moved your heart, let your tongue now be moved, and let your hand be moved also. Put on your sword, the sword of the Spirit, which is the word of God. Glorify your hand and your right arm in dealing out vengeance to the nations and punishment to the peoples, and by binding their kings in chains and their nobles in fetters of iron."[22] And these things which we have now said are sufficient to show the fulness of the power of the Vicar of Christ.

---

21. *De consid.* IV,VII,23 (PL 182,788).
22. *De consid.* II,VI,13 (PL 182,749); Cf. *Ephes.* VI,17.

X

Containing certain objections relating to the foregoing remarks, and the
solutions to these objections

Finally, then, it remains to touch upon certain objections and doubts which
arise in relation to some of the foregoing remarks, and to furnish solutions
and responses to those objections in order to make the arguments set forth
above more plainly evident. For, as the Philosopher attests, the solution of
doubts is the most fruitful method of investigating the truth.[1] And although
the doubts and objections which arise in this matter could be resolved by
those arguments which we have already considered, it is nonetheless well to
bring to mind further doubts for the sake of a fuller understanding, so that
the truth may appear more readily from their solution.

The first doubt to arise in relation to what we have said above, then, is as
follows. There are two powers: namely, the spiritual, which is called
priestly, and the temporal, which is called royal; but it seems that the royal
power is not necessary in the Church, nor is it instituted by the will of God.
For at *Matthew* VI it is said: "No man can serve two masters."[2] Since
spiritual lordship is necessary to the salvation of the faithful, therefore, [it
seems that] there should be no other lordship in the Church; and this is
especially so in that temporal lordship seems to stand in opposition to
spiritual, since spiritual ends are often impeded by temporal ones.

Again, even though there were good kings amongst them, royal lordship
was granted to the people of Israel by divine permission only, and not by
injunction or commission.[3] But that which arises only from the permission
of God seems to be unlawful and worthy of blame; for evils are permitted
by God. [It seems that] royal power, therefore, as evil, is not of benefit to
the Church, nor is it instituted by God.

To this doubt, we must reply that both powers come from God, not only by
His permission but also by His act; and this is clear enough in the case of
the spiritual power. As to the temporal, however, this may be proved by
what is written at *Proverbs* VIII: "By me, kings reign, and lawgivers decree

---

1. See, perhaps, *Metaphysics* I,2 (983a10ff).
2. *Matt.* VI,24.
3. Cf. *I Reg.* VIII,7ff; XII,12ff.

just things."[4] And at *Wisdom* VI it is said to kings themselves: "Power is given you by the Lord, and strength by the Most High."[5] Moreover, the same might be shown from many other authorities. And because God and nature make nothing in vain, both powers are therefore ordained of God for the benefit of the human multitude.

According to some, however, the need and reason for the distinction between the two powers arises from the fact that there are two peoples, that is, the clergy and the laity, who are, as it were, the two flanks of the ecclesiastical body. The spiritual power, therefore, governs clerics, and the temporal lay persons. This distinction is doubtful, however; because, although clerics are subject to spiritual government in a more particular sense, in that it pertains to their office to perform those tasks which belong to the spiritual life, laymen must also be no less subject to the spiritual power. And this is especially so in spiritual cases, which are weightier than the temporal ones in respect of which they are immediately subject to the temporal power.

Again, the distinction between the two powers is also attributed to the fact that life is of two kinds: namely, spiritual and earthly; for to the spiritual power pertain those things which belong to the spiritual life, and to the temporal those which are necessary to earthly life. But the life of man is called spiritual because the soul derives its life from God, and it is called earthly because the body derives its life from the earth; and, as we have shown above, this is a suitable distinction if it is properly understood. And there are also other appropriate ways, of which we have treated above, of distinguishing between these powers.

But as to what we said at the beginning concerning the two masters, we must reply that "no man can serve two masters" when they are opposed to one another. Hence Chrysostom, expounding this verse, says: "He is speaking of two masters who command contradictory things."[6] Royal power, however, when it is properly ordered, is in no way discordant with priestly power, but is in agreement and concord with it. And just as the earthly life supplies aid to the spiritual and the spiritual life works together with the earthly, so royal power serves the priestly, and the latter guides and directs the former.

Moreover, as to what was also said concerning the opposition of these two powers, this is in one way true and in another way not true. For the powers discussed above are opposites in the sense that they divide between them one common thing, which is power; but they are not opposites in the sense that the one strives against the other and excludes or impedes it. On the contrary, the one assists the other, as we have said. And if any who hold temporal power oppose the spiritual power or impede it, this arises from the disorder of their wills in abusing the power granted to them, and not from

---

4. *Prov.* VIII,15.
5. *Sap.* VI,4.
6. *In Mattheum* VI,24 (*Homilia* XXI) (PG 57,295).

the condition of the power itself, which is ordained of God to serve the spiritual.

As to the second objection that was made, that royal power exists by the permission, but not by the commission, of God, we must reply that royal power is a good in itself and is ordained of God for the benefit of human society. This is clear from the fact that God Himself set Moses over the people of Israel, who, though he was not called a king, nonetheless exercised a royal office. David also was endued with royal power by divine election; and many others have achieved the power of government by the divine will. Royal power or lordship is indeed said to have been permitted to the people of Israel at the time of Samuel; not, however, as an evil which was to blame for their wickedness, but as an evil which was a punishment for their wickedness, given as a burden and a punishment because of the fault of those who asked to be given a king out of a disordered will which trusted less in God than in man. This was said to Samuel himself by God, when the children of Israel asked for a king: "They have not rejected thee, but me, that I should not reign over them."[7] And that this was then permitted as a punishment is clear from the rule of the kings which, as Samuel foretold for them,[8] was indeed a rule secured not by righteous government but by tyrannical dominion and, by the same token, by the oppression of subjects.

A further doubt arises in connexion with the fact that spiritual power is said to be superior to temporal and that the former institutes and judges the latter; for it seems that this is not true. For on that verse of the psalm, "Against Thee only have I sinned",[9] the Gloss says that the king is above all others, and so is to be punished only by God, Who is greater than he. If any one of the people sins, he sins against God and the king; but the king has no man to judge what he does.[10] [It seems that] the spiritual power therefore cannot judge the temporal. Also, at I Peter II it is said: "Submit yourself to every ordinance of man for the Lord's sake: whether it be to the king, as supreme," [and so on.][11] If, therefore, the king is supreme, he is not subject to the judgment of anyone. Moreover, granted that the temporal power is subject to the spiritual in spiritual matters, it nonetheless does not seem to be subject to it in temporal cases and in the judgment of earthly matters. Hence, Hugh, in his book *De sacramentis*, says: "The spiritual power does not, therefore, rule in such a way as to prejudice the right of the earthly by what it does, just as the earthly power itself never usurps what is due to the spiritual without blame."[12] Again, in the Old Testament, which prefigures the New, the priests were subject to the kings, at any rate in temporal matters; and so, in the same way, [it seems that] the temporal power will in

7. *I Reg.* VIII,7.
8. *I Reg.* VIII, 11ff.
9. *Psalm.* L,6.
10. *Glossa ordinaria,* PL 113,919
11. *I Pet.* II,13.
12. *De sacramentis* II,II,VII (PL 176,420).

the New be superior to the spiritual in secular cases, even though it is inferior to it in spiritual cases.

To this doubt, we must reply that the spiritual power is beyond question superior to the temporal in every way, as we have shown above. And so Hugh says in the book *De sacramentis*: "Just as the spiritual life is greater in dignity than the earthly, and the spirit than the body, so also does the spiritual power precede the secular power in honour and dignity."[13]

As to the first objection that was made, therefore, that the king has no man to pass judgment on what he does, we must reply that, when the temporal power is judged by the spiritual, it is not judged by man, but by God, on Whose behalf the spiritual power acts. Alternatively, it can be said that the king who has no one to pass judgment on what he does is the highest spiritual king: that is, the Supreme Pontiff, who, as of right, is judged by God alone, and not by man; although from time to time he submits himself to the judgment of others by reason of his humility.

As to the second objection that was made, concerning the supremacy of the king, we must say that the king is supreme, not in an absolute sense, but in the order of temporal powers. For just as something is said to be foremost in an absolute sense, as God is, so something is also said to be the foremost of its kind, as is the highest kind of body, which is foremost in the order of bodies. And so someone is said to be supreme in an absolute sense in the Church, as is the Supreme Pontiff, the Vicar of Christ; but someone is also said to be supreme in a certain order, as is an archpriest in his college and the king in the order of powers subject to him.

As to the third objection that was made, that the spiritual power does not act in such a way as to prejudice the right of the temporal, we must say that if the spiritual power judges the earthly power by reason of the latter's fault - that is, because it has abused its power - it does not act in such a way as to prejudice it: rather, it does what it should. For just as the spirit is appointed for the direction of the body, so the spiritual power is appointed for the direction of the temporal. But the prejudice of which Hugh speaks must be understood in relation to the temporal possessions which the spiritual power has, which, as Hugh says, can never be prejudicially withheld from the royal power. For if reason and necessity require it, and the earthly power owes protection to those possessions, and the possessions are themselves owed to the earthly power by the necessity of service, now, therefore, the spiritual power would act to the prejudice of the temporal if this service which is owed to the royal power for the protection of those possessions was denied when it was needed. For it is fitting to "render to Caesar the things that are Caesar's and to God the things that are God's."[14] If, however, the spiritual power judges the temporal by reason of its fault, whether the fault be temporal or spiritual, it does nothing to prejudice it,

---

13. *De sacramentis* II,II,IV (PL 176,418).
14. *Matt.* XXII,21.

because it is doing what it can and must do as of right, and no one does injustice who makes use of his own right.

As to the fourth objection that was made, concerning the Old Testament, we must say that the priesthood of the Old Testament was carnal and was passed on by carnal procreation, even though it was ordained to spiritual service and prefigured the spiritual priesthood of the New Testament which is not passed on by carnal succession. To the extent, therefore, that the former priesthood was carnal and earthly, it was subject to the earthly - that is, to the royal - power; but insofar as it was spiritual in its service and in what it prefigured, it surpassed the earthly power. Hence, kings were anointed, instituted and censured by the priests. Alternatively, we must say that, in the Old Testament, the priests were permitted to have only temporal things as their reward, and so the earthly power was then the highest power. In the New Testament, however, the spiritual power is the highest power, for, in the New Testament, the priests are promised both spiritual and earthly things as their reward, because temporal things are added to them for their sustenance and need, according to that verse of *Matthew*: "Seek ye first the kingdom of God and His righteousness, and all things will be added unto you."[15] Hence, in the New Testament, the temporal power is placed under the spiritual, not only in spiritual things, but also in temporal things, which are directed towards spiritual ends. For this reason, the spiritual power can judge and punish the earthly both spiritually and temporally when the latter uses its power ill by acting against God and the Church. It is clear from this that the opinion of those is false who say that the pope, because he rules in spiritual matters, can indeed reign on earth and excommunicate a man subject to him in spiritual matters and, if he is a heretic, judge him and expel him from the Church, but cannot take away temporal power from him nor expel him from a temporal kingdom, because he is not subject to him in temporal matters.

But these persons are moved to say this by two things. The first is that no power extends itself to those things which do not fall within its own order. Temporal things, however, are outside the order of the spiritual power and pertain to the order of the temporal power. [It seems that] the spiritual power therefore cannot judge anyone in temporal matters. The second is that, as they say, unbelievers can have lordship over believers. Those who say this, however, do not understand their own utterance; for if the spiritual power can expel an earthly king from the Church, it can also release the believers who are subject to him from his lordship. As to what they maintain concerning the two orders of power, we must reply that the orders do not, in fact, differ in this way, because the one is subordinated to the other just as, even though the order of corporeal things is different from the order of spiritual things, the corporeal order is nonetheless subject to the spiritual order. And as to what they say concerning unbelieving princes, we must reply that learned men argue as follows: that in no way may

15. *Matt*. VI,33.

unbelievers be newly appointed over the faithful, for this would be an occasion of scandal and danger to the faith; but the lordship of unbelievers which already exists must be tolerated by the faithful for the sake of avoiding scandal.[16] It could, however, be taken away by the Church, because the unbelievers might rightly deserve to lose their power over the faithful because of their unbelief.

A further doubt arises when it is said that the spiritual power is not subject to the temporal. For it seems that the former is subject to the latter because, as can be gathered from many authorities, service and tribute are due to the temporal power from the earthly things which the priestly power possesses. To this doubt, we must reply that, in one way, the spiritual power can be considered with respect to the things which it possesses, and, in another way, with respect to the persons who are sharers in spiritual power. As to the things which it possesses, however, we must make a distinction, because certain of the Church's possessions are spiritual in kind and are held under divine law, such as first-fruits, tithes, offerings, and those things which are given as burial fees. These things must be reckoned as sustaining the ministers of divine worship, and so the spiritual power is not subject to the temporal in respect of them because neither tribute nor any service is owed to the temporal power from these things and for them; for these things are in a certain sense spiritual, because they are annexed and attached by divine law to the spiritual office.

Other of her possessions, however, are temporal in kind, and are held under human law: such as the right to sell or grant without violating the obligation of service; and for these things the spiritual power owes customary service and tribute to temporal princes. With regard to these things, however, we must, according to Hugh, make a distinction; for: "Sometimes only the fruits of possession are granted to the Church for her use, but the power of executing justice is not granted. Sometimes again, use and power are granted together, although, even then, though the Church receives the fruits of earthly possessions for her use, the power of executing justice is wielded not by ecclesiastical persons, but by laymen."[17] As to the persons themselves, however, it must be said absolutely that all persons deputed to the care of the spiritual life are in no way subject to the earthly power, nor may the earthly power judge them.

As to the objection which was made concerning tribute, we must reply that the spiritual power does not pay tribute to the temporal as to a superior and in recognition of its lordship, but as a payment for the peace and quiet secured by that power, which must protect and defend the Church and the Church's goods.

Another doubt arises when it is said that the spiritual power already has temporal power under divine law; for there seem to be many objections to this saying. The first, indeed, is that, since these powers are distinct, they

---

16. Cf. Aquinas, *Summa theol.* IIaIIae,q.10,a.10.

17. *De sacramentis* II,II,VII (PL 176,420).

cannot belong to the same person. Furthermore, it is the task of the temporal power to use the material sword; and so the Apostle says to the Romans: "He beareth not the sword in vain";[18] that is, according to the Gloss, he has a judicial power to inflict bodily punishment upon the wicked.[19] But the material sword does not belong to the spiritual power, and therefore it [seems that it] is not proper for it to have temporal power. Moreover, Christ did not have temporal power. On the contrary, He avoided it; and so, therefore, [it seems that] His vicar does not have it. Again, as the blessed Bernard says in the fourth book of *De consideratione*, speaking to Eugenius of the imperial insignia and adornments or trappings: "In these things, you are the successor, not of Peter, but of Constantine."[20] [It seems,] therefore, [that] temporal power does not belong to Peter by divine law, nor to his successors. Hence, we do not read that Christ gave temporal power to Peter or that Peter exercised such power.

To this doubt, we must reply that it has been made sufficiently clear above that the spiritual power already has temporal power in a higher and more excellent fashion. As to the first objection that was made, concerning the distinctness of the powers, we must say that these powers are distinct, but that the one nonetheless pre-exists in the other in a more excellent fashion, just as the powers of lower bodies are distinct from the powers of higher bodies yet nonetheless pre-exist in them in a nobler way. Alternatively, we must say that although these powers are distinct, they can nonetheless belong to the same person, just as, within the same intellectual power, there are distinct sciences which indeed, in a certain sense, have opposing characters, as do the speculative and practical sciences. And although the same person may have both powers, he does not, however, exercise both of them in the same way, as has sufficiently appeared from what we have said above. Also, it can be said that royal power over spiritual things and over temporal things are not two powers, but two parts of the one perfect royal power, of which only one part resides in earthly kings, and in an inferior fashion, whereas both parts reside in the holders of spiritual power, and in a more excellent fashion. In the prelates of the Church, therefore, and especially in the Supreme Prelate, there is an entire and perfect and full royal power; whereas in the princes of this world it exists in a partial and diminished form.

As to the second objection that was made, concerning the swords, we must reply that, just as the spiritual power has a twofold power, so does it have a twofold sword; for by the word 'sword' is to be understood a power of judgment. For it has a spiritual sword for the infliction of spiritual punishment, and it has a material sword for the infliction of bodily punishment. But just as it has spiritual power according to immediate execution and temporal power according to authority and direction, so it is

18. *Rom.* XIII,4.
19. *Glossa interlinearis* on *Rom.* XIII,4.
20. *De consid.* IV,III,6 (PL 182,776).

said to hold the two swords in different ways. For it holds the spiritual according to use and the temporal according to command; and this is to hold the latter in a manner having the greater dignity. Hence, the blessed Bernard, speaking to Eugenius in the fourth book of *De consideratione*, says: "Why should you again try to usurp the sword which you were once commanded to put back into its sheath? He who denies that that sword is yours, however, seems to me not to pay sufficient attention to the words of the Lord when He says, 'Put up thy sword into the sheath.'[21] This sword is also yours, therefore, and is to be drawn from its sheath at your command, although not by your hand. Otherwise, if that sword in no way belonged to you, the Lord would not have replied, 'It is enough', but 'It is too much', when the apostles said, 'Behold, here are two swords.'[22] Both swords, therefore - that is, the spiritual and the material - belong to you. But the latter is to be drawn for the Church and the former by the Church: the former by the priest, and the latter by the hand of the knight, but clearly at the bidding of the priest and at the command of the emperor."[23] What is it, then, to hold the material sword as its commander? Certain persons explain this by saying that the spiritual power which holds it can exhort the secular prince, to whom is entrusted the material sword, to take up arms against malefactors, and can expound and interpret the divine law in which it is enjoined: "Thou shalt not suffer malefactors to live."[24] The sign [which the spiritual power gives to the temporal of what the latter is to do] is therefore nothing other than an interpretation of the divine law and an exhortation to princes to obey the divine law. And such an explanation is apt enough; for this sign is an indication of what is desired, and, by interpreting and exhorting in this way, the spiritual power indicates that it desires that punishment be inflicted upon evildoers, and this indication is a kind of command. In addition to this command, however, there is required the command of the secular prince, whose task it is to use the material sword, requiring his soldiers or his minister to act. Hence, just as, in any operation which we perform by means of our external members, there is required a universal will as the prime and remote mover, and a particular will as the immediate mover, and the motive force of the members in order to bring about the action, so too, in the infliction of bodily punishment, the spiritual power is as it were the prime mover, and so is said to indicate its desire, and the temporal power is as it were the immediate mover, and so gives the command, because it directly commands the armies to act; and the prince's minister executes the act of punishment.

As to the third objection that was made, concerning Christ, we must reply that Christ was appointed king as much in temporal as in spiritual things, but that while He lived on earth He declined to administer the temporal affairs

---

21. *Joan.* XVIII,11.
22. *Luc.* XXII,38.
23. *De consid.* IV,III, 7 (PL182,776).
24. Cf. *Exod.* XXII,18.

of an earthly kingdom. Hence, it is said in *John*: "My kingdom is not of this world."[25] Similarly, He declined to exercise judicial power over temporal things. But He declined to exercise temporal power in order to teach us by example that we should avoid involvement with temporal concerns and anxiety for them, and in order to show that those who must strive after greater things should not occupy themselves with lesser ones. Hence, on that verse of *Luke* XII, where Christ says, "Who made me a judge or a divider over you?"[26] - that is, of your riches - Ambrose says in a gloss: "Well does He avoid earthly things, Who has descended for the sake of heavenly; and He does not deign to be the judge of quarrels and an arbiter of property, having the judgment of the living and dead and the arbitration of merits. You should consider, therefore, not what you seek, but of whom you ask it; nor should you, in your eagerness of spirit, suppose that the greater are to be disturbed by the less."[27] In *John* VI, we gather that, after Christ had fed the multitude, in which act he exercised a royal office, He withdrew to a mountain because they wanted to make Him a king,[28] and, by this, as the Gloss says, He teaches us to despise worldly dignities.[29] And although Christ did not exercise a royal power over temporal things, it does not follow from this that His vicar may not exercise it, especially in necessary cases. For there are also many other things which Christ did not do which He had the power to do, which His vicar may nonetheless do. For we do not read that Christ baptized with the baptism of water, yet He nonetheless had a pre-eminent power in all the sacraments. Nor do we read that He spoke in different tongues, yet He nonetheless had the gift of tongues, and all the gifts of grace were given to Him together. But the apostles baptized and spoke in tongues. Also, the apostles themselves refrained from doing some things which they had the power to do, so that they should not be impeded in weightier matters; and for this reason the Apostle says: "God sent me not to baptize, but to preach the gospel."[30] For Christ sent forth the apostles to do and ordain many things in the Church that He did not do or ordain Himself. And from all these things it can be inferred that, even though Christ did not exercise temporal power, His vicar can nonetheless exercise it; although by Christ's example, he should not involve himself in the judgment of temporal things regularly, but only in certain cases and for necessary causes, as has been shown above.

As to the fourth objection that was made, that in temporal things the pope is not the successor of Peter but of Constantine, we must reply that he is the successor of Peter in temporal power insofar as Peter held it under the divine law and he himself holds it in the same way. Insofar as the pope has such power under human law, however, he is the successor of Constantine; and

---

25. *Joan.* XVIII,36.
26. *Luc.* XII,14.
27. *Expositio in Evang. secund. Luc.* VII (PL 15,1730).
28. *Joan.* VI,15.
29. Chrysostom, in Aquinas, *Catena Aurea* on *Joan.* VI,15.
30. *I Cor.* I,17.

we have said above how human law may here operate in addition to the divine law. And as to what was further said, that we do not read that Christ gave temporal power to Peter, we must reply that when a principal power is entrusted to someone, what is accessory to it is understood to be entrusted also. Hence, when Christ entrusted spiritual power, which is a principal power, to Peter, it is understood that He entrusted temporal power also, because temporal power pre-exists in the spiritual as a lower power does in a higher; and so, in conferring the keys of the kingdom of Heaven and entrusting His sheep, it is understood that Christ gave to Peter spiritual and temporal power and jurisdiction simultaneously.

As to what was said in addition concerning Peter, that he did not exercise temporal power, we must reply that, just as Christ left many things for the apostles to do and to ordain which He did not do Himself, so also have the apostles left many things for their successors to do which they did not do themselves; for different things are appropriate and expedient according to the different conditions of the Church and the different times. In the primitive Church, there was a need for preaching and miracles to convert and convince unbelievers; also, there was a need for patience against the persecution of tyrants, so that the faith should not fail, but might grow strong. Later, however, the need was for argument and exposition of the scriptures against the spread of heresies in the Church. And now that she is established and strong, she must bring power to bear against rebellious men and the adversaries of the Church, against whom the spiritual power can and must require the aid and service of the temporal power of the faithful over which the latter has authority. Hence, the blessed Augustine, in a letter to his colleague Boniface, deals with a certain objection raised by the heretics, that the Church may not call upon the king to aid her against anyone because the apostles did not do this; and he answers this objection by saying that it is appropriate to act in different ways at different times. And in order to make this clearer, we here quote the actual words of Augustine, who speaks as follows. "For as to what those persons say who desire not to have just laws enacted against their ungodly doings: when they say that the apostles never petitioned the kings of the earth for such laws, they do not consider that the times were then different and that all things are done in their proper season. For, at that time, what emperors had believed in Christ, so as to serve Him in godliness by enacting laws against ungodliness? For, then, the words of the prophet still had force: 'Why do the heathen rage, and the people imagine a vain thing? The kings of the earth set themselves, and their rulers take counsel together, against the Lord and against His anointed.'[31] That which is spoken a little later in the same psalm was not yet fulfilled: 'Be wise now, therefore, O ye kings; be instructed, ye judges of the earth. Serve the Lord with fear, and rejoice with trembling.'[32] How, therefore, are kings to serve the Lord with fear, if not by forbidding, and

---

31. *Psalm.* II,1f.
32. *Psalm.* II,10f.

chastising with religious severity, those things which are done contrary to the Lord's commandments? For a man serves Him in one way inasmuch as he is a man, and in another inasmuch as he is a king. Inasmuch as he is a man, he serves Him by living faithfully; whereas, inasmuch as he is a king, he serves Him by enforcing with due severity laws which enjoin what is righteous and forbid what is the reverse: just as Hezekiah served Him when he destroyed the groves and temples of the idols and the high places which had been built contrary to God's commandments.[33] In this way, therefore, do kings serve the Lord inasmuch as they are kings, when they do in His service those things which they could not do if they were not kings. Since, then, the kings of the earth were not yet serving the Lord in the time of the apostles, but were still imagining vain things against the Lord and against His anointed, acts of ungodliness could not then by any means be forbidden, but were, rather, performed under the laws. For the order of the times was then unfolding in such a way that even the Jews were slaying those who proclaimed Christ, believing themselves to be thereby serving God, just as Christ had foretold; and the heathen were raging against the Christians, so that the suffering of the martyrs might overcome all. But as soon as what is written elsewhere began to be fulfilled - 'All kings shall fall down before Him; all nations shall serve Him'[34] - what man of sound mind could say to the kings: 'Let not any thought trouble you within your kingdom as to who hinders or opposes the Church of our Lord; it is not your business to care who may choose to be religious or sacrilegious', given that he cannot say to them, 'It is not your business to care who in your kingdom may choose to be chaste or unchaste'?"[35]

By these words, therefore, Augustine clearly shows that there are many things which the apostles did not do which their successors must and can do, and this by reason of the different conditions of the times. Hence, if those who hold spiritual power at the present time make use of temporal power in the manner shown above, and of the insignia and instruments of that power, they do not do what is not lawful for them; rather, they do that which they can do as of right, and which we must believe to be for the benefit of the Church, according to the infallible ordinance of the providence of God, Who rules and directs the Church with special care. Sometimes, however, it comes about that certain persons, in the use which they make of such power, are inordinate both in what they do and in what they desire, just as not a few also use spiritual power unworthily.

A further doubt arises in connexion with what was said above: that the pope institutes royal power. For what we gather from the law seems to tell against this: namely, that empire comes only from God.[36] Also, the Apostle says: "There is no power but of God."[37] [It seems that] royal or

---

33. *IV Reg.* XVIII,4.
34. *Psalm.* LXXI,11.
35. *De correctione Donatistarum* V (PL 33,801f).
36. Cf. Justinian, *Codex* I,XVII,1; 2; 18; *Novella* VI.
37. *Rom.* XIII,1.

imperial power, therefore, is not instituted by the pope. Moreover, although a superior art may make use of an inferior one in its service, it does not institute it; and so, in the same way, the spiritual power may make use of the temporal in its service, but it does not institute it.

To this doubt, we must reply, just as we have said above, that it falls to the spiritual power to institute the temporal and to judge it if it is not good.[38] As to the objection that empire comes from God alone, therefore, without the intermediate co-operation of any nature: this is not true. On the contrary, it comes from God through the intermediate institution of human beings, whose nature is inclined towards government, just as it is also towards social life. Hence, it can be said to come from God, but through the intermediate co-operation of natural inclination and institution. For government was introduced amongst men by human law, which arises from nature. If, however, we are to understand that it comes from God alone because it arises only from the law of nature and is not instituted by the spiritual power, we must reply, just as we have said above, that it comes from God alone insofar as it is unformed and unperfected, but, insofar as it is formed and perfected, it comes from God through the mediation of those who hold spiritual power in the Church, for she proceeds from grace and is ordained to grace.

Alternatively, it can be said that the institution of the temporal power has its being from human law inasmuch as the prince is set over men, but that the institution of the temporal prince inasmuch as he is a Christian prince over Christian men is by the spiritual power. For just as someone is made a Christian through the ministry of the spiritual power, so someone is made a Christian prince through the ministry of that same power, to which every Christian is subject by divine law. And it must be known that, since spiritual power is of two kinds - that is, of orders and of jurisdiction - each is in a certain way required for the institution of Christian princes. For he is chosen by the power of jurisdiction, so that he may be a prince and have power; but it is by the power of orders that the anointing and consecration are administered which designate the firmness and sanctity of his power.

As to what was said in addition, that "there is no power but of God", we must reply that without doubt every power comes from God, but that human co-operation is not excluded by this fact. For insofar as its being is imperfect, it comes from God naturally through the mediation of human institution; but insofar as its being is perfected, it comes from God supernaturally through the mediation of human institution. With regard to this saying of the Apostle, however, it must be known that all powers come from God in the same way, but that some arise by natural human institution, as with human communities of whatever rite; and others by the spiritual ordinance of God, as was the case with the Israelite people; or by the formation of spiritual ministers, as with the Christian people; or by the just permission of God, and of this kind is the power of wicked princes who

---

38. Cf. Hugh of Saint Victor, *De sacramentis* II,II,IV (PL 176,418).

usurp power to themselves by force or cunning. And from this can be resolved the contradiction which seems to exist as between the words of the apostle just quoted - that is, that there is no power but of God - and the words of the prophet Hosea, speaking in the person of God of certain princes: "They have reigned, but not by me."[39] For every power comes either from an act of God, as does the power of good princes who receive their power rightly, or by His permission, as does the power of the wicked, who usurp power to themselves; and it is these latter who are said to reign, but not by God, because they do not reign by His act, but only by His permission. And this permission is just, for, as the Gloss[40] on the verse of the Apostle just cited says, it is not unjust for evil men to receive the power to do harm, so that the patience of the good may be tested and the iniquity of the wicked punished. For by the power given to the Devil, Job was tested so that he should be seen to be just; and Peter was tempted so that he should not trust in himself; and Paul was beaten so that he should not exalt himself; and Judas was condemned so that he should hang himself. And so it is that God permits the unjust as well as the just to have power, provided that some good comes from it; and it is in this sense that even the power of the wicked comes from the ordinance of God. For although God does not do evil, he nonetheless ordains it, for, as the blessed Augustine says, God assists men of good will, judges wicked men, and ordains all men.[41]

Alternatively, we must say that power is one thing and the use of power another. Power, therefore, is entirely good, and is therefore from God. The use of power, however, is sometimes evil. It, therefore, is not from God; and, because to make use of power is to reign, it is said of certain persons, "They have reigned, but not by me." Hence, the Gloss on that same verse of the Apostle says that no power is given either to a good man or to a bad other than by God.[42] And so the Lord said to Pilate; "Thou couldest have no power at all against me, except it were given thee from above."[43] The malice of men, then, has in itself the desire to do harm; but it does not have the power to do so if God does not give it. For the will to do harm can arise from the soul of man, but "there is no power but of God." So, therefore, the wicked use of power does not come from God, whereas power itself, because it is a good, is of God; and so he who holds power wickedly is said to reign, but not by God, because he uses his power ill. The good man, by contrast, reigns by God because he uses his power well, imitating God in this respect.

For as Gregory says on that verse of Job, "God doth not cast away the mighty, for He Himself also is mighty":[44] "He desires to imitate God who, at the height of his power, governs in order to secure the advantage of others

---

39. *Osee* VIII,4.
40. *Glossa ordinaria*, PL 114,512; Peter Lombard, *Collectanea* PL 191,1504.
41. *De civ. Dei* V,9 (CC XLVII,139).
42. *Glossa ordinaria*, PL 114,512; Cf. Peter Lombard, *Collectanea*, PL 191,1504.
43. *Joan.* XIX,11.
44. *Job* XXXVI,5.

and not to magnify his own glory; who wishes rather to promote the welfare of others than to rule them."[45] And this is to use power well.

Or, again, we must say, as Isidore says in the third book of his work on the Supreme Good: "God ordains both good and evil powers, but he favours the good and hates the evil. For when kings are good, this is by divine favour; but, when they are wicked, this is because of the wickedness of the people. As Job attests, the lives of rulers are disposed according to the merits of the people: 'He maketh a man who is a hypocrite to reign for the sins of the people.'[46] For when God is angry, nations receive such a ruler as they deserve for their sins."[47]

As to the further objection that a superior art does not institute an inferior, we must reply that, although the superior art does not institute the inferior art in every way, it nonetheless institutes it in the sense of perfecting it, insofar as it gives to it a mode of operation and a form appropriate to the needs of the end which the superior art seeks; and, by the same token, the spiritual power institutes the temporal in the sense of perfecting it, as we have said above.

Alternatively, we can say that the superior art, although it does not institute the inferior art, nonetheless institutes certain persons to have and exercise that art. Similarly, the spiritual power does not institute temporal power as such, because, in this sense, temporal power comes only from God. It does, however, institute it to its task, in the sense that it institutes those who must have and exercise such power. And when it is said that the spiritual power has the task of instituting the temporal power, this is to be taken to mean the man who has such power; for, as the Gloss says on that verse of the Apostle, "there is no power but of God": "The word 'power' sometimes applies to power itself, which is given to someone by God, and sometimes to the man who has the power."[48] It is in this way, therefore, that we are to interpret the statement that the spiritual power institutes the temporal power: that the man who has spiritual power works together with God so that some men may have and exercise temporal power. And, according to this, we can interpret in another way the statement introduced above: that is, that empire comes only from God. For this is true to the extent that the word 'empire' is taken to mean imperial power as such. If, however, it is taken to mean the man who has such power, then it does not come from God alone: for the fact that such a man has and exercises imperial power comes from God by the intermediate co-operation of a man having spiritual power.

Another doubt arises when it is said that the spiritual power has in relation to the temporal the nature of both an efficient and a final cause. Against this would seem to be the fact that cause and purpose do not coincide in the same entity amongst created things, but only in God; and so, if the spiritual

---

45. *Moralia* XXVI (PL 76,378).
46. *Job* XXXIV,30.
47. *Sentent.* III,XLVIII (PL 83,720).
48. *Glossa ordinaria*, PL 114,512

power has the nature of an end in relation to the temporal, it cannot also have the nature of an efficient or motive cause, and so it neither institutes nor judges it. To this, we must reply that, although some persons rely upon this argument to show that the spiritual power is in no way related to the temporal as an efficient and motive cause, but only as an end, this argument is in itself false, as is clear from what we have discussed above and from the reason that we now adduce: that the premise upon which it rests is false, when it is said that efficient and final causes do not coincide in the same creature. For, in relation to those arts which are subservient to it, the art of architecture has the nature of a prime mover insofar as it governs them, and it has the nature of a final cause insofar as it directs their work to its own purpose. And, in the same way, he who rules according to spiritual power has the nature of an efficient and motive cause and of an end also, in relation to him who rules according to temporal power.

Another doubt arises when it is said that the blessed Peter has received "the laws of an earthly empire",[49] and that kings preside over the earthly kingdom; for against the first of these sayings seems to be the fact that the Lord said to Peter: "I will give unto thee the keys of the kingdom of Heaven"; for He did not say, "of the kingdom of earth." And against the second of these sayings seems to be the fact that the earthly kingdom is the kingdom of this world, which is set over against the kingdom of Christ, and is the kingdom of the Devil, so that all kings are ministers of the Devil, and not of God: for why, therefore, is it said in *Wisdom* that kings are the ministers of God?[50] To these two objections we must reply at once that the phrase 'earthly kingdom' is used in two senses. For, in one sense, we say of the earthly kingdom that it appoints earthly things as its end; and the earthly kingdom is in that sense evil and diabolic and opposed to the heavenly kingdom which has celestial things as its end. In another sense, however, the earthly kingdom is the same as the heavenly: that is, it is the congregation or fellowship of good men who are pilgrims upon the earth. For it is called the kingdom of Heaven from the fact that it is directed towards heavenly goods as its final end; but it is called the earthly kingdom from the fact that it is, as yet, still turned towards earthly things and makes use of earthly things themselves. And it is in this second sense that the blessed Peter and each of his successors has the laws of the earthly empire; and, similarly, it is in this sense that Christian kings govern the earthly kingdom. In this respect, then, what Christ said to Peter - "I will give unto thee the keys of the kingdom of Heaven" - is to be taken to mean that He entrusted to him the laws of the earthly kingdom because that same kingdom is called earthly by reason of its use of temporal and earthly things, and it is called heavenly by reason of its hope and love for things heavenly. Hence also, Christ then said: "Whatsoever thou shalt bind on earth shall be bound in Heaven." So also, the secular prince, though he may be said to preside

---

49. *Dist*. XXII,c.1 (CIC I,73).
50. *Sap*. VI,5.

over the earthly kingdom, nonetheless has heavenly authority in a certain sense. For although he does not have immediate power over the spiritual things by which man is made heavenly, he nonetheless does have an immediate power over the temporal and earthly things which are directed towards spiritual ends and serve them. We therefore said above that royal power over temporal things is called spiritual according to a certain sense; and it follows that it can in the same sense be called heavenly. For although, in its own nature, it may not be directed towards anything but its natural end, nonetheless, inasmuch as it is guided by the authority of the spiritual power, it is directed towards the supernatural end which the spiritual power itself directly seeks.

Another doubt arises when it is said that the pope has temporal power under human law - that is, by the grant of Constantine. For against this seems to be what the blessed Augustine says at *De civitate Dei* IV: that kingdoms without justice are nothing but great bands of robbers.[51] Rather, as the same Augustine says at *De civitate Dei* II, there is no true justice where Christ is not ruler.[52] It seems, then, that the kingdom or empire of the Romans was a band of robbers at the time when Constantine acquired it, because it was not then subject to Christ through faith; and so Constantine could not rightly grant the empire [to Pope Sylvester] because he did not justly possess it himself. Through the grant of Constantine, therefore, the pope did not receive anything under human law; rather, he received only by human fact what he held in any case under divine law.

In order to resolve this doubt, we must consider which kingdoms are good and just and which are not. In this connexion, it must be known that, according to the blessed Augustine, at *De civitate Dei* IV and V, kingdoms do not come into being through fate or chance or from false gods, but are ordained by the providence of the one true God, in Whose hands are all powers and all the laws of all kingdoms.[53] But because not only the good but also the wicked are under the providence of God (albeit in different ways, because He sustains the good and tolerates the wicked, from whom He brings forth good), we must further consider whether the laws of both wicked and good kingdoms are under the providence of God. It must be known, therefore, that it is good for there to be kingdoms and royal power amongst men, and expedient for the human race. For because of the ignorance which is in human nature, the rule of reason alone is not sufficient for mankind; and, for this reason, it is expedient that the society of men, who are in many respects not adequate to govern themselves, should be ruled and directed by some person or persons esteemed above others for their prudence of intellect. Moreover, because of human malice, men do evil and injure one another, and so it is expedient for some to be the rulers of others, by whom men may be restrained from wickedness. Again,

---

51. *De civ. Dei* IV,4 (CC XLVII,101).
52. *De civ. Dei* II,21 (CC XLVII,55).
53. *De civ. Dei* IV,33 (CC XLVII,126); V,21 (XLVII,157).

because of the self-love of men, each seeks his own advantage, and so it is fitting that there should be certain governors of the community who seek and procure the common good. Furthermore, in every multitude it is appropriate that there should be some ruling principle, as we see in the various parts of nature; and so it is appropriate that there should be something in the human multitude by which the multitude may be ruled: particularly since man is by nature a social and communal animal. For society and community would not be preserved but scattered if there were not someone who had the care of the common good of the multitude and the society. As Solomon says: "Where there is no governor, the people shall fall."[54] Amongst men, therefore, it is expedient that some should be the rulers of others, by whom the ignorant are directed, offenders restrained and punished, the innocent defended, the common good procured, and the society itself preserved.

Some, however, acquire ruling power by rightful means and some by wicked ones. Certain persons, indeed, acquire ruling power rightly, appointed either by the agreement and common consent of the multitude or, beyond this, by the special ordinance of God Himself, as was done in the case of the Israelite people; or by the institution of those who act on God's behalf, as must be the case amongst the Christian people. He achieves ruling power wickedly, however, who, from love of mastery, or by force or deceit, or by any other unworthy means, usurps ruling power to himself. Someone may, however, achieve princely power unworthily yet subsequently be made a true ruler either by the consent of his subjects or by the authority of a superior. And just as the mode of acquiring power can be rightful or wicked, so can be the use of power once obtained; for some use the power which they have rightly, and some wickedly.

From these considerations there arises a fourfold distinction. For the rule of some persons is rightful both in the manner of its acquisition and in its use; whereas, on the other hand, the rule of some is wicked in the manner of its acquisition but righteous in its use; and the rule of some is wicked in both the ways of which we have spoken; and the rule of some is rightful in the manner of its acquisition but wicked in its use, although this last occurs more rarely. Those kingdoms are just and legitimate, therefore, in which both the manner of acquiring power and the use of power - or, at any rate, the manner of acquiring it - are rightful; and such kingdoms are under the providence of God as good. Those are unjust, however, in which one or both of the things of which we have spoken are lacking, and these are under the providence of God as evil; for God permits such kingdoms to exist either to prove the good or to punish the wicked, or for other purposes known to Him.

And, following from these conclusions, we must say that because, amongst the gentiles, some kings have acquired power rightly and have indeed made right use of such power, there are, therefore, some legitimate and just kingdoms amongst them. In order to come specifically to the kingdom or

---

54. *Prov.* XI,14.

empire of the Romans, however, over which Constantine held sway, we must say that that kingdom was broader and loftier than all the kingdoms of the gentiles and indeed began unjustly, because by robbery and violence, but, in its progress, was governed according to good morals, and, because of this, deserved to become so broad and mighty, as the blessed Augustine says.[55] And because of the good rule of that empire, it was made pleasing to many nations, so that they willingly submitted themselves to the Roman empire or tolerated its dominion; and so it became, in a certain sense, just and legitimate. It was not just in every sense, however, because it began evilly, and it lacked the Christian faith and worshipped false gods, to whom the Romans attributed the power of that kingdom, and it made wicked use of that power. For many of those who held sway in that kingdom or empire were tyrants, who used the power of government ill. And those who were good did not use their power well in all things, but only in some.

Constantine, however, stands out from amongst the others for many reasons, as is clear from the writings in which the achievements of the rulers of Rome are recorded. Hence, it can be said that Constantine attained the empire justly under human law, and therefore that he could grant what he held under that law. And the Roman Pontiff received the dignity of the Roman empire from Constantine under human law; and we have described above how human law may operate in addition to the divine. To the objection, therefore, that the Roman kingdom was a band of robbers because it was without justice, we must reply that a kingdom is a band of robbers when justice of every kind whatsoever is absent from it. In the Roman kingdom, however, especially after it had begun to grow great, there was indeed some justice, albeit not that which is formed by the faith of Christ, which alone is called true justice; and therefore the kingdom of Rome was not at that time a band of robbers. It was not, however, just in every sense, because the kingdom which lacks the faith of Christ cannot be just in every sense.

Hence, it must be known that, amongst the gentiles who had the faith [which prefigured that] of Christ, it was possible for there to be, and there certainly was, just kingship; and this is clear from the examples of Melchizedek and Job. Amongst the Jews also, just kingship could and did exist, for God provided a special kingship for the people of Israel in whom there would indeed be the faith of Christ in time to come. And just kingship can and does beyond doubt exist amongst Christians. Amongst unbelievers, however, there can be just kingship in a certain degree, to the extent that they live rightly, but not in every sense. Moreover, kingship might and can be, and sometimes is, unjust in every sense, amongst both believers and unbelievers.

Another doubt arises when it is said that those who have spiritual power can possess temporal things. For against this seems to be the fact that, when He sent them out to preach, God said to the apostles: "Thou shalt possess

---

55. *De civ. Dei* V,12 (CC XLVII,142ff).

neither gold nor silver",[56] and so on. To this doubt, we must reply that the prelates of the Church can possess temporal things both in order to sustain their lives and to distribute to the poor, and for other pious uses; not only as users, but they can also have lordship over temporal things. The care of those temporal things, however, they must entrust to others, so that they may be the more free to attend to spiritual tasks. Hence, we read that Christ possessed a money-bag and entrusted it to Judas; and in this it was prefigured that the Church was to have temporal possessions.[57] The apostles also had temporal things, because those who were converted to Christ sold their possessions and laid the price before the feet of the apostles, who distributed to each according to his need.[58] Nonetheless, they later entrusted the care of such distribution to the seven deacons.[59]

To the objection concerning Christ's words to the apostles, therefore, we must reply that Christ commanded this not so that it should be unlawful to possess gold and silver, but so that others, seeing the contempt in which the apostles held temporal things, should be the more readily moved to conversion. Alternatively, He said this in order to teach that, for the sake of carrying out the duty of preaching, every other care and anxiety must be laid aside; or He said this because it was expedient at that time; or He said it so that the preachers might know that other men are their debtors in temporal things by reason of their office, for "the labourer is worthy of his hire."[60]

Another doubt arises when it is said that Peter was the head of the apostles and of all the faithful, and, similarly, that his successors are the heads of the Church. For against this seems to be that fact that there is only one head of one body, and Christ is the head of the Church. Peter and his successors, therefore, cannot properly be heads of the Church. To this doubt, we must add that certain persons assert that Peter was not the head of the Church because there was not in him a fulness of spiritual understanding; and because she is not called Petrine from Peter, but Christian from Christ; and because spiritual power does not devolve from him to others, for it was not he alone who received the keys, but the whole Church in him, because he signified the whole Church. Hence, Isidore says that the other apostles were made Peter's peers in honour and power.[61] This assertion, however, is not true. On the contrary, Peter is truly called the head of the Church, and so too is each of his successors. Nonetheless, we must note that, just as fulness of power does not belong to Christ and His vicar in the same way, so also the nature of a head does not belong to Christ and His vicar in the same way; for it belongs to Christ principally and pre-eminently, but to His vicar as a minister and secondarily. And so the Church is not called Petrine from

---

56. Cf. *Matt*. X,9f; *Marc*. VI,8; *Luc*. IX,3; X,4.
57. *Joan*. XII,6.
58. *Act*. IV,35.
59. *Act*. VI,1ff.
60. *Luc*. X,7.
61. This statement is not found in the works of Isidore, who, indeed, in a letter to Eugenius, Bishop of Toledo (*Epist*. VIII (PL 83,908)) expresses exactly the opposite view.

Peter, but Christian from Christ, because she is named from [Him Who is her head in] the more excellent and principal sense.

And what is said concerning the equality of the power [given to the apostles] is not true. For the Church has received the power of the keys in such a way that it may be devolved from one to others, and, although Christ conferred power upon all the apostles, He nonetheless willed that Peter should have primacy in this power, as we have shown above: so that, although the apostles received power from Christ at the beginning, they nonetheless soon received it from Peter, His prelate, also. When Isidore says that the apostles had parity of power with Peter, then, this parity is to be understood as similarity, but not as equality. Alternatively, we must say that they had parity of power with respect to the action and effect of their power, but not with respect to the institution of their power and their mode of having it. For they were not all instituted to it equally; rather, one of them was placed above the others.

And as to the objection that there is one head of one body, we must reply that Christ and His vicar are not said to be two heads, but one; for the pope is not called a head for any other reason than that he acts on Christ's behalf and represents His person.

The final doubt arises when it is said that the pope has fulness of power. For against this seems to be the fact that the pope is called the Vicar of Christ, since he who is the vicar of another does not have the fulness of power which is in him whose vicar he is. To this doubt, we must reply that, granted that the title of vicar does not [necessarily] imply fulness of power, we must not for this reason say that the pope, who is the Vicar of Christ, may not have fulness of power; for this fulness is to be understood and described in terms of the other titles which belong to him, such as 'head' and 'shepherd' and many others. Or, alternatively, we must say that it is one thing to consider the proper use of a title with respect to the primary meaning which attaches to that title, and another to consider its use with respect to the secondary meanings to which it is adapted. If, then, we consider the proper meaning of the word 'vicar', this title does not imply any diminution of power. For the word 'vicar' is derived from *vicis*, which word means 'task' and 'duty': a vicar is said to be one who performs the task of another; and, in this sense, all the apostles are said to be vicars of Christ, as in the Preface, where it is said: ["May Thy flock be governed] by those whom Thou hast chosen to be the vicars and shepherds of the same",[62] that is, of Thy flock. And, consequently, the successors of the apostles are called vicars of Christ.

In the singular sense, however, the Supreme Pastor of the ecclesiastical flock - that is, the successor of Peter - is called the Vicar of Christ; but this is in the sense in which anything at all which is the equivalent of something else is called a 'vicar'. Hence, it is said in *Leviticus*: "He that killeth a beast shall render a substitute [*vicarium*]", which is to say that he is to render an

---

62. *Missale Romanum*, Preface of the Apostles.

equivalent, "that is, beast for beast",[63] by which, clearly, we are to understand an entire, that is, an equally good, animal: otherwise there would not be due restitution of the kind which the law intends. And so, having regard to the proper meaning of the title, when someone is said to be the vicar of another in office or power, this suggests that the power which he has is not diminished, but equal. If, however, we consider the title of vicar with respect to the other uses to which it is applied as it were by adaptation, the title may then sometimes be taken to designate a power which is not full; and so, in this sense, someone may be called the vicar of another to whom, however, the other's power has not been entrusted fully and totally. We have an example of this in *Exodus*, where, at the advice of Jethro, Moses chose able men from the people, to whom he entrusted the judgment of small and easier matters, reserving the greater and more weighty to be referred to himself.[64] And the prelates of the Church themselves act in imitation of this, appointing certain persons, who are called vicars by some and officials by others, to the conduct of daily affairs and business and to the smaller tasks; but they perform the greater tasks themselves.

Or, again, we must reply to this objection that, even supposing that a vicar can do less than he whose vicar he is, the pope is still rightly called the Vicar of Christ. For, as we have shown above, he does not have the whole of that fulness of power which Christ has; but he does have the fulness of spiritual and temporal power which has been communicated to him for the government of the Church Militant by the Lord Jesus Christ Himself, Whose power and rule endures for ever and ever. Amen.

Here ends the short work on Christian government composed by Brother James of Viterbo of the Order of Hermits of Saint Augustine.

oOo

---

63. *Levit.* XXIV,18.
64. *Exod.* XVIII,14ff.

BIBLIOGRAPHY

(a) Primary sources

De regimine Christiano was first published in modern times by G.-L. Perugi, *Il De regimine christiano di Giacomo Capocci, Viterbese* (Rome, 1914). This is a printing of one late manuscript only, and not a critical edition. The only critical edition is by H.-X. Arquillière, *Le plus ancien traité de l'Église: Jacques de Viterbe, De regimine christiano* (Paris, 1926). This is, however, a strangely slapdash piece of editing. The long Introduction is worth reading (Professor Arquillière describes the manuscript tradition on pp. 17ff); but the text is very unsatisfactory. It contains many transcriptional and other errors; a number of readings have been allowed to stand which are clearly incorrect; and the notes are scanty, inaccurate and inconsistently presented.

Two other papalist tracts must be mentioned in connexion with the events of 1296-1303: Henry of Cremona, *De potestate papae* (ed. R. Scholz, *Die Publizistik*, 459ff) and Aegidius Romanus, *De ecclesiastica potestate* (ed. G. Boffito and G.U. Oxilia, *Un Trattato Inedito di Egidio Colonna* (Florence, 1908); also by R. Scholz, *Aegidius Romanus de ecclesiastica potestate* (Weimar, 1929; repr. Aalen, 1961); English translation by R.W. Dyson, *Giles of Rome on Ecclesiastical Power* (Woodbridge, Suffolk, and Dover, New Hampshire, 1986)). The Boffito and Oxilia version has a useful Introduction, but is not a critical edition.

With one exception, the writings of Philip the Fair's supporters are much less impressive than those of his opponents. The following may be noted:

Anonymous, *Antequam essent clerici* (Dupuy, *Histoire du différend d'entre le Pape Boniface VIII et Philippe le Bel Roy de France* (Paris, 1655), 21ff.

Anonymous, *Disputatio inter clericum et militem* (M. Goldast, *Monarchia sancti imperii Romani* (Frankfurt and Hanover, 1612-14), I, 13ff).

157

BIBLIOGRAPHY

Anonymous, *Quaestio disputata in utramque partem pro et contra pontificiam potestatem* (Goldast, II, 95ff. Goldast's attribution of this work to Aegidius Romanus is plainly wrong).

Anonymous, *Quaestio de potestate papae*, also known as *Rex pacificus*; printed in Dupuy, but in a seriously mutilated form. See W. Ullmann, "A Medieval Document on Papal Theories of Government", *English Historical Review*, LXI (1946), 180ff.

John [Quidort] of Paris, *Tractatus de potestate regia et papale* (ed. J. Leclerq, *Jean de Paris et l'ecclésiologie du XIIIe siécle* (Paris, 1942). This is the exception mentioned above. The work has been translated into English twice (both times as *On Royal and Papal Power*): by J.A. Watt (Toronto, 1971) and A.P. Monahan (New York and London, 1974).

There are several useful anthologies of primary sources in translation. The following are especially recommended:

Brian Tierney, *The Crisis of Church and State, 1050-1300* (Englewood Cliffs, New Jersey, 1980).

Ewart Lewis, *Medieval Political Ideas* (2 vols., New York, 1954).

(b) Selected secondary sources

The following list includes the standard works on the subject, but it is certainly not exhaustive.

H.-X. Arquillière	:	*L'Augustinisme politique* (Paris, 1955).
A. Black	:	*Political Thought in Europe 1250-1450* (Cambridge, 1992).
T.S.R. Boase	:	*Boniface VIII* (London, 1933).
Christopher Brooke	:	*Europe in the Central Middle Ages, 962-1154* (London, 1964).
J.H. Burns, *et al.*	:	*The Cambridge History of Medieval Political Thought* (Cambridge, 1988).
R.W. and A.J. Carlyle	:	*A History of Medieval Political Theory in the West* (6 vols., Edinburgh and London, 1903-36).

BIBLIOGRAPHY

G.A.L. Digard : *Philippe le Bel et le Saint Siège de 1285 à 1304* (Paris 1936).

W.K. Ferguson : *Europe in Transition, 1300-1520* (Boston, 1962).

H. Finke : *Aus den Tagen Bonifaz VIII* (Münster, 1902).

J.-P. Genet : *Le Monde au Moyen Age* (Paris, 1991).

E. Gilson : *Christian Philosophy in the Middle Ages* (London, 1955).

P. Hughes : *A History of the Church* (3 vols., London, 1934-37).

G. Ladner : "The Concepts of *ecclesia* and *christianitas* and their relation to the idea of papal *plenitudo potestatis* from Gregory VII to Boniface VIII", *Miscellanea historicae pontificiae*, XVIII (1954), 9ff.

Lagarde, G. de : *La naissance de l'esprit laïque au déclin du moyen âge* (6 vols., Paris, 1948).

W.D. McCreedy, : "Papal *plenitudo potestatis* and the Source of Temporal Authority in Later Medieval Papal Hierocratic Theory", *Speculum*, XLVIII (1973), 654ff.

C.H. McIlwain : *The Growth of Political Ideas in the West* (New York, 1932).

H.K. Mann : *The Lives of the Popes in the Middle Ages* (18 vols., London, 1906-32).

J.H. Mundy : *Europe in the High Middle Ages, 1150-1309* (London, 1973).

S.R. Packard : *Europe and the Church under Innocent III* (New York, 1927).

159

BIBLIOGRAPHY

J. Rivière	:	*Le problème de l'église et de l'état au temps de Philippe le Bel* (Paris, 1926).
R. Scholz	:	*Die Publizistik zur Zeit Philipps des Schönen und Bonifaz VIII* (Stuttgart, 1903).
J.R. Strayer	:	*On the Medieval Origins of the Modern State* (Princeton, 1970).
H. Tillmann	:	*Pope Innocent III* (Amsterdam, 1978).
W. Ullmann	:	*Medieval Papalism: The Political Theories of the Medieval Canonists* (London, 1949).
W. Ullmann	:	*The Growth of Papal Government in the Middle Ages* (London, 1955).
W. Ullmann	:	*Principles of Government and Politics in the Middle Ages* (London, 1961).
W. Ullmann	:	*A History of Political Thought: The Middle Ages* (Harmondsworth, 1965).
J. A. Watt	:	*The Theory of Papal Monarchy in the Thirteenth Century* (London, 1965).
M.J. Wilks	:	*The Problem of Sovereignty in the Later Middle Ages* (Cambridge, 1963).
C.T. Wood	:	*Philip the Fair and Boniface VIII* (New York, 1967).

oOo